Robert Baylor
Brenda Stokes
Mt. San Antonio College

FINE FRENZY
Enduring Themes in Poetry

SECOND EDITION

McGraw-Hill Book Company

New York St. Louis San Francisco Auckland
Bogotá Düsseldorf London Madrid
Mexico Montreal New Delhi Panama Paris
São Paulo Singapore Sydney Tokyo Toronto

This book was set in Palatino by Monotype Composition Company, Inc.
The editors were Donald W. Burden and Phyllis T. Dulan;
the cover was designed by Joan E. O'Connor;
the production supervisor was Dominick Petrellese.
It was printed and bound by The Book Press.

FINE FRENZY
Enduring Themes in Poetry

10 11   BKP BKP   8 9

**Library of Congress Cataloging in
Publication Data**

Baylor, Robert, comp.
    Fine frenzy.

    Includes index.
    1. English poetry.
    2. American poetry.
I. Stokes, Brenda. II. Title.
PR1175.B277 1978   821'.008
77-5605
ISBN 0-07-004160-1

To Mary and Stan

CONTENTS

Childhood, Youth, Maturity, Old Age 31

Social Conscience   53

Alienation   77

Love

Illusion/Reality   145

Faith   171

Order   205

Marriage   229

War   249

Mutability and Death   275

Insight   313

PREFACE

The second edition of *Fine Frenzy* follows the first in format and approach. Changes, additions, and deletions have been based on our own experience with the text and helpful suggestions from teachers and students who have used it. Our original intention remains the same: to produce a text which will lessen the frustration teachers and students often feel when confronting poetry anthologies that contain too much teaching apparatus (editorial comments, questions, footnotes, etc.), too few poems, and too many irrelevant poems.

During years of teaching we have found that apparatus tends to limit rather than enhance student response. The student is often so busy answering questions that he or she misses the poem. This edition contains almost 400 poems presented with minimal footnotes of references in text not readily found in a college dictionary. The table of contents lists the poems thematically, while the index catalogs poets, poems, and first lines in alphabetical order. An essay on prosody and a glossary, each fully illustrated by excerpts from poems in the text, complete the apparatus. A substantial teacher's manual is also available. It provides explications, teaching suggestions, and information about records and films. In the text, the poetry speaks for itself.

The poems provide a wide choice. In addition to those 100 poems which have come to form the traditional base of the introductory course, the teacher may choose from some 80 traditional poems less widely anthologized and more than 200 poems by modern and contemporary poets. Every major form and type of poem in English are included: sonnet, vilanelle, rondeau, ballad, limerick, lyric, narrative, reflective, etc. The thrust of poetry written since World War II is well represented. The teacher who wishes to use a formal approach may do so; a historical approach is not precluded.

Poetry seems irrelevant to many students because their only exposure has been to obvious or didactic verse. They don't need to be told a sunset is beautiful, they know it already; and they want to discover their own moral truths. As W. H. Auden has written, "When we read Kipling we can usually say, 'That is just how I feel.' Of course there is nothing wrong with that, but when we read a great poet, we say, 'I never realized before what I felt. From now on, thanks to this poem, I shall feel differently.'"

This text not only provides poetry relevant to contemporary experience, but its thematic arrangement shows that great poetry is always relevant. The discovery that Shakespeare and Shelley were sociopolitical animals; that Pete Seeger did not write "Turn, Turn, Turn" (Ecclesiastes did!); that man has always searched for a sustaining faith, felt his isolation, reveled in love, and sought for beauty reveals to students the relevance of the entire range of human experience.

We have reduced the number of thematic sections from fifteen to twelve. Each is arranged alphabetically to give a random mix of traditional, modern, and contemporary poems which reveal the continuity between one generation and the next and show that student concerns have always been the concerns of the poet. Most of the new poems are by contemporary or modern poets.

In sum, *Fine Frenzy* is based on three corollary premises: that the contents of a poetry anthology should be poetry; that teachers desire a large selection of poems from which to choose; and that students demand poems that are relevant to their interests and experience.

The editors wish to acknowledge the assistance courteously extended during the production of this book by Donald Keran, Lawrence Ferguson, and the staffs of Pomona Public and Mt. San Antonio College Libraries. A note of special appreciation also to Mary Baylor, who ordered the chaos when the frenzy became too fine.

Robert Baylor
Brenda Stokes

EXUBERANCE

Inebriate of Air—am I

Emily Dickinson

If all be true that I do think

Henry Aldrich (1647–1710)

If all be true that I do think,
There are five reasons we should drink:
Good wine, a friend, or being dry,
Or lest we should be by and by,
Or any other reason why.

Auto Mobile

A. R. Ammons (1926–   )

For the bumps bangs & scratches of
collisive encounters
madam
I through time's ruts and weeds
sought you, metallic, your
stainless steel flivver:
I have banged you, bumped
and scratched, side-swiped,
momocked & begommed you &
your little flivver still   10
works so well.

I'd have you, quoth he

Anonymous

I'd have you, quoth he,
Would you have me, quoth she,
   O where, Sir?

In my Chamber, quoth he,
In your Chamber, quoth she,
   Why there, Sir?

To kiss you, quoth he,
To kiss me, quoth she,
   O why, Sir?

Cause I love it, quoth he,   10
Do you love it? quoth she,
   So do I, Sir.

Sumer Is Icumen In

Anonymous

Sumer is icumen in,
   Lhudé[1] sing cuccu;
Groweth sed and bloweth[2] med[3]
   And springth the wudé nu.[4]
     Sing cuccu!
Awé[5] bleteth after lomb,
   Lhouth[6] after calvé cu;[7]
Bulluc sterteth, bucké verteth;
   Murie sing cuccu.
     Cuccu, cuccu,   10
   Wel singés thu, cuccu,
   Ne swik[8] thu naver nu.[9]

Sing cuccu nu! Sing cuccu!
Sing cuccu! Sing cuccu nu!

1 Loud. 2 Blossoms. 3 Meadow. 4 Wood now. 5 Ewe. 6 Lows.
7 Cow. 8 Stop. 9 Now.

from Homage to Mistress Bradstreet
John Berryman (1914–1972)

19

So squeezed, wince you I scream? I love you & hate
off with you. Ages! *Useless.* Below my waist
he has me in Hell's vise.
Stalling. He let go. Come back: brace
me somewhere. No. No. Yes! everything down
hardens I press with horrible joy down
my back cracks like a wrist
shame I am voiding oh behind it is too late

20

hide me forever I work thrust I must free
now I all muscles & bones concentrate   10
what is living from dying?
Simon I must leave you so untidy
Monster you are killing me Be sure
I'll have you later Women do endure
I can *can* no longer
and it passes the wretched trap whelming and I am me

21

drencht & powerful, I did it with my body!
One proud tug greens Heaven. Marvellous,
unforbidding Majesty.
Swell, imperious bells. I fly.   20
Mountainous, woman not breaks and will bend:
sways God nearby: anguish comes to an end.
Blossomed Sarah, and I
blossom. Is that thing alive? I hear a famisht howl.

Soft Snow
William Blake (1757–1827)

I walked abroad in a snowy day;
I asked the soft snow with me to play;
She played and she melted in all her prime,
And the winter called it a dreadful crime.

To H
William Blake (1757–1827)

Thy friendship oft has made my heart to ake:
Do be my Enemy for Friendship's sake.

Jabberwocky
Lewis Carroll (1832–1898)

'Twas brillig, and the slithy toves
   Did gyre and gimble in the wabe;
All mimsy were the borogoves,
   And the mome raths outgrabe.

"Beware the Jabberwock, my son!
   The jaws that bite, the claws that catch!
Beware the Jubjub bird, and shun
   The frumious Bandersnatch!"

He took his vorpal sword in hand;
   Long time the manxome foe he sought—
So rested he by the Tumtum tree,
   And stood awhile in thought.

10

And, as in uffish thought he stood,
   The Jabberwock, with eyes of flame,
Came whiffling through the tulgey wood,
   And burbled as it came!

One, two! One, two! And through and through
   The vorpal blade went snicker-snack!
He left it dead, and with its head
   He went galumphing back.   20

"And hast thou slain the Jabberwock?
   Come to my arms, my beamish boy!
O frabjous day! Callooh! Callay!"
   He chortled in his joy.

'Twas brillig, and the slithy toves
   Did gyre and gimble in the wabe;
All mimsy were the borogoves,
   And the mome raths outgrabe.

Good Times

Lucille Clifton (1937–   )

My Daddy has paid the rent
and the insurance man is gone
and the lights is back on
and my uncle Brud has hit
for one dollar straight
and they is good times
good times
good times

My Mamma has made bread
and Grampaw has come   10
and everybody is drunk
and dancing in the kitchen

and singing in the kitchen
oh these is good times
good times
good times

oh children think about the
good times

The Music Crept by Us

Leonard Cohen (1934–   )

I would like to remind
the management
that the drinks are watered
and the hat-check girl
has syphilis
and the band is composed
of former SS monsters
However since it is
New Year's Eve
and I have lip cancer
I will place my
paper hat on my
concussion and dance

10

Old Movies

John Cotton (1925–   )

How I loved those old movies
they would show in the Roxys
and Regals amongst all that
gilt plaster, or in the Bijou
flea-pits smelling of Jeyes.[1]
The men sleek haired and suited,
with white cuffs and big trilbies,
their girls all pushovers,
wide-eyed with lashes
like venus fly traps and their   10
clouds of blonde candyfloss
for hair.   Oh those bosoms, hips
and those long long legs
I never saw in daylight!
And their apartments,
vast as temples,
full of unused furniture,
the sideboards bending with booze,
and all those acres of bed!
She, in attendance, wearing   20
diaphanous, but never quite
diaphanous enough, nightwear.
And their lives!
Where the baddies only,
if not always, stopped one,
and they loved and loved
and never ended up married.
Every time I get a whiff
of that disinfectant
I feel nostalgic.   30

1 Trade name for a British disinfectant.

going uptown to visit miriam

Victor Hernandez Cruz (1949–   )

on the train
old ladies playing football
going for empty seats

very funny persons

the train riders
        are silly people
        i am a train rider

but no one knows where i am
going to take this train

to take this train   10
to take this train

the ladies   read popular
paperbacks   because they
are popular   they get off
at 42 to change for the
westside line   or off
59 for the department store

the train pulls in & out
the white walls   dark-
ness   white walls dark-   20
ness

ladies looking up   i
wonder where they going
the dentist   pick up

husband pick up wife
pick up kids
pick up?grass?
to library   to museum
to laundromat   to school

but no one knows where i am   30
going to take this train

to take this train

to visit miriam
to visit miriam

& to kiss her
on the cheek
& hope i don't
see sonia on the
street

But no one knows where i'm taking   40
this train
       taking this train
        to visit miriam.

nobody loses all the time

e. e. cummings (1894–1962)

nobody loses all the time

i had an uncle named
Sol who was a born failure and
nearly everybody said he should have gone
into vaudeville perhaps because my Uncle Sol could
sing McCann He Was a Diver on Xmas Eve like Hell Itself which
may or may not account for the fact that my Uncle

Sol indulged in that possibly most inexcusable
of all to use a highfalootin phrase
luxuries that is or to   10
wit farming and be
it needlessly
added

my Uncle Sol's farm
failed because the chickens
ate the vegetables so
my Uncle Sol had a
chicken farm till the
skunks ate the chickens when

my Uncle Sol   20
had a skunk farm but
the skunks caught cold and
died and so
my Uncle Sol imitated the
skunks in a subtle manner

or by drowning himself in the watertank
but somebody who'd given my Uncle Sol a Victor
Victrola and records while he lived presented to
him upon the auspicious occasion of his decease a
scrumptious not to mention splendiferous funeral with   30
tall boys in black gloves and flowers and everything and

i remember we all cried like the Missouri
when my Uncle Sol's coffin lurched because
somebody pressed a button
(and down went
my Uncle
Sol

and started a worm farm)

A Bird came down the Walk

Emily Dickinson (1830–1886)

A Bird came down the Walk—
He did not know I saw—
He bit an Angleworm in halves
And ate the fellow, raw,

And then he drank a Dew
From a convenient Grass—
And then hopped sidewise to the Wall
To let a Beetle pass—

He glanced with rapid eyes
That hurried all around—   10
They looked like frightened Beads, I thought—
He stirred his Velvet Head

Like one in danger, Cautious,
I offered him a Crumb
And he unrolled his feathers
And rowed him softer home—

Than Oars divide the Ocean,
Too silver for a seam—
Or Butterflies, off Banks of Noon
Leap, plashless as they swim.   20

I taste a liquor never brewed

Emily Dickinson (1830–1886)

I taste a liquor never brewed—
From Tankards scooped in Pearl—
Not all the Vats upon the Rhine
Yield such an Alcohol!

Inebriate of Air—am I—
And Debauchee of Dew—
Reeling—thro endless summer days—
From inns of Molten Blue—

When "Landlords" turn the drunken Bee
Out of the Foxglove's door—   10
When Butterflies—renounce their "drams"—
I shall but drink the more!

Till Seraphs swing their snowy Hats—
And Saints—to windows run—
To see the little Tippler
Leaning against the—Sun—

A Lame Beggar
John Donne (1572–1631)

"I am unable," yonder beggar cries,
"To stand or move!" If he say true, he lies.

Calm was the even, and clear was the sky
from AN EVENING'S LOVE

John Dryden (1631–1700)

I

Calm was the even, and clear was the sky,
  And the new-budding flowers did spring,
When all alone went Amyntas and I
  To hear the sweet nightingal sing.
I sate, and he laid him down by me,
  But scarcely his breath he could draw;
For when with a fear, he began to draw near,
  He was dashed with: "A ha ha ha ha!"

II

He blushed to himself, and lay still for a while,
  And his modesty curbed his desire;   10
But straight I convinced all his fear with a smile,
  Which added new flames to his fire.

"O Sylvia," said he, "you are cruel,
    To keep your poor lover in awe;"
Then once more he pressed with his hand to my breast,
    But was dashed with: "A ha ha ha ha!"

III

I knew 'twas his passion that caused all his fears,
    And therefore I pitied his case;
I whispered him softly: "There's nobody near,"
    And laid my cheek close to his face: 20
But as he grew bolder and bolder,
    A shepherd came by us and saw,
And just as our bliss we began with a kiss,
    He laughed out with "A ha ha ha ha!"

Dirge

Kenneth Fearing (1902–1961)

1–2–3 was the number he played but today the number came
   3–2–1;
   bought his Carbide at 30 but it went to 29; had the favorite
   at Bowie but the track was slow—

O, executive type, would you like to drive a floating power,
   knee action, silk-upholstered six? Wed a Hollywood star?
   Shoot the course in 58? Draw to the ace, king, jack?
O, fellow with a will who won't take no, watch out for three
   cigarettes on the same, single match; O democratic voter
   born in August under Mars, beware of liquidated rails—   10

Dénouement to dénouement, he took a personal pride in the
   certain, certain way he lived his own, private life,
   but nevertheless, they shut off his gas; nevertheless,
   the bank foreclosed; nevertheless, the landlord called;
   nevertheless, the radio broke,

And twelve o'clock arrived just once too often,
   just the same he wore one gray tweed suit, bought one
      straw hat, drank one straight Scotch, walked one short
      step, took one long look, drew one deep breath,
   just one too many,   20

And wow he died as wow he lived,
   going whop to the office and blooie home to sleep and
      biff got married and bam had children and oof got fired,
   zowie did he live and zowie did he die,

With who the hell are you at the corner of his casket,
   and where the hell we going on the right hand silver
   knob, and who the hell cares walking second from the
   end with an American Beauty wreath from why the hell
   not.

Very much missed by the circulation staff of the New York   30
   Evening Post; deeply, deeply mourned by the B.M.T.,

Wham, Mr. Roosevelt; pow, Sears Roebuck; awk, big dipper;
    bop, summer rain;
  bong, Mr., bong, Mr., bong, Mr., bong.

Crazy

Lawrence Ferlinghetti (1919–   )

                crazy
                    to be alive in such a strange
                                    world
    with the band playing schmaltz
                        in the classic bandshell
                                        and the people
            on the benches under the clipped trees
                                    and girls
            on the grass
                    and the breeze blowing and the streamers   10
    streaming
                    and a fat man with a graflex
                    and a dark woman with a dark dog she called Lucia
                    and a cat on a leash
                    and a pekinese with a blond baby
                    and a cuban in a fedora
                    and a bunch of boys posing for a group
                                        picture
            and just then
                    while the band went right on playing   20
                                    schmaltz
    a midget ran past shouting and waving his hat
                                    at someone
                and a young man with a gay campaignbutton
    came up and said
                    Are you by any chance a registered
                            DEMOCRAT?

This morning
Javier Gálvez (1937–   )

This morning
The sun broke
my window
and came in laughing

His Return to London
Robert Herrick (1591–1674)

From the dull confines of the drooping West,
To see the day spring from the pregnant East,
Ravished in spirit, I come, nay more, I fly
To thee, blest place of my nativity!
Thus, thus with hallowed foot I touch the ground
With thousand blessings by thy fortune crowned.
O fruitful genius! that bestowest here
An everlasting plenty, year by year;
O place! O people! Manners framed to please
All nations, customs, kindreds, languages!   10
I am a free-born Roman;[1] suffer then
That I amongst you live a citizen.
London my home is: though by hard fate sent
Into a long and irksome banishment;
Yet since called back; henceforward let me be,
O native country, repossessed by thee!
For, rather than I'll to the West return,
I'll beg of thee first here to have mine urn.
Weak I am grown, and must in short time fall;
Give thou my sacred relics burial.   20

1 He equates present day London (seventeenth century) with ancient Rome
as the center of the world.

Midnight Dancer
Langston Hughes (1902–1967)

Wine-maiden
Of the jazz-tuned night,
Lips
Sweet as purple dew,
Breasts
Like the pillows of all sweet dreams,
Who crushed
The grapes of joy
And dripped their juice
On you?

Rondeau
Leigh Hunt (1784–1859)

Jenny kissed me when we met,
   Jumping from the chair she sat in;
Time, you thief, who love to get
   Sweets into your list, put that in:
Say I'm weary, say I'm sad,
   Say that health and wealth have missed me,
Say I'm growing old, but add,
   Jenny kissed me.

The Bagel
David Ignatow (1914–   )

I stopped to pick up the bagel
rolling away in the wind,
annoyed with myself
for having dropped it
as it were a portent.
Faster and faster it rolled,
with me running after it
bent low, gritting my teeth,
and I found myself doubled over
and rolling down the street   10
head over heels, one complete somersault
after another like a bagel
and strangely happy with myself.

Variations on a Theme by William Carlos Williams[1]
Kenneth Koch (1925–   )

1

I chopped down the house that you had been saving
        to live in next summer.
I am sorry, but it was morning, and I had nothing to do
and its wooden beams were so inviting.

2

We laughed at the hollyhocks together
and then I sprayed them with lye.
Forgive me. I simply do not know what I am doing.

1 See "This Is Just to Say" by Williams on page 29.

I gave away the money that you had been saving to live
    on for the next ten years.
The man who asked for it was shabby
and the firm March wind on the porch was so juicy and cold.

Last evening we went dancing and I broke your leg.   10
Forgive me. I was clumsy, and
I wanted you here in the wards, where I am the doctor!

Gratitude

Annette Lynch (1922–   )

And should I thank you, my dear skin,
For holding me in,
For holding me in?

When all the while I want to shout
Let me out,
Let me out!

Look Closely

Morton Marcus (1936–   )

I hold in my hands
one invaluable, unusually large, circular,
hydrated, cellular, fish-spined, shell-pasted,
molecular, wood-fitted, lilac scented, pollenated,
earth-colored, Katanga-mined, Bantu-smelted,
cleaned, polished, rough-edged, curved,

granite, gold-encrusted, filigreed, stamped,
platinum inlaid, green embossed, diamond-tipped,
rectangular, sculpted, Polynesian carved,
interconnecting, figure-locking,   10
beaten, Persian hammered, sheeted,
fur covered, feathered,
braided, Inca woven, lace trimmed,
stitched, beaded, Navajo embroidered,
Chinese inspired, Japanese designed, Brahmanic,
blue lacquered, hand painted, red enamelled,
impenetrable, soaring, mythic, hermaphroditic,
Hebraic, gothic,
mobile, eurythmic, mechanical,
non-plastic, free-spinning,   20
winged, elevated,
piece of myself.

If you look closely
you can see it.

Lucinda Matlock

Edgar Lee Masters (1868–1950)

I went to the dances at Chandlerville,
And played snap-out at Winchester.
One time we changed partners,
Driving home in the moonlight of middle June,
And then I found Davis.
We were married and lived together for seventy years,
Enjoying, working, raising the twelve children,
Eight of whom we lost
Ere I had reached the age of sixty.
I spun, I wove, I kept the house, I nursed the sick,   10
I made the garden, and for holiday
Rambled over the fields where sang the larks,
And by Spoon River gathering many a shell,
And many a flower and medicinal weed—

Shouting to the wooded hills, singing to the green valleys,
At ninety-six I had lived enough, that is all,
And passed to a sweet repose.
What is this I hear of sorrow and weariness,
Anger, discontent and drooping hopes?
Degenerate sons and daughters,   20
Life is too strong for you—
It takes life to love Life.

First Fig
Edna St. Vincent Millay (1892–1950)

My candle burns at both ends;
    It will not last the night;
But ah, my foes, and oh, my friends—
    It gives a lovely light!

Ancient Music[1]
Ezra Pound (1885–1972)

Winter is icummen in,
Lhude sing Goddamm,
Raineth drop and staineth slop,
And how the wind doth ramm!
        Sing: Goddamm.

Skiddeth bus and sloppeth us,
An ague hath my ham.
Freezeth river, turneth liver,
        Damm you, sing: Goddamm.

1 See "Summer Is Icumen In" on page 4.

Goddamm, Goddamm, 'tis why I am, Goddamm, 10
    So 'gainst the winter's balm.
Sing goddamm, damm, sing Goddamm,
Sing goddamm, sing goddamm, DAMM.

Skirt Dance

Ismael Reed (1938–   )

i am to my honey what marijuana is
to tiajuana. the acapulco of her
secret harvest. up her lush coasts i
glide at midnight bringing a full boat.
(that's all the Spanish i know.)

The master, the swabber, the boatswain, and I

from THE TEMPEST (II, 2)

William Shakespeare (1564–1616)

The master, the swabber, the boatswain, and I,
    The gunner, and his mate,
Loved Mall, Meg, and Marian, and Margery,
    But none of us cared for Kate.
    For she had a tongue with a tang,
    Would cry to a sailor "Go hang!"
She loved not the savor of tar nor of pitch;
Yet a tailor might scratch her where'er she did itch.
Then to sea, boys, and let her go hang!

Sigh No More, Ladies

from MUCH ADO ABOUT NOTHING (II, 3)

William Shakespeare (1564–1616)

Sigh no more, ladies, sigh no more!
  Men were deceivers ever,
One foot in sea, and one on shore;
  To one thing constant never.
    Then sigh not so,
    But let them go,
  And be you blithe and bonny,
Converting all your sounds of woe
  Into Hey nonny, nonny.

Sing no more ditties, sing no moe,   10
  Of dumps so dull and heavy!
The fraud of men was ever so,
  Since summer first was leavy.
    Then sigh not so,
    But let them go,
  And be you blithe and bonny,
Converting all your sounds of woe
  Into Hey nonny, nonny.

When Icicles Hang

from LOVE'S LABOUR'S LOST (V, 2)

William Shakespeare (1564–1616)

When icicles hang by the wall,
  And Dick the shepherd blows his nail,
And Tom bears logs into the hall,
  And milk comes frozen home in pail,

When blood is nipped and ways be foul,
    Then nightly sings the staring owl:
        "Tu-whit, tu-who!"
        A merry note,
While greasy Joan doth keel[1] the pot.

When all aloud the wind doth blow,   10
    And coughing drowns the parson's saw,[2]
And birds sit brooding in the snow,
    And Marian's nose looks red and raw,
When roasted crabs hiss in the bowl,
    Then nightly sings the staring owl:
        "Tu-whit, tu-who!"
        A merry note,
While greasy Joan doth keel the pot.

1 Stir.   2 Cliché.

Adults Only

William Stafford (1914–   )

Animals own a fur world;
people own worlds that are variously, pleasingly, bare.
And the way these worlds *are* once arrived for us kids with a jolt,
that night when the wild woman danced
in the giant cage we found we were all in
at the state fair.

Better women exist, no doubt, than that one,
and occasions more edifying, too, I suppose.
But we have to witness for ourselves what comes for us,
nor be distracted by barkers of irrelevant ware;   10
and a pretty good world, I say, arrived that night
when that woman came farming right out of her clothes,
by God,

At the state fair.

The Plot against the Giant

Wallace Stevens (1879–1955)

First Girl

When this yokel comes maundering,
Whetting his hacker,
I shall run before him,
Diffusing the civilest odors
Out of geraniums and unsmelled flowers.
It will check him.

Second Girl

I shall run before him,
Arching cloths besprinkled with colors
As small as fish-eggs.
The threads
Will abash him.

10

Third Girl

Oh, la . . . le pauvre![1]
I shall run before him,
With a curious puffing.
He will bend his ear then.
I shall whisper
Heavenly labials in a world of gutturals.
It will undo him.

1 The poor thing.

Poets to Come
Walt Whitman (1819–1892)

Poets to come! orators, singers, musicians to come!
Not to-day is to justify me and answer what I am for,
But you, a new brood, native, athletic, continental, greater than
      before known,
Arouse! for you must justify me.

I myself but write one or two indicative words for the future,
I but advance a moment only to wheel and hurry back in the
      darkness.

I am a man who, sauntering along without fully stopping, turns a
      casual look upon you and then averts his face.
Leaving it to you to prove and define it,
Expecting the main things from you.

I hear America Singing
Walt Whitman (1819–1892)

I HEAR America singing, the varied carols I hear,
Those of mechanics, each one singing his as it should be blithe
   and strong,
The carpenter singing his as he measures his plank or beam,
The mason singing his as he makes ready for work, or leaves
   off work,
The boatman singing what belongs to him in his boat,
   the deck-hand singing on the steamboat deck,
The shoemaker singing as he sits on his bench, the hatter
   singing as he stands,
The wood-cutter's song, the plowboy's on his way in the
   morning, or at noon intermission or at sundown,
The delicious singing of the mother, or of the young wife
   at work, or of the girl sewing or washing,

Each singing what belongs to him or her and to none else,
The day what belongs to the day—at night the party of young
    fellows, robust, friendly,   10
Singing with open mouths their strong melodious songs.

This Is Just to Say[1]
William Carlos Williams (1883–1962)

I have eaten
the plums
that were in
the icebox

and which
you were probably
saving
for breakfast

Forgive me
they were delicious   10
so sweet
and so cold.

1 See "Variations on a Theme by William Carlos Williams" on page 20.

CHILDHOOD, YOUTH, MATURITY, OLD AGE

Boyhood was a crime he had once committed.

Norman MacCaig

The Ball Poem
John Berryman (1914–1972)

What is the boy now, who has lost his ball,
What what is he to do? I saw it go
Merrily bouncing, down the street, and then
Merrily over—there it is in the water!
No use to say "O there are other balls":
An ultimate shaking grief fixes the boy
As he stands rigid, trembling, staring down
All his young days into the harbour where
His ball went. I would not intrude on him,
A dime, another ball, is worthless. Now   10
He senses first his responsibility
In a world of possessions. People will take balls,
Balls will be lost always, litte boy,
And no one buys a ball back. Money is external.
He is learning, far behind his desperate eyes,
The epistemology of loss, how to stand up.
Knowing what every man must one day know
And most know many days, how to stand up.
And gradually light returns to the street,
A whistle blows, the ball is out of sight,   20
Soon part of me will explore the deep and dark
Floor of the harbour. I am everywhere,
I suffer and move, my mind and my heart move
With all that move me, under the water
Or whistling, I am not a little boy.

Nurse's Song
William Blake (1757–1827)

When the voices of children are heard on the green
And whisp'rings are in the dale,
The days of my youth rise fresh in my mind,
My face turns green and pale.

Then come home, my children, the sun is gone down
And the dews of night arise;
Your spring and your day are wasted in play,
And your winter and night in disguise.

So we'll go no more a-roving

George Gordon, Lord Byron (1788–1824)

So we'll go no more a-roving
  So late into the night,
Though the heart be still as loving,
  And the moon be still as bright.

For the sword outwears its sheath,
  And the soul wears out the breast,
And the heart must pause to breathe,
  And Love itself have rest.

Though the night was made for loving,
  And the day returns too soon,   10
Yet we'll go no more a-roving
  By the light of the moon.

If I could only live at the pitch that is near madness

Richard Eberhart (1904–   )

If I could only live at the pitch that is near madness
When everything is as it was in my childhood
Violent, vivid, and of infinite possibility:
That the sun and the moon broke over my head.

Then I cast time out of the trees and fields,
Then I stood immaculate in the Ego;
Then I eyed the world with all delight,
Reality was the perfection of my sight.

And time has big handles on the hands,
Fields and trees a way of being themselves.   10
I saw battalions of the race of mankind
Standing stolid, demanding a moral answer.

I gave the moral answer and I died
And into a realm of complexity came
Where nothing is possible but necessity
And the truth wailing there like a red babe.

Those Winter Sundays

Robert Hayden (1913–   )

Sundays too my father got up early
and put his clothes on in the blueblack cold,
then with cracked hands that ached
from labor in the weekday weather made
banked fires blaze. No one ever thanked him.

I'd wake and hear the cold splintering, breaking.
When the rooms were warm, he'd call,
and slowly I would rise and dress,
fearing the chronic angers of that house,

Speaking indifferently to him,   10
who had driven out the cold
and polished my good shoes as well.
What did I know, what did I know
of love's austere and lonely offices?

Spring and Fall: To a Young Child

Gerard Manley Hopkins (1844–1889)

Margaret, are you grieving
Over Goldengrove unleaving?
Leaves, like the things of man, you
With your fresh thoughts care for, can you?
Ah! as the heart grows older
It will come to such sights colder
By and by, nor spare a sigh
Though worlds of wanwood leafmeal lie;
And yet you will weep and know why.
Now no matter, child, the name: 10
Sorrow's springs are the same.
Nor mouth had, no nor mind, expressed
What heart heard of, ghost guessed:
It is the blight man was born for,
It is Margaret you mourn for.

Loveliest of Trees

A. E. Housman (1859–1936)

Loveliest of trees, the cherry now
Is hung with bloom along the bough,
And stands about the woodland ride,
Wearing white for Eastertide.

Now, of my threescore years and ten,
Twenty will not come again,
And take from seventy springs a score,
It only leaves me fifty more.

And since to look at things in bloom
Fifty springs are little room,   10
About the woodlands I will go
To see the cherry hung with snow.

To Autumn

John Keats (1795–1821)

Season of mists and mellow fruitfulness,
  Close bosom-friend of the maturing sun;
Conspiring with him how to load and bless
  With fruit the vines that round the thatch-eves run;
To bend with apples the mossed cottage-trees,
  And fill all fruit with ripeness to the core;
    To swell the gourd, and plump the hazel shells
With a sweet kernel; to set budding more,
  And still more, later flowers for the bees,
  Until they think warm days will never cease,   10
    For Summer has o'er-brimmed their clammy cells.

Who hath not seen thee oft amid thy store?
  Sometimes whoever seeks abroad may find
Thee sitting careless on a granary floor,
  Thy hair soft-lifted by the winnowing wind;
Or on a half-reaped furrow sound asleep,
  Drowsed with the fume of poppies, while thy hook
    Spares the next swath and all its twinèd flowers:
And sometimes like a gleaner thou dost keep
  Steady thy laden head across a brook;   20
  Or by a cider-press, with patient look,
    Thou watchest the last oozings hours by hours.

Where are the songs of Spring? Ay, where are they?
  Think not of them, thou hast thy music too,—
While barrèd clouds bloom the soft-dying day,
  And touch the stubble-plains with rosy hue;
Then in a wailful choir the small gnats mourn
  Among the river sallows,[1] borne aloft
    Or sinking as the light wind lives or dies;
And full-grown lambs loud bleat from hilly bourn,[2]   30
  Hedge-crickets sing; and now with treble soft
  The red-breast whistles from a garden-croft;
    And gathering swallows twitter in the skies.

1 Willows. 2 Boundary.

Family
Norman MacCaig (1910–   )

The father raised words
like gentle whiplashes. His eyes
were Mosaic with a dubious wisdom. Boyhood
was a crime he had once committed.

The mother wept secretly inside
her joy. She knew every new word
was an argument against her, that the first steps
were the beginning of a long journey.

The little boy's eyes were frightened
but would not close. He stared   10
beyond the serpent in the apple tree
to the round sweet dangerous apple.

"Dover Beach"—a Note to That Poem[1]
Archibald MacLeish (1892–   )

                          The wave withdrawing
Withers with seaward rustle of flimsy water
Sucking the sand down, dragging at empty shells,
The roil after it settling, too smooth, smothered . . .

After forty a man's fool to wait in the
Sea's face for the full force and the roaring of
Surf to come over him: droves of careening water.
After forty the tug's out and the salt and the
Sea follow it: less sound and violence.
Nevertheless the ebb has its own beauty—   10
Shells sand and all and the whispering rustle.
There's earth in it then and the bubbles of foam gone.

1 See "Dover Beach" by Matthew Arnold, p. 177.

Moreover—and this too has its lovely uses—
It's the outward wave that spills the inward forward
Tripping the proud piled mute virginal
Mountain of water in wallowing welter of light and
Sound enough—thunder for miles back. It's a fine and a
Wild smother to vanish in: pulling down—
Tripping with outward ebb the urgent inward.

Speaking alone for myself it's the steep hill and the 20
Toppling lift of the young men I am toward now—
Waiting for that as the wave for the next wave.
Let them go over us all I say with the thunder of
What's to be next in the world. It's we will be under it!

How Soon Hath Time

John Milton (1608–1674)

How soon hath Time, the subtle thief of youth,
  Stolen on his wing my three and twentieth year!
  My hasting days fly on with full career,
  But my late spring no bud or blossom show'th.
Perhaps my semblance might deceive the truth,
  That I to manhood am arrived so near,
  And inward ripeness doth much less appear,
  That some more timely-happy spirits endu'th.
Yet be it less or more, or soon or slow,
  It shall be still in strictest measure even 10
  To that same lot, however mean or high,
Toward which Time leads me, and the will of heaven;
  All is, if I have grace to use it so,
  As ever in my great Taskmaster's eye.

Like Any Other Man

Gregory Orr (1947–   )

Like any other man

I was born with a knife
in one hand
and a wound in the other.

In the house where I lived
all the mirrors
were painted black.

So many years
before the soft key of your tongue
unlocked my body.

Mr. Flood's Party

Edwin Arlington Robinson (1869–1935)

Old Eben Flood, climbing alone one night
Over the hill between the town below
And the forsaken upland hermitage
That held as much as he should ever know
On earth again of home, paused warily.
The road was his with not a native near;
And Eben, having leisure, said aloud,
For no man else in Tilbury Town to hear:

"Well, Mr. Flood, we have the harvest moon
Again, and we may not have many more;   10
The bird is on the wing, the poet says,
And you and I have said it here before.
Drink to the bird." He raised up to the light
The jug that he had gone so far to fill,

And answered huskily: "Well, Mr. Flood,
Since you propose it, I believe I will."

Alone, as if enduring to the end
A valiant armor of scarred hopes outworn,
He stood there in the middle of the road
Like Roland's ghost winding a silent horn.   20
Below him, in the town among the trees,
Where friends of other days had honored him,
A phantom salutation of the dead
Rang thinly till old Eben's eyes were dim.

Then, as a mother lays her sleeping child
Down tenderly, fearing it may awake,
He set the jug down slowly at his feet
With trembling care, knowing that most things break;
And only when assured that on firm earth
It stood, as the uncertain lives of men   30
Assuredly did not, he paced away,
And with his hand extended paused again:

"Well, Mr. Flood, we have not met like this
In a long time; and many a change has come
To both of us, I fear, since last it was
We had a drop together. Welcome home!"
Convivially returning with himself,
Again he raised the jug up to the light;
And with an acquiescent quaver said:
"Well, Mr. Flood, if you insist, I might.   40

"Only a very little, Mr. Flood—
For auld lang syne. No more, sir; that will do."
So, for the time, apparently it did,
And Eben evidently thought so too;
For soon amid the silver loneliness
Of night he lifted up his voice and sang,
Secure, with only two moons listening,
Until the whole harmonious landscape rang—

"For auld lang syne." The weary throat gave out,
The last word wavered; and the song being done,   50

He raised again the jug regretfully
And shook his head, and was again alone.
There was not much that was ahead of him,
And there was nothing in the town below—
Where strangers would have shut the many doors
That many friends had opened long ago.

My Papa's Waltz
Theodore Roethke (1908–1963)

The whiskey on your breath
Could make a small boy dizzy;
But I held on like death:
Such waltzing was not easy.

We romped until the pans
Slid from the kitchen shelf;
My mother's countenance
Could not unfrown itself.

The hand that held my wrist
Was battered on one knuckle;   10
At every step I missed
My right ear scraped a buckle.

You beat time on my head
With a palm caked hard by dirt,
Then waltzed me off to bed
Still clinging to your shirt.

Rondel

Muriel Rukeyser (1913–   )

Now that I am fifty-six
Come and celebrate with me—

What happens to song and sex
Now that I am fifty-six

They dance, but differently,
Death and distance in the mix;
Now that I'm fifty-six
Come and celebrate with me.

Her Kind

Anne Sexton (1928–1974)

I have gone out, a possessed witch,
haunting the black air, braver at night;
dreaming evil, I have done my hitch
over the plain houses, light by light:
lonely thing, twelve-fingered, out of mind.
A woman like that is not a woman, quite.
I have been her kind.

I have found the warm caves in the woods,
filled them with skillets, carvings, shelves,
closets, silks, innumerable goods;   10
fixed the suppers for the worms and the elves:
whining, rearranging the disaligned.
A woman like that is misunderstood.
I have been her kind.

I have ridden in your cart, driver,
waved my nude arms at villages going by,

learning the last bright routes, survivor
where your flames still bite my thigh
and my ribs crack where your wheels wind.
A woman like that is not ashamed to die.
I have been her kind.

20

That time of year thou mayst in me behold
Sonnet 73
William Shakespeare (1564–1616)

That time of year thou mayst in me behold
When yellow leaves, or none, or few, do hang
Upon those boughs which shake against the cold,
Bare ruined choirs, where late the sweet birds sang;
In me thou see'st the twilight of such day
As after sunset fadeth in the west.
Which by and by black night doth take away,
Death's second self, that seals up all in rest.
In me thou see'st the glowing of such fire
That on the ashes of its youth doth lie,
As the death-bed whereon it must expire,
Consumed with that which it was nourished by.
This thou perceiv'st, which makes thy love more strong,
To love that well which thou must leave ere long.

10

Looking at Pictures to Be Put Away
Gary Snyder (1930–   )

Who was this girl
In her white night gown
Clutching a pair of jeans

On a foggy redwood deck.
She looks up at me tender.
Calm, surprised,

What will we remember
Bodies thick with food and lovers
After twenty years.

as i look out

Laura St. Martin (1957–   )

as i look out from the desk window
fingering the new books
i see a quiet afternoon
caught in a crack between summer and fall
summer is evaporating on the lawns
and i watch in deep brown anticipation
as the fog which held that last warm night
takes away the flowered dresses
suntanned legs and swimming pools
thin clouds and sunlight argued over the morning   10
mornings that still whisper bandanas and beaches
but Fall will have it all soon
when her sharp breath blows away any lingering
and sends us scurrying back to schoolhouses all bundled up
scurrying back to realities and glories on the wane

In the Orchard

Muriel Stuart (1889–   )

'I THOUGHT you loved me.' 'No, it was only fun.'
'When we stood there, closer than all?' 'Well, the harvest moon
Was shining and queer in your hair, and it turned my head.'
'That made you?' 'Yes.' 'Just the moon and the light it made
Under the tree?' 'Well, your mouth, too.' 'Yes, my mouth?'
'And the quiet there that sang like the drum in the booth.
You shouldn't have danced like that.' 'Like what?' 'So close,
With your head turned up, and the flower in your hair, a rose
That smelt all warm.' 'I loved you. I thought you knew
I wouldn't have danced like that with any but you.'   10
'I didn't know. I thought you knew it was fun.'
'I thought it was love you meant.' 'Well, it's done.' 'Yes, it's done.
I've seen boys stone a blackbird, and watched them drown
A kitten . . . it clawed at the reeds, and they pushed it down
Into the pool while it screamed. Is that fun, too?'
'Well, boys are like that . . . Your brothers . . .' 'Yes, I know.
But you, so lovely and strong! Not you! Not you!'
'They don't understand it's cruel. It's only a game.'
'And are girls fun, too?' 'No, still in a way it's the same.
It's queer and lovely to have a girl . . .' 'Go on.'   20
'It makes you mad for a bit to feel she's your own,
And you laugh and kiss her, and maybe you give her a ring,
But it's only in fun.' 'But I gave you everything.'
'Well, you shouldn't have done it. You know what a fellow thinks
When a girl does that.' 'Yes, he talks of her over his drinks
And calls her a—' 'Stop that now. I thought you knew.'
'But it wasn't with anyone else. It was only you.'
'How did I know? I thought you wanted it too.
I thought you were like the rest. Well, what's to be done?'
'To be done?' 'Is it all right?' 'Yes.' 'Sure?' 'Yes, but why?'   30
'I don't know. I thought you were going to cry.
You said you had something to tell me.' 'Yes, I know.
It wasn't anything really . . . I think I'll go.'
'Yes, it's late. There's thunder about, a drop of rain
Fell on my hand in the dark. I'll see you again
At the dance next week. You're sure that everything's right?'
'Yes.' 'Well, I'll be going.' 'Kiss me . . .' 'Good night.' . . . 'Good
    night.'

Ulysses

Alfred, Lord Tennyson (1809–1892)

It little profits that an idle king,
By this still hearth, among these barren crags,
Matched with an aged wife, I mete and dole
Unequal laws unto a savage race
That hoard, and sleep, and feed, and know not me.
I cannot rest from travel: I will drink
Life to the lees: all times I have enjoyed
Greatly, have suffered greatly, both with those
That loved me, and alone; on shore, and when
Through scudding drifts the rainy Hyades   10
Vexed the dim sea: I am become a name;
For always roaming with a hungry heart
Much have I seen and known; cities of men
And manners, climates, councils, governments,
Myself not least, but honored of them all;
And drunk delight of battle with my peers,
Far on the ringing plains of windy Troy.
I am a part of all that I have met;
Yet all experience is an arch wherethrough
Gleams that untravelled world, whose margin fades   20
For ever and for ever when I move.
How dull it is to pause, to make an end,
To rust unburnished, not to shine in use!
As though to breathe were life. Life piled on life
Were all too little, and of one to me
Little remains: but every hour is saved
From that eternal silence, something more,
A bringer of new things; and vile it were
For some three suns to store and hoard myself,
And this gray spirit yearning in desire   30
To follow knowledge like a sinking star,
Beyond the utmost bound of human thought.
    This is my son, mine own Telemachus,
To whom I leave the scepter and the isle—
Well-loved of me, discerning to fulfil
This labor, by slow prudence to make mild
A rugged people, and through soft degrees

Subdue them to the useful and the good.
Most blameless is he, centered in the sphere
Of common duties, decent not to fail   40
In offices of tenderness, and pay
Meet[1] adoration to my household gods
When I am gone. He works his work, I mine.
   There lies the port: the vessel puffs her sail;
There gloom the dark broad seas. My mariners,
Souls that have toiled, and wrought, and thought with me—
That ever with a frolic welcome took
The thunder and the sunshine, and opposed
Free hearts, free foreheads—you and I are old;
Old age hath yet his honor and his toil;   50
Death closes all: but something ere the end,
Some work of noble note, may yet be done,
Not unbecoming men that strove with gods.
The lights begin to twinkle from the rocks:
The long day wanes: the slow moon climbs: the deep
Moans round with many voices. Come, my friends,
'Tis not too late to seek a newer world.
Push off, and sitting well in order smite
The sounding furrows; for my purpose holds
To sail beyond the sunset and the baths   60
Of all the western stars, until I die.
It may be that the gulfs will wash us down:
It may be we shall touch the Happy Isles
And see the great Achilles, whom we knew.
Though much is taken, much abides; and though
We are not now that strength which in old days
Moved earth and heaven, that which we are, we are;
One equal temper of heroic hearts,
Made weak by time and fate but strong in will
To strive, to seek, to find, and not to yield.   70

1 Suitable, proper.

The Retreat

Henry Vaughan (1622–1695)

Happy those early days, when I
Shined in my angel-infancy!
Before I understood this place
Appointed for my second race,
Or taught my soul to fancy aught
But a white, celestial thought;
When yet I had not walked above
A mile or two from my first love,
And looking back—at that short space—
Could see a glimpse of his bright face;   10
When on some gilded cloud or flower
My gazing soul would dwell an hour,
And in those weaker glories spy
Some shadows of eternity;
Before I taught my tongue to wound
My conscience with a sinful sound,
Or had the black art to dispense
A several sin to every sense,
But felt through all this fleshly dress
Bright shoots of everlastingness.   20
   O, how I long to travel back,
And tread again that ancient track!
That I might once more reach that plain
Where first I left my glorious train;
From whence the enlightened spirit sees
That shady city of palm trees.
But ah! my soul with too much stay
Is drunk, and staggers in the way!
Some men a forward motion love,
But I by backward steps would move;   30
And when this dust falls to the urn,
In that state I came, return.

Anne and the Peacock
Noel Welch

Infant she played in the shadow
of its vigilant fan.

At twelve discovered, by accident,
why fans are spread.

At nineteen her dress swept the lawn
as elegantly as any tail.

At twenty-eight for one dazzling moment
she rivalled its splendor.

At forty followed the disappearing glory
down long walks between formal hedges.   10

Now watched by a hundred callous eyes
she sits in a high-backed wicker chair

twisting the emerald rings on her thin fingers:
dead leaves pile round her feet.

Politics
William Butler Yeats (1865–1939)

In our time the destiny of man presents its meaning in political terms.
                                                    Thomas Mann

How can I, that girl standing there,
My attention fix
On Roman or on Russian
Or on Spanish politics?
Yet here's a travelled man that knows
What he talks about,

And there's a politician
That has read and thought,
And maybe what they say is true
Of war and war's alarms,
But O that I were young again
And held her in my arms!

SOCIAL CONSCIENCE

*when the sign
says DONT WALK
crawl*

Robert Hershon

West London

Matthew Arnold (1822–1888)

Crouched on the pavement close by Belgrave Square,
A tramp I saw, ill, moody, and tongue-tied;
A babe was in her arms, and at her side
A girl; their clothes were rags, their feet were bare.
Some labouring men, whose work lay somewhere there,
Passed opposite; she touched her girl, who hied
Across and begged, and came back satisfied.
The rich she had let pass with frozen stare.
Thought I: Above her state this spirit towers;
She will not ask of aliens, but of friends,   10
Of sharers in a common human fate.
She turns from that cold succor, which attends
The unknown little from the unknowing great,
And points us to a better time than ours.

The Unknown Citizen

(To JS/07/M378
This Marble Monument
Is Erected by the State)

W. H. Auden (1907–1973)

He was found by the Bureau of Statistics to be
One against whom there was no official complaint,
And all the reports on his conduct agree
That, in the modern sense of an old-fashioned word, he was a
    saint,
For in everything he did he served the Greater Community.
Except for the War till the day he retired
He worked in a factory and never got fired,
But satisfied his employers, Fudge Motors Inc.
Yet he wasn't a scab or odd in his views,

For his Union reports that he paid his dues, 10
(Our report on his Union shows it was sound)
And our Social Psychology workers found
That he was popular with his mates and liked a drink.
The Press are convinced that he bought a paper every day
And that his reactions to advertisements were normal in every
way.
Policies taken out in his name prove that he was fully insured,
And his Health-card shows he was once in hospital but left it
cured.
Both Producers Research and High-Grade Living declare
He was fully sensible to the advantages of the Instalment Plan
And had everything necessary to the Modern Man, 20
A phonograph, a radio, a car and a frigidaire.
Our researchers into Public Opinion are content
That he held the proper opinions for the time of year;
When there was peace, he was for peace; when there was war,
he went.
He was married and added five children to the population,
Which our Eugenist[1] says was the right number for a parent
of his generation,
And our teachers report that he never interfered with their
education.
Was he free? Was he happy? The question is absurd:
Had anything been wrong, we should certainly have heard.

1 Eugenicist.

Formal Application
Donald W. Baker (1923–   )

"The poets apparently want to rejoin the human race."   Time

I shall begin by learning to throw
the knife, first at trees, until it sticks
in the trunk and quivers every time;

next from a chair, using only wrist

and fingers, at a thing on the ground,
a fresh ant hill or a fallen leaf,

then at a moving object, perhaps
a pieplate swinging on twine, until
I pot it at least twice in three tries.

Meanwhile, I shall be teaching the birds
that the skinny fellow in sneakers
is a source of suet and bread crumbs,

first putting them on a shingle nailed
to a pine tree, next scattering them
on the needles, closer and closer

to my seat, until the proper bird,
a towhee, I think, in black and rust
and gray, takes tossed crumbs six feet away.

Finally, I shall coordinate
conditioned reflex and functional
form and qualify as Modern Man.

You see the splash of blood and feathers
and the blade pinning it to the tree?
It's called an "Audubon Crucifix."

The phrase has pleasing (even pious)
connotations, like *Arbeit Macht Frei*,[1]
"Molotov Cocktail," and *Enola Gay*.[2]

10

20

1 The slogan of the Nazi party: "Labor liberates."   2 The American plane
that dropped the A-bomb on Hiroshima.

Holy Thursday
William Blake (1757–1827)

Is this a holy thing to see
In a rich and fruitful land,
Babes reduced to misery,
Fed with cold and usurous hand?

Is that trembling cry a song?
Can it be a song of joy?
And so many children poor?
It is a land of poverty!

And their sun does never shine,
And their fields are bleak and bare,   10
And their ways are filled with thorns:
It is eternal winter there.

For where'er the sun does shine,
And where'er the rain does fall,
Babe can never hunger there,
Nor poverty the mind appall.

London
William Blake (1757–1827)

I wander through each chartered[1] street,
Near where the chartered Thames does flow,
And mark in every face I meet
Marks of weakness, marks of woe.

In every cry of every man
In every infant's cry of fear,
In every voice, in every ban,[2]
The mind-forged manacles I hear.

1 Incorporated, constricted.   2 Prohibited activity.

How the chimney-sweeper's cry
Every black'ning church appalls;
And the hapless soldier's sigh
Runs in blood down palace walls.

But most through midnight streets I hear
How the youthful harlot's curse
Blasts the new-born infant's tear,
And blights with plagues the marriage hearse.

10

Rotation

Julian Bond (1940–   )

Like plump green floor plans
the pool tables squat
Among fawning mahogany Buddhas with felt heads.
Like clubwomen blessed with adultery
The balls dart to kiss
and tumble erring members into silent oblivion.
Right-angled over the verdant barbered turf
Sharks point long fingers at the multi-colored worlds
and play at percussion
Sounding cheap plastic clicks
in an 8-ball universe built for ivory.

10

Incident

Countee Cullen (1903–1946)

Once riding in old Baltimore,
    Heart-filled, head-filled with glee,
I saw a Baltimorean
Keep looking straight at me.

Now I was eight and very small,
   And he was no whit bigger,
And so I smiled, but he poked out
   His tongue and called me, "Nigger."

I saw the whole of Baltimore
   From May until December: 10
Of all the things that happened there
   That's all that I remember.

In Goya's Greatest Scenes
Lawrence Ferlinghetti (1919–   )

In Goya's greatest scenes we seem to see
                  the people of the world
    exactly at the moment when
        they first attained the title of
                'suffering humanity'
      They writhe upon the page
            in a veritable rage
                of adversity
     Heaped up
       groaning with babies and bayonets   10
               under cement skies
   in an abstract landscape of blasted trees
     bent statues bats wings and beaks
       slippery gibbets
    cadavers and carnivorous cocks
    and all the final hollering monsters
       of the
           'imagination of disaster'
   they are so bloody real
          it is as if they really still existed   20

    And they do

> Only the landscape is changed
> They still are ranged along the roads
> plagued by legionaires
> false windmills and demented roosters

> They are the same people
> only further from home
> on freeways fifty lanes wide
> on a concrete continent
> spaced with bland billboards
> illustrating imbecile illusions of happiness   30

> The scene shows fewer tumbrils
> but more maimed citizens
> in painted cars
> and they have strange license plates
> and engines
> that devour America

Uptown

Allen Ginsberg (1926–   )

Yellow-lit Budweiser signs over oaken bars,
"I've seen everything"—the bartender handing me change of $10,
I stared at him amiably eyes thru an obvious Adamic beard—
with Montana musicians homeless in Manhattan, teen age
curly hair themselves—we sat at the antique booth & gossiped,
Madame Grady's literary salon a curious value in New York—
"If I had my way, I'd cut off your hair and send you to
    Vietnam"—
"Bless you then" I replied to a hatted thin citizen hurrying to the
    barroom door
upon wet dark Amsterdam Avenue decades later—
"And if I couldn't do that I'd cut your throat" he snarled
    farewell,   10
and "Bless you sir" I added as he went to his fate in the rain,
    dapper Irishman.

Night, Death, Mississippi

Robert Hayden (1913–   )

I.

A quavering cry. Screech-owl?
Or one of them?
The old man in his reek
and gauntness laughs—

One of them, I bet—
and turns out the kitchen lamp,
limping to the porch to listen
in the windowless night.

Be there with Boy and the rest
if I was well again.   10
Time was. Time was.
White robes like moonlight

In the sweetgum dark.
Unbucked that one then
and him squealing bloody Jesus
as we cut it off.

Time was. A cry?
A cry all right.
He hawks and spits,
fevered as by groinfire.   20

Have us a bottle,
Boy and me—
he's earned him a bottle—
when he gets home.

II.

Then we beat them, he said,
beat them till our arms was tired
and the big old chains
messy and red.

O Jesus burning on the lily cross

Christ, it was better
than hunting bear
which don't know why
you want him dead.

O night, rawhead and bloodybones night

You kids fetch Paw
some water now so's he
can wash that blood
off him, she said.

O night betrayed by darkness not its own

How to Walk in a Crowd
Robert Hershon (1936–   )

never pass a nun
on the left

never walk behind
children
they hold hands

never look up
you'll trip
on the blind man's
dog

watch for people
growing apart

10

never be afraid
of gutters holes
cracks pale canes
sleeping cops

never stop
for greetings
it's a plot

when the sign
says DONT WALK
crawl

20

the woman beside
you at the curb
has fallen dead
she'll get
a ticket

I, Too

Langston Hughes (1902–1967)

I, too, sing America.

I am the darker brother.
They send me to eat in the kitchen
When company comes,
But I laugh
And eat well,
And grow strong.

Tomorrow,
I'll be at the table
When company comes.

10

Nobody'll dare
Say to me,
"Eat in the kitchen,"
Then.

Besides,
They'll see how beautiful I am
And be ashamed—

I, too, am America.

Shine, Perishing Republic
Robinson Jeffers (1887–1962)

While this America settles in the mould of its vulgarity, heavily
   thickening to empire,
And protest, only a bubble in the molten mass, pops and sighs
   out, and the mass hardens,

I sadly smiling remember that the flower fades to make fruit, the
   fruit rots to make earth.
Out of the mother; and through the spring exultances, ripeness
   and decadence; and home to the mother.

You making haste haste on decay: not blameworthy; life is good,
   be it stubbornly long or suddenly   10
A mortal splendor: meteors are not needed less than mountains:
   shine, perishing republic.

But for my children, I would have them keep their distance from
   the thickening center; corruption
Never has been compulsory, when the cities lie at the monster's
   feet there are left the mountains.

And boys, be in nothing so moderate as in love of man, a clever
   servant, insufferable master.
There is the trap that catches noblest spirits, that caught—they
   say—God, when he walked on earth.   20

The Warden Said to Me the Other Day
Etheridge Knight (1933–   )

The warden said to me the other day
(innocently, I think), "Say, etheridge,
why come the black boys don't run off
like the white boys do?"
I lowered my jaw and scratched my head
and said (innocently, I think), "Well, suh,
I ain't for sure, but I reckon it's cause
we ain't got no wheres to run to."

The Plot to Assassinate the Chase Manhattan Bank

Carl Larsen (1935–   )

To assassinate the Chase Manhattan Bank
Is not as easy as you'd think.
I walked in, see, and yelled "Kings-X!"
and saw what looked like great machines
come rumbling to a halt, and I thought,
fine—I'm halfway home. Then God rose from
the Office of the President,
a little miffed, I think, and said,
"What's on your mind?"
"I came up from the Coast," I said,   10
"to blow this pad to—if you will
excuse my pun—to Kingdom Come."
"You can't do that, my Son," he said,
and that's how I knew he was God,
although he looked a great deal
like John Wayne. "You wouldn't want,"
he said, "to do away with this—"
and from each teller's cage, a flock
of rainbow doves flew up, and settled
near the roof. "Put down your bomb,   20
let's have a talk," he said, and smiled.
I laid aside the bomb and followed him
into his office, and sat down.
"The Proletariat demands," I said,
"You cease this madness"; And he
smiled again. I saw he had a golden tooth.
"Some for the glories of this world,"
God said, then showed a picture of his family,
and then his house, a nice split-level
place up in the Bronx. His wife,   30
a pleasant-looking woman,
had inscribed it: "Love, In God We Trust."
He wiped away the tears that gathered
in the corners of his steely eyes,
choked back a sob, and called The Fuzz.
Inside a minute, forty cops popped from
the walls and drawers, came running from

the vault where God kept love, and
clamped the irons around my feet.
"Now Jean Valjean,"[1] God shouted,   40
gaining his composure, "now you'll
face the rack!" I pleaded it was all
a joke. I said I'd be a good li'l boy
and stay home playing with my spiders
if he'd let me go. But his bit was not
forgiveness, and they locked me in
a dungeon full of nasty things he had
discarded, like the stars,
and sea-foam, and the earth.

1 The protagonist of Victor Hugo's novel *Les Misérables*, the theme of
which is the injustice of justice implacably applied.

Assassination

Don L. Lee (1942–   )

it was wild.
the
bullet hit high.
                    (the throat-neck)
& from everywhere,
        the motel, from under bushes and cars,
        from around corners and across streets,
        out of the garbage cans and from rat holes
        in the earth
they came running.   10
with
guns
    drawn
    they came running
toward the King—
                    all of them
                    fast and sure—

as if
the King
was going to fire back.   20
they came running,
fast and sure,
in the
wrong
direction.

Auto Wreck

Karl Shapiro (1913–   )

Its quick soft silver bell beating, beating
And down the dark one ruby flare
Pulsing out red light like an artery,
The ambulance at top speed floating down
Past beacons and illuminated clocks
Wings in a heavy curve, dips down,
And brakes speed, entering the crowd.
The doors leap open, emptying light;
Stretchers are laid out, the mangled lifted
And stowed into the little hospital.   10
Then the bell, breaking the hush, tolls once,
And the ambulance with its terrible cargo
Rocking, slightly rocking, moves away,
As the doors, an afterthought, are closed.

We are deranged, walking among the cops
Who sweep glass and are large and composed.
One is still making notes under the light.
One with a bucket douches ponds of blood
Into the street and gutter.
One hangs lanterns on the wrecks that cling,   20
Empty husks of locusts, to iron poles.

Our throats were tight as tourniquets,
Our feet were bound with splints, but now
Like convalescents intimate and gauche,

We speak through sickly smiles and warn
With the stubborn saw of common sense,
The grim joke and the banal resolution.
The traffic moves around with care,
But we remain, touching a wound
That opens to our richest horror.   30

Already old, the question Who shall die?
Becomes unspoken Who is innocent?
For death in war is done by hands;
Suicide has cause and stillbirth, logic.
But this invites the occult mind,
Cancels our physics with a sneer,
And spatters all we knew of dénouement
Across the expedient and wicked stones.

England in 1819
Percy Bysshe Shelley (1792–1822)

An old, mad, blind, despised, and dying king,[1]
Princes, the dregs of their dull race, who flow
Through public scorn—mud from a muddy spring:
Rulers who neither see, nor feel, nor know,
But leech-like to their fainting country cling,
Till they drop, blind in blood, without a blow;
A people starved and *stabbed in the untilled field*,[2]
An army, which liberticide and prey
Makes as a two-edged sword to all who wield;
Golden and sanguine laws which tempt and slay;   10
Religion Christless, Godless—a book sealed;
A Senate—Time's worst statute unrepealed,—
Are graves, from which a glorious Phantom may
Burst to illumine our tempestuous day.

1 George III. 2 A reference to Peterloo, the Manchester massacre in
which over 600 people, men, women, and children, were killed by the
Yeomenry called out to arrest the speakers addressing a large, wholly
peaceful crowd demanding parliamentary reform. Countrywide indignation
eventually contributed largely to the success of the reform movement.

An Elementary School Classroom in a Slum
Stephen Spender (1909–   )

Far far from gusty waves, these children's faces.
Like rootless weeds the torn hair round their paleness.
The tall girl with her weighed-down head. The paper-
seeming boy with rat's eyes. The stunted unlucky heir
Of twisted bones, reciting a father's gnarled disease,
His lesson from his desk. At back of the dim class,
One unnoted, sweet and young: his eyes live in a dream
Of squirrels' game, in tree room, other than this.

On sour cream walls, donations. Shakespeare's head
Cloudless at dawn, civilized dome riding all cities.   10
Belled, flowery, Tyrolese valley. Open-handed map
Awarding the world its world. And yet, for these
Children, these windows, not this world, are world,
Where all their future's painted with a fog,
A narrow street sealed in with a lead sky,
Far far from rivers, capes, and stars of words.

Surely Shakespeare is wicked, the map a bad example
With ships and sun and love tempting them to steal—
For lives that slyly turn in their cramped holes
From fog to endless night? On their slag heap, these children   20
Wear skins peeped through by bones and spectacles of steel
With mended glass, like bottle bits in slag.
All of their time and space are foggy slum
So blot their maps with slums as big as doom.

Unless, governor, teacher, inspector, visitor,
This map becomes their window and these windows
That open on their lives like crouching tombs
Break, O break open, till they break the town
And show the children to the fields and all their world
Azure on their sands, to let their tongues   30
Run naked into books, the white and green leaves open
The history theirs whose language is the sun.

A Description of the Morning
Jonathan Swift (1667–1745)

Now hardly here and there an hackney-coach
Appearing, showed the ruddy morn's approach.
Now Betty from her master's bed had flown,
And softly stole to discompose her own.
The slipshod 'prentice from his master's door,
Had pared the dirt, and sprinkled round the floor.
Now Moll had whirled her mop with dext'rous airs,
Prepared to scrub the entry and the stairs.
The youth with broomy stumps began to trace
The kennel edge, where wheels had worn the place.   10
The small-coal man was heard with cadence deep,
'Till drowned in shriller notes of chimney sweep,
Duns at his lordship's gate began to meet,
And brickdust Moll had screamed through half a street.
The turnkey now his flock returning sees,
Duly let out a-nights to steal for fees.
The watchful bailiffs take their silent stands;
And schoolboys lag with satchels in their hands.

Epitaph on the World
Henry David Thoreau (1817–1862)

Here lies the body of this world,
Whose soul alas to hell is hurled.
This golden youth long since was past,
Its silver manhood went as fast,
And iron age drew on at last;
'Tis vain its character to tell,
The several fates which it befell,
What year it died, when 'twill arise,
We only know that here it lies.

Tract

William Carlos Williams (1883–1962)

I will teach you my townspeople
how to perform a funeral—
for you have it over a troop
of artists—
unless one should scour the world—
you have the ground sense necessary.

See! the hearse leads.
I begin with a design for a hearse.
For Christ's sake not black—
nor white either—and not polished!   10
Let it be weathered—like a farm wagon—
with gilt wheels (this could be
applied fresh at small expense)
or no wheels at all:
a rough dray to drag over the ground.

Knock the glass out!
My God—glass, my townspeople!
For what purpose? Is it for the dead
to look out or for us to see
how well he is housed or to see   20
the flowers or the lack of them—
or what?
To keep the rain and snow from him?
He will have a heavier rain soon:
pebbles and dirt and what not.
Let there be no glass—
and no upholstery phew!
and no little brass rollers
and small easy wheels on the bottom—
my townspeople what are you thinking of?   30
A rough plain hearse then
with gilt wheels and no top at all.
On this the coffin lies
by its own weight.
                  No wreaths please—

especially no hot house flowers.
Some common memento is better,
something he prized and is known by:
his old clothes—a few books perhaps—
God knows what! You realize   40
how we are about these things
my townspeople—
something will be found—anything
even flowers if he had come to that.
So much for the hearse.

For heaven's sake though see to the driver!
Take off the silk hat! In fact
that's no place at all for him—
up there unceremoniously
dragging our friend out to his own dignity!   50
Bring him down—bring him down!
Low and inconspicuous! I'd not have him ride
on the wagon at all—damn him—
the undertaker's understrapper!
Let him hold the reins
and walk at the side
and inconspicuously too!

Then briefly as to yourselves:
Walk behind—as they do in France,
seventh class, or if you ride   60
Hell take curtains! Go with some show
of inconvenience; sit openly—
to the weather as to grief.
Or do you think you can shut grief in?
What—from us? We who have perhaps
nothing to lose? Share with us
share with us—it will be money
in your pockets.
                    Go now   70
I think you are ready.

London, 1802
William Wordsworth (1770–1850)

Milton! thou shouldst be living at this hour:
England hath need of thee: she is a fen
Of stagnant waters: altar, sword, and pen,
Fireside, the heroic wealth of hall and bower,
Have forfeited their ancient English dower
Of inward happiness. We are selfish men;
Oh! raise us up, return to us again;
And give us manners, virtue, freedom, power.
Thy soul was like a star, and dwelt apart;
Thou hadst a voice whose sound was like the sea: 10
Pure as the naked heavens, majestic, free,
So didst thou travel on life's common way,
In cheerful godliness; and yet thy heart
The lowliest duties on herself did lay.

Ghetto Summer School
Douglas Worth (1940–   )

They'd learn more playing stickball in the street.

Here their gnawed pencils scratch silence
while the teacher, for forty-point-one bucks a day
fingers his crewcut and his manual
through six weeks' planned assault
on ignorance.

Only the fan, from the antiseptic hall
muzzled, grinding its metal teeth
has anything worth writing down to say.

The Great Day
William Butler Yeats (1865–1939)

Hurrah for revolution and more cannon-shot!
A beggar upon horseback lashes a beggar on foot.
Hurrah for revolution and cannon come again!
The beggars have changed places, but the lash goes on.

The Second Coming
William Butler Yeats (1865–1939)

Turning and turning in the widening gyre.[1]
The falcon cannot hear the falconer;
Things fall apart; the centre cannot hold;
Mere anarchy is loosed upon the world,
The blood-dimmed tide is loosed, and everywhere
The ceremony of innocence is drowned;
The best lack all conviction, while the worst
Are full of passionate intensity.

Surely some revelation is at hand;
Surely the Second Coming is at hand.   10
The Second Coming! Hardly are those words out
When a vast image out of *Spiritus Mundi*[2]
Troubles my sight: somewhere in sands of the desert
A shape with lion body and the head of a man,
A gaze blank and pitiless as the sun,
Is moving its slow thighs, while all about it
Reel shadows of the indignant desert birds.
The darkness drops again; but now I know
That twenty centuries of stony sleep
Were vexed to nightmare by a rocking cradle,   20
And what rough beast, its hour come round at last,
Slouches towards Bethlehem to be born?

1 A spiraling, circling path upward and outward from the center.   2 The
racial memory.

ALIENATION

He stopped living his life
As the people on the
television did it much better.

Howard Byatt

Chicken-Licken

Maya Angelou (1928–   )

She was afraid of men,
sin and the humors
of the night.
When she saw a bed
locks clicked
in her brain.

She screwed a frown
around and plugged
it in the keyhole.
Put a chain across   10
her door and closed
her mind.

Her bones were found
round thirty years later
when they razed
her building to
put up a parking lot.

Autopsy: read
dead of acute peoplelessness.

Lord Randal

Anonymous

"O where hae ye been, Lord Randal, my son?
O where hae ye been, my handsome young man?"
"I hae been to the wild wood; mother, make my bed soon,
For I'm weary wi hunting, and fain wald lie down."

"Where gat ye your dinner, Lord Randal, my son?
Where gat ye your dinner, my handsome young man?"

"I dined wi my true-love; mother, make my bed soon,
For I'm weary wi hunting, and fain wald lie down."

"What gat ye to your dinner, Lord Randal, my son?
What gat ye to your dinner, my handsome young man?"   10
"I gat eels boiled in broo; mother, make my bed soon,
For I'm weary wi hunting, and fain wald lie down."

"What became of your bloodhounds, Lord Randal, my son?
What became of your bloodhounds, my handsome young man?"
"O they swelld and they died; mother, make my bed soon,
For I'm weary wi hunting, and fain wald lie down."

"O I fear ye are poisond, Lord Randal, my son!
O I fear ye are poisond, my handsome young man!"
"O yes! I am poisond; mother, make my bed soon,
For I'm sick at the heart, and I fain wald lie down."   20

Blues and Bitterness

(for BILLIE HOLIDAY)

Lerone Bennett (1928–   )

Ice tinkled in glasses,
froze and rolled away
from hearts
in tombs where she slept.
Smoke noosed,
coiled and dangled from ceilings
in caves where she wept.

I woke up this morning
Just befo' the break of day.
I was bitter, blue and black, Lawd.   10
There ain't nothing else to say.

In saloons
festooned with trumpets
she prayed—sang
love songs to dead men
waiting with hammers
at the bottom of syringes.
She sang it in a song
before Sartre put it into a book.
She was Bigger[1]   20
before Wright wrote,
was with Nekeela
in a slave coffle,[2]
was stripped, branded
and eaten by the sharks
and rose again
on the third day in Georgia.

I wondered why God made me.
I wondered why He made me black.
I wondered why Mamma begat me—   30
And I started to give God His ticket back.

1 Protagonist of Richard Wright's novel *Native Son.* 2 A file of slaves
chained together.

Death

Howard Byatt (1953–   )

They gave my father a television
        when he retired
Thinking it would pass the time
        better than a watch.

        His first television
He would watch it all the day.
        He stopped living his life
As the people on the television
        did it much better.

He was dispersed
Amongst a hundred shadows.

But gradually his eyes clouded
          their sparkle absorbed
In the valves and microcircuits.
I wish he would rebel against this death
          Curse, bless me, but not deny me.

He did not
          and one day returning
From work
I found him sitting there
Dead eyes gaping at a dead television.

10

20

A Man Said to the Universe

Stephen Crane (1871–1900)

A man said to the universe:
"Sir, I exist!"
"However," replied the universe,
"The fact has not created in me
A sense of obligation."

Yet Do I Marvel

Countee Cullen (1903–1946)

I doubt not God is good, well-meaning, kind,
And did He stoop to quibble could tell why
The little buried mole continues blind,
Why flesh that mirrors Him must some day die,

Make plain the reason tortured Tantalus[1]
Is baited by the fickle fruit, declare
If merely brute caprice dooms Sisyphus[2]
To struggle up a never-ending stair.
Inscrutable. His ways are, and immune
To catechism by a mind too strewn   10
With petty cares to slightly understand
What awful brain compels His awful hand.
Yet do I marvel at this curious thing:
To make a poet black, and bid him sing!

1 A Greek king who was doomed in Hades to stand in water that receded
when he tried to drink and under branches bearing fruit he could never
reach.   2 Sisyphus was condemned in Hades to roll a rock uphill only to
have it roll down again.

Winter's Onset from an Alienated Point of View

Alan Dugan (1923–   )

The first cold front came in
whining like a carpenter's plane
and curled the warm air
up the sky: winter is
for busy work, summer
for construction. As for
spring and fall, ah, you
know what we do then:
sow and reap. I want
never to be idle or by plumb   10
or level to fear death,
so I do none of this
in offices away from weather.

We Wear the Mask
Paul Laurence Dunbar (1872–1906)

We wear the mask that grins and lies,
It hides our cheeks and shades our eyes,—
This debt we pay to human guile;
With torn and bleeding hearts we smile,
And mouth with myriad subtleties.

Why should the world be over-wise,
In counting all our tears and sighs?
Nay, let them only see us, while
    We wear the mask.

We smile, but, O great Christ, our cries   10
To thee from tortured souls arise.
We sing, but oh the clay is vile
Beneath our feet, and long the mile;
But let the world dream otherwise,
    We wear the mask!

The Love Song of J. Alfred Prufrock
T. S. Eliot (1888–1965)

S'io credesse che mia risposta fosse
A persona che mai tornasse al mondo,
Questa fiamma staria senza piu scosse.
Ma perciocche giammai di questo fondo
Non torno vivo alcun, s'i' odo il vero,
Senza tema d'infamia ti rispondo.[1]

1 Epigraph from Dante's *Inferno*, Canto 27: "If I thought my answer were/to one who ever would return to the world,/this flame should shake no more./But since none from this depth/ever did return alive, if what I hear be true,/without fear of infamy I answer thee."

Let us go then, you and I,
When the evening is spread out against the sky
Like a patient etherised upon a table;
Let us go, through certain half-deserted streets,
The muttering retreats
Of restless nights in one-night cheap hotels
And sawdust restaurants with oyster-shells:
Streets that follow like a tedious argument
Of insidious intent
To lead you to an overwhelming question . . .   10
Oh, do not ask, "What is it?"
Let us go and make our visit.

In the room the women come and go
Talking of Michelangelo.

The yellow fog that rubs its back upon the window-panes,
The yellow smoke that rubs its muzzle on the window-panes
Licked its tongue into the corners of the evening,
Lingered upon the pools that stand in drains,
Let fall upon its back the soot that falls from chimneys,
Slipped by the terrace, made a sudden leap,   20
And seeing that it was a soft October night,
Curled once about the house, and fell asleep.

And indeed there will be time
For the yellow smoke that slides along the street,
Rubbing its back upon the window-panes;
There will be time, there will be time
To prepare a face to meet the faces that you meet;
There will be time to murder and create,
And time for all the works and days of hands
That lift and drop a question on your plate;   30
Time for you and time for me,
And time yet for a hundred indecisions,
And for a hundred visions and revisions,
Before the taking of a toast and tea.

In the room the women come and go
Talking of Michelangelo.

And indeed there will be time
To wonder, "Do I dare?" and, "Do I dare?"
Time to turn back and descend the stair,
With a bald spot in the middle of my hair— 40
[They will say: "How his hair is growing thin!"]
My morning coat, my collar mounting firmly to the chin,
My necktie rich and modest, but asserted by a simple pin—
[They will say: "But how his arms and legs are thin!"]
Do I dare
Disturb the universe?
In a minute there is time
For decisions and revisions which a minute will reverse.

For I have known them all already, known them all:—
Have known the evenings, mornings, afternoons, 50
I have measured out my life with coffee spoons;
I know the voices dying with a dying fall
Beneath the music from a farther room.
    So how should I presume?

And I have known the eyes already, known them all—
The eyes that fix you in a formulated phrase,
And when I am formulated, sprawling on a pin,
When I am pinned and wriggling on the wall,
Then how should I begin
To spit out all the butt-ends of my days and ways? 60
    And how should I presume?

And I have known the arms already, known them all—
Arms that are braceleted and white and bare
[But in the lamplight, downed with light brown hair!]
Is it perfume from a dress
That makes me so digress?
Arms that lie along a table, or wrap about a shawl.
    And should I then presume?
    And how should I begin?

    .   .   .   .   .

Shall I say, I have gone at dusk through narrow streets 70
And watched the smoke that rises from the pipes
Of lonely men in shirt-sleeves, leaning out of windows? . . .

I should have been a pair of ragged claws
Scuttling across the floors of silent seas.

.   .   .   .   .

And the afternoon, the evening, sleeps so peacefully!
Smoothed by long fingers,
Asleep . . . tired . . . or it malingers,
Stretched on the floor, here beside you and me.
Should I, after tea and cakes and ices,
Have the strength to force the moment to its crisis?   80
But though I have wept and fasted, wept and prayed,
Though I have seen my head [grown slightly bald] brought in
    upon a platter,
I am no prophet—and here's no great matter;
I have seen the moment of my greatness flicker,
And I have seen the eternal Footman hold my coat, and snicker,
And in short, I was afraid.

And would it have been worth it, after all,
After the cups, the marmalade, the tea,
Among the porcelain, among some talk of you and me,
Would it have been worth while,   90
To have bitten off the matter with a smile,
To have squeezed the universe into a ball
To roll it toward some overwhelming question,
To say: "I am Lazarus, come from the dead,
Come back to tell you all, I shall tell you all"—
If one, settling a pillow by her head,
    Should say: "That is not what I meant at all.
    That is not it, at all."

And would it have been worth it, after all,
Would it have been worth while,   100
After the sunsets and the dooryards and the sprinkled streets,
After the novels, after the teacups, after the skirts that trail
    along the floor—
And this, and so much more?—
It is impossible to say just what I mean!
But as if a magic lantern threw the nerves in patterns on a
    screen:
Would it have been worth while

If one, settling a pillow or throwing off a shawl,
And turning toward the window, should say:
  "That is not it at all,
  That is not what I meant, at all."   110

.   .   .   .   .   .

No! I am not Prince Hamlet, nor was meant to be;
Am an attendant lord, one that will do
To swell a progress, start a scene or two,
Advise the prince; no doubt, an easy tool,
Deferential, glad to be of use,
Politic, cautious, and meticulous;
Full of high sentence, but a bit obtuse;
At times, indeed, almost ridiculous—
Almost, at times, the Fool.

I grow old . . . I grow old . . .   120
I shall wear the bottoms of my trousers rolled

Shall I part my hair behind? Do I dare to eat a peach?
I shall wear white flannel trousers, and walk upon the beach.
I have heard the mermaids singing, each to each.

I do not think that they will sing to me.

I have seen them riding seaward on the waves
Combing the white hair of the waves blown back
When the wind blows the water white and black.

We have lingered in the chambers of the sea
By sea-girls wreathed with seaweed red and brown   130
Till human voices wake us, and we drown.

The Stranger

William Everson (1912–   )

(Brother Antoninus)

Pity this girl.
At callow sixteen,
Glib in the press of rapt companions,
She bruits[1] her smatter,[2]
Her bed-lore brag.
She prattles the lip-learned, light-love list.
In the new itch and squirm of sex,
How can she foresee?

How can she foresee the thick stranger,
Over the hills from Omaha,   10
Who will break her across a hired bed,
Open the loins,
Rive the breach,
And set the foetus wailing within the womb,
To hunch toward the knowledge of its disease,
And shamble down time to doomsday?

1 Talks about.   2 Small amount of knowledge.

St. Louis Blues

W. C. Handy (1873–1958)

Ah hate to see de evenin' sun go down,
Hate to see de evenin' sun go down—
'Cause my baby—he done lef' dis town
Feelin' tomorrow lak Ah feel today,
Feel tomorrow lak Ah feel today,
Ah'll pack mah trunk, make mah getaway.

St. Louis 'oman wid her di'mon' rings
Pulls dat man 'roun' by her apron strings;
'Twant for powder an' for store-bought hair
De man Ah love would not gone nowhere.   10

You ought to see dat stove-pipe brown of mine
Lak he own de Di'mon' Joseph Line;
He'd make a cross-eyed 'oman go stone blin'.
Blacker than midnight, teeth lak flags of truce,
Blackest man in de whole St. Louis,
Blacker de berry—sweeter is de juice.
About a crap game he knows a pow'ful lot
But when work-time comes he's on de dot;
Gwine to ask him for a cold ten spot;
What it takes to git it, he's cert'nly got.   20

    Got de St. Louis Blues, jes' blue as Ah can be
    Dat man got a heart lak a rock cast in de sea
    Or else he wouldn't gone so far from me.

Epitaph on a Pessimist
Thomas Hardy (1840–1928)

I'm Smith of Stoke, aged sixty-odd,
    I've lived without a dame
From youth-time on; and would to God
    My dad had done the same.

Of Misery
Thomas Howell (c. 1568–1581)

Corpse, clad with carefulness,
Heart, heaped with heaviness,
Purse, poor and penniless,
Back, bare in bitterness,
Lips, laide[1] with loathsomeness;
Oh, get my grave in readiness,
Fain would I die to end this stress,
       Remédiless.

1 Hideous.

Counting the Mad
Donald Justice (1925–   )

This one was put in a jacket,
This one was sent home,
This one was given bread and meat
But would eat none,
And this one cried No No No No
All day long.

This one looked at the window
As though it were a wall,
This one saw things that were not there,
This one things that were,   10
And this one cried No No No No
All day long.

This one thought himself a bird,
This one a dog,
And this one thought himself a man,
An ordinary man,
And cried and cried No No No No
All day long.

As You Leave Me

Etheridge Knight (1933–   )

Shiny record albums scattered over
the livingroom floor, reflecting light
from the lamp, sharp reflections that hurt
my eyes as I watch you, squatting among the platters,
the beer foam making mustaches on your lips.

And, too,
the shadows on your cheeks from your long lashes
fascinate me—almost as much as the dimples:
in your cheeks, your arms and your legs:
dimples . . . dimples . . . dimples . . .   10

You
hum along with Mathis—how you love Mathis!
with his burnished hair and quicksilver voice that dances
among the stars and whirls through canyons
like windblown snow. sometimes I think that Mathis
could take you from me if you could be complete
without me. I glance at my watch. it is now time.

You rise,
silently, and to the bedroom and the paint:
on the lips red, on the eyes black,   20
and I lean in the doorway and smoke, and see you
grow old before my eyes, and smoke. why do you
chatter while you dress, and smile when you grab
your large leather purse? don't you know that when you
leave me I walk to the window and watch you? and light
a reefer as I watch you?   and I die as I watch you
disappear in the dark streets
to whistle and to smile at the johns.

In the Cage
Robert Lowell (1917–   )

The Lifers file into the hall,
According to their houses—twos
Of laundered denim. On the wall
A colored fairy tinkles blues
And titters by the balustrade;   5
Canaries beat their bars and scream.
We come from tunnels where the spade
Pick-axe and hod for plaster steam
In mud and insulation. Here
The Bible-twisting Israelite   10
Fasts for his Harlem. It is night,
And it is vanity, and age
Blackens the heart of Adam. Fear,
The yellow chirper, beaks its cage.

What Do You Say When A Man Tells You,
You Have the Softest Skin
Mary Mackey

do you say
its progesterone, progesterone makes it soft?
when he says
you have big brown eyes
do you say
of course
I'm nearsighted?

my body grew in rings
like a tree trunk
at the center I'm always 10   10
at the center I'm always wearing
pink plastic glasses

braces
wire wrapped around my head
a mouth full of rubber bands
I have buck teeth I can spit through
corrective shoes
pimples
no legs
no butt 20
no breasts

one day my mother buys me falsies
overnight I grow from 28AA to 36D
I look down and notice I can't see my feet
I feel like a fork-lift
I imagine they are realies

in gym the girls steal my bra
and throw it in the pool
my rubber breasts float away
like humpbacked whales 30
I dive for them
over and over
I dive for my breasts
and come up flat

what do you say when a man tells you
you're beautiful?
do you tell him,
"I'm still fishing
I'm still fishing for my body."

The Harlem Dancer
Claude McKay (1890–1948)

Applauding youths laughed with young prostitutes
And watched her perfect, half-clothed body sway;
Her voice was like the sound of blended flutes
Blown by black players upon a picnic day.

She sang and danced on gracefully and calm,
The light gauze hanging loose about her form;
To me she seemed a proudly-swaying palm
Grown lovelier for passing through a storm.
Upon her swarthy neck black shiny curls
Luxuriant fell; and tossing coins in praise,　　　　　　　10
The wine-flushed, bold-eyed boys, and even the girls,
Devoured her shape with eager, passionate gaze;
But looking at her falsely-smiling face,
I knew her self was not in that strange place.

In The Snack-Bar

Edwin Morgan (1920–　　)

A cup capsizes along the formica,
slithering with a dull clatter.
A few heads turn in the crowded evening snack-bar.
An old man is trying to get to his feet
from the low round stool fixed to the floor.
Slowly he levers himself up, his hands have no power.
He is up as far as he can get. The dismal hump
looming over him forces his head down.
He stands in his stained beltless gaberdine
like a monstrous animal caught in a tent　　　　　　　10
in some story. He sways slightly,
the face not seen, bent down
in shadow under his cap.
Even on his feet he is staring at the floor
or would be, if he could see.
I notice now his stick, once painted white
but scuffed and muddy, hanging from his right arm.
Long blind, hunchback born, half paralysed
he stands
fumbling with the stick　　　　　　　20
and speaks:
'I want—to go to the—toilet.'

It is down two flights of stairs, but we go.
I take his arm. 'Give me—your arm—it's better,' he says.
Inch by inch we drift towards the stairs.
A few yards of floor are like a landscape
to be negotiated, in the slow setting out
time has almost stopped. I concentrate
my life to his: crunch of spilt sugar,
slidy puddle from the night's umbrellas, 30
table edges, people's feet,
hiss of the coffee-machine, voices and laughter,
smell of a cigar, hamburgers, wet coats steaming,
and the slow dangerous inches to the stairs.
I put his right hand on the rail
and take his stick. He clings to me. The stick
is in his left hand, probing the treads.
I guide his arm and tell him the steps.
And slowly we go down. And slowly we go down.
White tiles and mirrors at last. He shambles 40
uncouth into the clinical gleam.
I set him in position, stand behind him
and wait with his stick.
His brooding reflection darkens the mirror
but the trickle of his water is thin and slow, .
an old man's apology for living.
Painful ages to close his trousers and coat—
I do up the last buttons for him.
He asks doubtfully, 'Can I—wash my hands?'
I fill the basin, clasp his soft fingers round the soap. 50
He washes feebly, patiently. There is no towel.
I press the pedal of the drier, draw his hands
gently into the roar of the hot air.
But he cannot rub them together,
drags out a handkerchief to finish.
He is glad to leave the contraption, and face the stairs.
He climbs, and steadily enough.
He climbs, we climb. He climbs
with many pauses but with that one
persisting patience of the undefeated 60
which is the nature of man when all is said.
And slowly we go up. And slowly we go up.
The faltering, unfaltering steps

take him at last to the door
across that endless, yet not endless waste of floor.
I watch him helped on a bus. It shudders off in the rain.
The conductor bends to hear where he wants to go.

Wherever he could go it would be dark
and yet he must trust men.
Without embarrassment or shame 70
he must announce his most pitiful needs
in a public place. No one sees his face.
Does he know how frightening he is in his strangeness
under his mountainous coat, his hands like wet leaves
stuck to the half-white stick?
His life depends on many who would evade him.
But he cannot reckon up the chances,
having one thing to do,
to haul his blind hump through these rains of August.
Dear Christ, to be born for this! 80

The Misogynist
Jean Morgan

Better they never learned to read!
Better they build sand castles, and breed,
He said, and such was his line of conversation
        whenever anybody mentioned
        women's liberation.
Oh he protested much!

There was a woman once who knew him,
        saw right through him,
Found his tirades so transparent
        she could watch the very gears of his defense. 10
She never argued.
Hardly heard his words, in fact,
        (but loved to hear his accents fall).

It cramped his style to be forgiven.
How he hated talking to the wall!
He liked to see the taunted ladies
    coiling, bristling,
    serpents and cats,
    venomous, mewing.
The game, though dreary, reinforced his theory.   20

Games and arguments were not encounters of the kind
    she had in mind;
She looked to meeting-grounds
    beyond the barricades of barb and glib.
She cared (he knew); and he,
He felt some tremors in the shale
And then and there decided she was one he'd never call.

He was afraid to be loved, or to love.
A hand in winter, resisting the glove.

The Street[1]

Octavio Paz (1914–   )

The street is very long and filled with silence.
I walk in shadow and I trip and fall,
And then get up and walk with unseeing feet
Over the silent stones and the dry leaves,
And someone close behind, tramples them, too.
If I slow down and stop, he also stops.
If I run, so does he. I look. No one!
The whole street seems so dark, with no way out,
And though I turn and turn, I can't escape.
I always find myself on the same street   10
Where no one waits for me and none pursues.
Where I pursue, a man who trips and falls
Gets up and seeing me, keeps saying: "No one!"

1 Translated from the Spanish by Willis Knapp Jones.

Learning Experience
Marge Piercy (1936–   )

The boy sits in the classroom
in Gary, in the United States, in NATO, in SEATO
in the thing-gorged belly of the sociobeast
in fluorescent light in slowly moving time
in boredom thick and greasy as vegetable shortening.
The classroom has green boards and ivory blinds,
the desks are new and the teachers not so old.
I have come out on the train from Chicago to talk
about dangling participles. I am supposed
to teach him to think a little on demand.   10
The time of tomorrow's draft exam is written on the board.
The boy yawns and does not want to be in the classroom in Gary
where the furnaces that consumed his father seethe rusty smoke
and pour cascades of nerve-bright steel
while the slag goes out in little dumpcars smoking,
but even less does he want to be in Today's Action Army
in Vietnam, in the Dominican Republic, in Guatemala,
in death that hurts.
In him are lectures on small groups, Jacksonian democracy,
French irregular verbs, the names of friends   20
around him in the classroom in Gary in the pillshaped afternoon
where tomorrow he will try and fail his license to live.

Miniver Cheevy
Edwin Arlington Robinson (1869–1935)

Miniver Cheevy, child of scorn,
   Grew lean while he assailed the seasons;
He wept that he was ever born,
   And he had reasons.

Miniver loved the days of old
   When swords were bright and steeds were prancing;

The vision of a warrior bold
  Would set him dancing.

Miniver sighed for what was not,
  And dreamed, and rested from his labors;   10
He dreamed of Thebes and Camelot,
  And Priam's neighbors.

Miniver mourned the ripe renown
  That made so many a name so fragrant;
He mourned Romance, now on the town,
  And Art, a vagrant.

Miniver loved the Medici,
  Albeit he had never seen one;
He would have sinned incessantly
  Could he have been one.   20

Miniver cursed the commonplace
  And eyed a khaki suit with loathing;
He missed the medieval grace
  Of iron clothing.

Miniver scorned the gold he sought,
  But sore annoyed was he without it;
Miniver thought, and thought, and thought,
  And thought about it.

Miniver Cheevy, born too late,
  Scratched his head and kept on thinking;   30
Miniver coughed, and called it fate,
  And kept on drinking.

Richard Cory

Edwin Arlington Robinson (1869–1935)

Whenever Richard Cory went down town,
  We people on the pavement looked at him:
He was a gentleman from sole to crown,
  Clean favored, and imperially slim.

And he was always quietly arrayed,
  And he was always human when he talked;
But still he fluttered pulses when he said,
  "Good-morning," and he glittered when he walked.

And he was rich—yes, richer than a king,
  And admirably schooled in every grace: 10
In fine, we thought that he was everything
  To make us wish that we were in his place.

So on we worked, and waited for the light,
  And went without the meat, and cursed the bread;
And Richard Cory, one calm summer night,
  Went home and put a bullet through his head.

Tomorrow, and tomorrow, and tomorrow

from MACBETH (V, 3)

William Shakespeare (1564–1616)

To-morrow, and to-morrow, and to-morrow,
Creeps in this petty pace from day to day,
To the last syllable of recorded time;
And all our yesterdays have lighted fools
The way to dusty death. Out, out, brief candle!
Life's but a walking shadow; a poor player

That struts and frets his hour upon the stage
And then is heard no more. It is a tale
Told by an idiot, full of sound and fury,
Signifying nothing.   10

Lines

Percy Bysshe Shelley (1792–1822)

When the lamp is shattered
The light in the dust lies dead—
    When the cloud is scattered
The rainbow's glory is shed.
    When the lute is broken,
Sweet tones are remembered not;
    When the lips have spoken,
Loved accents are soon forgot.

    As music and splendour
Survive not the lamp and the lute,   10
    The heart's echoes render
No song when the spirit is mute:—
    No song but sad dirges,
Like the wind through a ruined cell,
    Or the mournful surges
That ring the dead seaman's knell.

    When hearts have once mingled
Love first leaves the well-built nest;
    The weak one is singled
To endure what it once possessed.   20
    O Love! who bewailest
The frailty of all things here,
    Why choose you the frailest
For your cradle, your home, and your bier?

Its passions will rock thee
As the storms rock the ravens on high;
   Bright reason will mock thee,
Like the sun from a wintry sky.
   From thy nest every rafter
Will rot, and thine eagle home   30
   Leave thee naked to laughter,
When leaves fall and cold winds come.

American Primitive

William Jay Smith (1918–   )

Look at him there in his stovepipe hat,
His high-top shoes, and his handsome collar;
Only my Daddy could look like that,
And I love my Daddy like he loves his Dollar.

The screen door bangs, and it sounds so funny—
There he is in a shower of gold;
His pockets are stuffed with folding money,
His lips are blue, and his hands feel cold.

He hangs in the hall by his black cravat,
The ladies faint, and the children holler: 10
Only my Daddy could look like that,
And I love my Daddy like he loves his Dollar.

Like as the culver on the barèd bough
Edmund Spenser (1551–1599)

Like as the culver on the barèd bough .
Sits mourning for the absence of her mate,
And in her moan sends many a wishful vow
For his return, that seems to linger late;
So I alone, now left disconsolate,
Mourn to myself the absence of my love,
And wandering here and there all desolate,
Seek with my plaints to match that mournful dove.
Ne joy of aught that under heaven doth hove[1]
Can comfort me, but her own joyous sight,   10
Whose sweet aspect both God and man can move,
In her unspotted pleasaunce to delight:
Dark is my day whiles her fair light I miss,
And dead my life, that wants such lively bliss.

1 Hover.

Break, Break, Break
Alfred, Lord Tennyson (1809–1892)

Break, break, break,
   On thy cold gray stones, O Sea!
And I would that my tongue could utter
   The thoughts that arise in me.

O, well for the fisherman's boy,
   That he shouts with his sister at play!
O, well for the sailor lad,
   That he sings in his boat on the bay!

And the stately ships go on
   To their haven under the hill;   10

But O for the touch of a vanished hand,
    And the sound of a voice that is still!

Break, break, break,
    At the foot of thy crags, O Sea!
But the tender grace of a day that is dead
    Will never come back to me.

Over

R. S. Thomas (1913–   )

I look. You look
Away. No colour,
No ruffling of the brow's
Surface betrays
Your feeling. As though I
Were not here; as
Though you were your own
Mirror, you arrange yourself
For the play. My eyes'
Adjectives; the way that   10
I scan you; the
Conjunction the flesh
Needs—all these
Are as nothing
To you. Serene, cool,
Motionless, no statue
Could show less
The impression of
My regard. Madam, I
Grant the artistry   20
Of your part. Let us
Consider it, then,
A finished performance.

Suicide

Alice Walker (1944–   )

First, suicide notes should be
(not long) but written
second,
all suicide notes
should be signed
in blood
by hand
and to the point—
that point being, perhaps,
that there is none.   10
Thirdly, if it is the thought
of rest that
fascinates
laziness should be admitted
in the clearest terms.
Then, all things done
ask those outraged
consider their happiest
summer
& tell if the days it   20
adds up to
is one.

The Only Bar in Dixon

James Welch (1940–   )

These Indians once imitated life.
Whatever made them warm
they called wine, song or sleep,
a lucky number on the tribal roll.

Now the stores have gone the gray

of this November sky.   Cars
whistle by, chrome wind, knowing
something lethal in the dust.

A man could build a reputation here.
Take that redhead at the bar—   10
she knows we're thugs, killers
on a fishing trip with luck.

No luck.   No room for those
sensitive enough to know they're beat.
Even the Flathead turns away,
a river thick with bodies,

Indians on their way to Canada.
Take the redhead—yours for just a word,
a promise that the wind will warm
and all the saints come back for laughs.   20

They Flee from Me

Sir Thomas Wyatt (c. 1503–1542)

They flee from me, that sometime did me seek
With naked foot, stalking in my chamber.
I have seen them gentle, tame, and meek
That now are wild, and do not remember
That sometime they put themselves in danger
To take bread at my hand; and now they range
Busily seeking with a continual change.

Thanked be fortune it hath been otherwise
Twenty times better; but once, in special,
In thin array, after a pleasant guise,   10
When her loose gown from her shoulders did fall,
And she me caught in her arms long and small,
Therewith all sweetly did me kiss
And softly said, "Dear heart, how like you this?"

It was no dream: I lay broad waking.
But all is turned, through my gentleness,
Into a strange fashion of forsaking;
And I have leave to go of her goodness,
And she also to use newfangleness.
But since that I so kindly am served,   20
I would fain know what she hath deserved.

LOVE

*If no love is, O God,
what fele I so?*

Geoffrey Chaucer

Black Is the Color
Anonymous

Black, black, black is the color of my true love's hair.
His lips are something wond'rous fair,
The purest eyes and the bravest hands,
I love the ground whereon he stands.
Black, black, black is the color of my true love's hair.

I love my love and well he knows,
I love the ground whereon he goes.
And if my love no more I see,
My life would quickly fade away.

Black, black, black is the color of my true love's hair.   10

Frankie and Johnny
Anonymous

Frankie and Johnny were lovers, great God how they could love!
Swore to be true to each other, true as the stars up above.
He was her man, but he done her wrong.

Frankie she was his woman, everybody knows.
She spent her forty dollars for Johnny a suit of clothes.
He was her man, but he done her wrong.

Frankie and Johnny went walking, Johnny in his brand new suit.
"O good Lawd," said Frankie, "but don't my Johnny look cute?"
He was her man, but he done her wrong.

Frankie went down to the corner, just for a bucket of beer.   10
Frankie said, "Mr. Bartender, has my loving Johnny been here?
He is my man, he wouldn't do me wrong."

"I don't want to tell you no story, I don't want to tell you no lie,
But your Johnny left here an hour ago with that lousy Nellie
  Blye.
He is your man, but he's doing you wrong."

Frankie went back to the hotel, she didn't go there for fun,
For under her red kimono she toted a forty-four gun.
He was her man, but he done her wrong.

Frankie went down to the hotel and looked in the window so
  high.
And there was her loving Johnny a-loving up Nellie Blye.   20
He was her man, but he was doing her wrong.

Frankie threw back her kimono, took out that old forty-four.
Root-a-toot-toot, three times she shot, right through the
  hardwood door.
He was her man, but he was doing her wrong.

Johnny grabbed off his Stetson, crying, "O, Frankie don't shoot!"
Frankie pulled that forty-four, went root-a-toot-toot-toot-toot.
He was her man, but he done her wrong.

"Roll me over gently, roll me over slow,
Roll me on my right side, for my left side hurts me so,
I was her man, but I done her wrong."   30

With the first shot Johnny staggered, with the second shot he
  fell;
When the last bullet got him, there was a new man's face in hell.
He was her man, but he done her wrong.

"O, bring out your rubber-tired hearses, bring out your
  rubber-tired hacks;
Gonna take Johnny to the graveyard and ain't gonna bring him
  back.
He was my man, but he done me wrong."

"O, put me in that dungeon, put me in that cell,
Put me where the northeast wind blows from the southeast
  corner of hell.
I shot my man, cause he done me wrong!"

My Love in Her Attire
Anonymous

My Love in her attire doth show her wit,
    It doth so well become her:
For every season she hath dressings fit,
    For winter, spring, and summer.
No beauty she doth miss
    When all her robes are on:
But Beauty's self she is
    When all her robes are gone.

Western Wind
Anonymous

Western wind, when will thou blow,
The small rain down can rain?
Christ, if my love were in my arms
And I in my bed again!

Soft Answers
Robert Bagg (1935–   )

Her wraithful turnings and her soft answers head
    Me off. The easiest allusion of her hips,
No matter how well spoken for, soon slips
    Her mind. I ask her long blond braids where they lead,

Hold them over her head, and let them fall.
    Even her breasts' tactfully gathered favor

Can't hold my hand's attention forever.
    Lazy as her love is, I have my hands full

With her, letting every beauty she owns
    Slip through my tongue and fingers, still hoping   10
For the whole of her, soon closing and opening
    Like a giant heart toying with my bones.

And Ruth Said . . .[1]

from THE KING JAMES BIBLE

Ruth (1:16–17)

And Ruth said, Intreat me not to leave thee, or to return from
following after thee: for whither thou goest, I will go; and where
thou lodgest, I will lodge: thy people shall be my people, and thy
God my God:
    Where thou diest, will I die, and there will I be buried: the
Lord do so to me, and more also, if ought but death part thee and
me.

1 Ruth is speaking to her mother-in-law.

I Am the Rose of Sharon

from THE KING JAMES BIBLE

Song of Solomon (2:1–6,10–13)

I am the rose of Sharon, and the lily of the valleys.
    As the lily among thorns, so is my love among the daughters.
    As the apple tree among the trees of the wood, so is my be-
loved among the sons. I sat down under his shadow with great
delight, and his fruit was sweet to my taste.

He brought me to the banqueting house, and his banner over me was love.

Stay me with flagons, comfort me with apples: for I am sick of love.

His left hand is under my head, and his right hand doth embrace me.

My beloved spake, and said unto me, Rise up, my love, my fair one, and come away.

For, lo, the winter is past, the rain is over and gone;

The flowers appear on the earth; the time of the singing of birds is come, and the voice of the turtle[1] is heard in our land;

The fig tree putteth forth her green figs, and the vines with the tender grape give a good smell. Arise, my love, my fair one, and come away.

1 Turtle dove.

When You Have Forgotten Sunday: The Love Story
Gwendolyn Brooks (1917–   )

—And when you have forgotten the bright bedclothes on a
    Wednesday and a Saturday,
And most especially when you have forgotten Sunday—
When you have forgotten Sunday halves in bed,
Or me sitting on the front-room radiator in the limping afternoon
Looking off down the long street
To nowhere,
Hugged by my plain old wrapper of no-expectation
And nothing-I-have-to-do and I'm-happy-why?
And if-Monday-never-had-to-come—   10
When you have forgotten that, I say,
And how you swore, if somebody beeped the bell,
And how my heart played hopscotch if the telephone rang;
And how we finally went in to Sunday dinner,

That is to say, went across the front-room floor to the ink-spotted
   table in the southwest corner
To Sunday dinner, which was always chicken and noodles
Or chicken and rice
And salad and rye bread and tea
And chocolate chip cookies—
I say, when you have forgotten that,
When you have forgotten my little presentiment   20
That e war would be over before they got to you;
And ho ' we finally undressed and whipped out the light and
   flowed into bed,
And lay loose-limbed for a moment in the week-end
Bright bedclothes,
Then gently folded into each other—
When you have, I say, forgotten all that,
Then you may tell,
Then I may believe
You have forgotten me well.

How Do I Love Thee?
Elizabeth Barrett Browning (1806–1861)

How do I love thee? Let me count the ways.
I love thee to the depth and breadth and height
My soul can reach, when feeling out of sight
For the ends of Being and ideal Grace.
I love thee to the level of every day's
Most quiet need, by sun and candlelight.
I love thee freely, as men strive for Right;
I love thee purely, as they turn from Praise;
I love thee with the passion put to use
In my old griefs, and with my childhood's faith.   10
I love thee with a love I seemed to lose
With my lost saints,—I love thee with the breath
Smiles, tears, of all my life!—and, if God choose,
I shall but love thee better after death.

Meeting at Night
Robert Browning (1812–1889)

The gray sea and the long black land;
And the yellow half-moon large and low;
And the startled little waves that leap
In fiery ringlets from their sleep,
As I gain the cove with pushing prow,
And quench its speed i' the slushy sand.

Then a mile of warm sea-scented beach;
Three fields to cross till a farm appears;
A tap at the pane, the quick sharp scratch
And blue spurt of a lighted match,   10
And a voice less loud, through its joys and fears,
Than the two hearts beating each to each!

Parting at Morning
Robert Browning (1812–1889)

Round the cape of a sudden came the sea,
And the sun looked over the mountain's rim:
And straight was a path of gold for him,
And the need of a world of men for me.

A Red, Red Rose
Robert Burns (1759–1796)

O my luve is like a red, red rose,
    That's newly sprung in June:
O my luve is like a melodie,
    That's sweetly played in tune.

As fair art thou, my bonie lass,
    So deep in luve am I;
And I will luve thee still, my dear,
    Till a' the seas gang dry.

Till a' the seas gang dry, my dear,
    And the rocks melt wi' the sun: 10
And I will luve thee still, my dear,
    While the sands o' life shall run.

And fare thee weel, my only luve!
    And fare thee weel a while!
And I will come again, my luve,
    Tho' it were ten thousand mile.

She Walks in Beauty

George Gordon, Lord Byron (1788–1824)

She walks in Beauty, like the night
    Of cloudless climes and starry skies;
And all that's best of dark and bright
    Meet in her aspect and her eyes:
Thus mellowed to that tender light
    Which Heaven to gaudy day denies.

One shade the more, one ray the less,
    Had half impaired the nameless grace
Which waves in every raven tress,
    Or softly lightens o'er her face;   10
Where thoughts serenely sweet express,
    How pure, how dear their dwelling-place.

And on that cheek, and o'er that brow,
    So soft, so calm, yet eloquent,
The smiles that win, the tints that glow,
    But tell of days in goodness spent,
A mind at peace with all below,
    A heart whose love is innocent!

Sleep, Angry Beauty, Sleep
Thomas Campion (1567–1620)

Sleep, angry beauty, sleep, and fear not me.
For who a sleeping lion dares provoke?
It shall suffice me here to sit and see
Those lips shut up, that never kindly spoke.
What sight can more content a lover's mind
Than beauty seeming harmless, if not kind?

My words have charmed her, for secure she sleeps;
Though guilty much of wrong done to my love;
And in her slumber, see! she, close-eyed, weeps!
Dreams often more than waking passions move.   10
Plead, Sleep, my cause, and make her soft like thee,
That she in peace may wake and pity me.

Envoi
Charles Causley (1917–   )

I am the Prince
I am the lowly
I am the damned
I am the holy.
My hands are ten knives.
I am the dove
Whose wings are murder.
My name is love.

Troilus Soliloquizes

from TROILUS AND CRISEYDE (I, 400–420)

Geoffrey Chaucer (1343–1400)

If no love is, O God, what fele I so?
And if love is, what thing and which is he?
If love be good, from whennes[1] com'th my wo?
If it be wikke,[2] a wonder thinketh me,
When every torment and adversitee
That com'th of him, may to me savory thinke;
For ay thurst I, the more that I it drinke.

And if that at myn owne lust I brenne,[3]
Fro whennes com'th my wailing and my pleynte?[4]
If harm agree me, wher-to pleyn I thenne?   10
I noot,[5] ne why unwery that I feynte.
O quikė deeth, O swetė harm so queynte,
How may of thee in me swich quantitee,
But-if that I consentė that it be?

And if that I consent, I wrongfully
Compleyn, y-wis;[6] thus possėd[7] to and fro,
Al sterėless[8] with-inn a boot[9] am I
A-mid the sea, by-twixen[10] windės two,
That in contrárie stonden ever-mo.
Allas, what is this wonder maladye?   20
For hete of cold, for cold of hete, I dye.

---

1 Whence. 2. Wicked. 3 Burn. 4 Complaint. 5 Know not. 6 I know.
7 Driven or thrust with violent impact. 8 Steerless (without rudder).
9 Boat. 10 Between.

may i feel said he

e. e. cummings (1894–1962)

may i feel said he
(i'll squeal said she
just once said he)
it's fun said she

(may i touch said he
how much said she
a lot said he)
why not said she

(let's go said he
not too far said she
what's too far said he
where you are said she)

may i stay said he
(which way said she
like this said he
if you kiss said she

may i move said he
is it love said she)
if you're willing said he
(but you're killing said she

but it's life said he
but your wife said she
now said he)
ow said she

(tiptop said he
don't stop said she
oh no said he)
go slow said she

(cccome? said he
ummm said she)
you're divine! said he
(you are Mine said she)

A Valediction Forbidding Mourning

John Donne (1572–1631)

As virtuous men pass mildly away
   And whisper to their souls to go,
Whilst some of their sad friends do say,
   "The breath goes now," and some say, "No":

So let us melt and make no noise,
   No tear-floods nor sigh-tempests move;
'Twere profanation of our joys
   To tell the laity our love.

Moving of th' earth brings harms and fears;
   Men reckon what it did and meant;   10
But trepidation of the spheres,
   Though greater far, is innocent.

Dull sublunary lovers' love
   (Whose soul is sense) cannot admit
Absence, because it doth remove
   Those things which elemented it.[1]

But we by a love so much refined
   That ourselves know not what it is,
Inter-assurèd of the mind,
   Care less, eyes, lips, and hands to miss.   20

Our two souls therefore, which are one,
   Though I must go, endure not yet
A breach, but an expansion,
   Like gold to airy thinness beat.

If they be two, they are two so
   As stiff twin compasses are two;
Thy soul, the fixed foot, makes no show
   To move, but doth, if th' other do.

1 Composed it.

And though it in the center sit,
   Yet when the other far doth roam,
It leans and hearkens after it
   And grows erect as that comes home.

Such wilt thou be to me, who must
   Like th' other foot, obliquely run;
Thy firmness makes my circle just
   And makes me end where I begun.

The Good-Morrow
John Donne (1572–1631)

I wonder, by my troth, what thou and I
Did till we loved? were we not weaned till then?
But sucked on country pleasures, childishly?
Or snorted we in the seven sleepers' den?
'Twas so; but this, all pleasures fancies be.
If ever any beauty I did see,
Which I desired, and got, 'twas but a dream of thee.

And now good-morrow to our waking souls,
Which watch not one another out of fear;
For love all love of other sights controls,
And makes one little room an everywhere.
Let sea-discoverers to new worlds have gone;
Let maps to other, worlds on worlds have shown;
Let us possess one world; each hath one, and is one.

My face in thine eye, thine in mine appears,
And true plain hearts do in the faces rest;
Where can we find two better hemispheres
Without sharp north, without declining west?
Whatever dies, was not mixed equally;
If our two loves be one, or thou and I
Love so alike that none do slacken, none can die.

The Sun Rising

John Donne (1572–1631)

Busy old fool, unruly Sun,
    Why dost thou thus,
Through windows, and through curtains, call on us?
Must to thy motions lovers' seasons run?
    Saucy pedantic wretch, go chide
    Late school-boys and sour prentices,[1]
  Go tell court-huntsmen that the king will ride,
  Call country ants to harvest offices;
Love, all alike, no season knows nor clime,
Nor hours, days, months, which are the rags of time.   10

    Thy beams so reverend and strong
    Why shouldst thou think?
I could eclipse and cloud them with a wink,
But that I would not lose her sight so long.
    If her eyes have not blinded thine,
    Look, and to-morrow late tell me,
  Whether both th' Indias of spice and mine
  Be where thou left'st them, or lie here with me.
Ask for those kings whom thou saw'st yesterday,
And thou shalt hear, "All here in one bed lay."   20

    She's all states, and all princes I;
    Nothing else is;
Princes do but play us; compared to this,
All honour's mimic, all wealth alchemy.
    Thou, Sun, art half as happy as we,
    In that the world's contracted thus;
  Thine age asks ease, and since thy duties be
  To warm the world, that's done in warming us.
Shine here to us, and thou art everywhere;
This bed thy centre is, these walls thy sphere.   30

1 Bad-tempered apprentices.

Whilst Alexis Lay Press'd
John Dryden (1631–1700)

    Whilst Alexis lay press'd
    In her arms he lov'd best,
With his hands round her neck, and his head on her breast,
He found the fierce pleasure too hasty to stay,
And his soul in the tempest just flying away.

    When Celia saw this,
    With a sigh and a kiss,
She cried: "O my dear, I am robb'd of my bliss!
'T is unkind to your love, and unfaithfully done,
To leave me behind you, and die all alone."   10

    The youth, tho' in haste,
    And breathing his last,
In pity died slowly, while she died more fast;
Till at length she cried: "Now, my dear, now let us go;
Now die, my Alexis, and I will die too!"

    Thus intranc'd they did lie,
    Till Alexis did try
To recover new breath, that again he might die:
Then often they died; but the more they did so,
The nymph died more quick, and the shepherd more slow.   20

Like Memnon's Rock[1]
Giles Fletcher (1548–1611)

Like Memnon's rock, touched with the rising sun,
Which yields a sound and echoes forth a voice;
But when it's drowned in western seas is done,
And drowsy-like leaves off to make a noise;

1 Reference is to a huge statue built to commemorate one of the Egyptian
Pharaohs.

So I, my love, enlightened with your shine,
A poet's skill within my soul I shroud—
Not rude, like that which finer wits decline,
But such as Muses to the best allowed.
But when your figure and your shape is gone,
I speechless am, like as I was before;   10
Or if I write, my verse is filled with moan,
And blurred with tears by falling in such store;
    Then muse not, Licia, if my muse be slack,
    For when I wrote I did thy beauty lack.

Beyond the Presidency

(for ROBERT BLY)

June 6, 1968

Morgan Gibson (1929–   )

Beginning my fortieth year
as Robert Kennedy sleeps beyond the presidency

all of us dream of doctors
like women in long labor.

How shall we bear our spirit
through bodyguards?

What last rite will open our arms
to the anarchy of love?

Questions [1]

Donald Hall (1928–   )

Why do you love her?

She loves me. I have never felt so valuable.

Why do you love her?

Her body is tender, like the color yellow.

Why do you love her?

I am with her, so totally. She teaches me about
feelings. One day she suddenly covered her eyes with her
hands. "What color are they?" They are light blue. I
know her eyes. I begin to see through them. She sees into
mine. Never before has inside spoken to inside.   10
We talk, we talk.

Where?

In the place we go to. It has flowers in it. On our trip
together, we talked all day and all night, sleeping and
waking.

What is the trouble between you?

The remainders of our lives. My expectations. Her
changeableness. My unchangingness.

Questions [2]

Donald Hall (1928–   )

How is it now?

The time of long days. Now I am accustomed to loving.

Why did you wait so long?

My fear.

What is it like, now?

Being together, just be-ing, not minds and not
bodies, but presences wholly aware of the other person,
which is almost not another person.

What do you feel like, when you are with her?

As if everything lost came back to me. I found a walled   10
garden where everything that I lost collected itself.
I walk among the model airplanes and the dead friends.

What are these walls?

Secrecy, privacy, and our troubles.

Troubles?

One day she is removed. We cannot find each others'
eyes. Another day she feels me removed. I plan, she finds
it constricting. I labor not to plan, she finds me distant.

Are the faults all hers?

She is angry and walks out slamming the door. She   20
takes our objects with her. I talk to her. She comes back.

Why is she angry?

Your voice on the telephone
Donald Hall (1928–   )

Your voice on the telephone
encloses itself
in the cell
of matter-of-fact.

Song
Ruth Herschberger (1917–   )

I said, I fear and resent men.
He said, I'm not a man, I'm a flower.

Sergei's a flower—
    What a flower!
       A broncho of a bloom.
Carnation, rose?
    A soft primrose?
       Chrysanthemum, or whom?
Sergei's a bower—
    What a bower!
       A grapevine of delight.
Sergei's a pose,   10
    A yellow rose,
       A stallion in the night.

Yes

from ULYSSES

James Joyce (1882–1941)

                                                    and Ronda with the old
windows of the posadas¹ glancing eyes a lattice hid for her lover
to kiss the iron and the wineshops half open at night and the
castanets and the night we missed the boat at Algeciras the
watchman going about serene with his lamp and O that awful
deepdown torrent O and the sea the sea crimson sometimes like
fire and the glorious sunsets and the figtrees in the Alameda
gardens yes and all the queer little streets and pink and blue and
yellow houses and the rosegardens and the jessamine and gera-
niums and cactuses and Gibraltar as a girl where I was a Flower   10
of the mountain yes when I put the rose in my hair like the
Andalusian girls used or shall I wear a red yes and how he kissed
me under the Moorish wall and I thought well as well him as
another and then I asked him with my eyes to ask again yes and
then he asked me would I yes to say yes my mountain flower and
first I put my arms around him yes and drew him down to me so
he could feel my breasts all perfume yes and his heart was going
like mad and yes I said yes I will Yes.

1 Inn. Ronda and Algeciras are cities in Spain.

The Passionate Shepherd to His Love
Christopher Marlowe (1564–1593)

Come live with me and be my love,
And we will all the pleasures prove,
That hills and valleys, dales and fields,
And all the craggy mountains yields.

There we will sit upon the rocks,

And see the shepherds feed their flocks,
By shallow rivers to whose falls
Melodious birds sing madrigals.

And I will make thee beds of roses
With a thousand fragrant posies,   10
A cap of flowers, and a kirtle[1]
Embroidered all with leaves of myrtle;

A gown made of the finest wool
Which from our pretty lambs we pull;
Fair lined slippers for the cold,
With buckles of the purest gold;

A belt of straw and ivy buds,
With coral clasps and amber studs:
And if these pleasures may thee move,
Come live with me and be my love.   20

The shepherds' swains shall dance and sing
For thy delight each May morning:
If these delights thy mind may move,
Then live with me and be my love.

1 A skirt or petticoat.

The Fickle One[1]
Pablo Neruda (1904–1973)

My eyes went away from me
following a dark girl
who went by.

She was made of black mother-of-pearl,

1 Translated by Donald D. Walsh.

made of dark-purple grapes,
and she lashed my blood
with her tail of fire.

After them all
I go.

A pale blonde went by   10
like a golden plant
swaying her gifts.
And my mouth went
like a wave
discharging on her breast
lightningbolts of blood.

After them all
I go.

But to you, without my moving,
without seeing you, distant you,   20
go my blood and my kisses,
my dark one and my fair one,
my tall one and my little one,
my broad one and my slender one,
my ugly one, my beauty,
made of all the gold
and of all the silver,
made of all the wheat
and of all the earth,
made of all the water   30
of the sea waves,
made for my arms,
made for my kisses,
made for my soul.

Love Poem

John Frederick Nims (1914–   )

My clumsiest dear, whose hands shipwreck vases,
At whose quick touch all glasses chip and ring,
Whose palms are bulls in china, burs in linen,
And have no cunning with any soft thing

Except all ill-at-ease fidgeting people:
The refugee uncertain at the door
You make at home; deftly you steady
The drunk clambering on his undulant floor.

Unpredictable dear, the taxi drivers' terror,
Shrinking from far headlights pale as a dime   10
Yet leaping before red apoplectic streetcars—
Misfit in any space. And never on time.

A wrench in clocks and the solar system. Only
With words and people and love you move at ease.
In traffic of wit expertly manoeuvre
And keep us, all devotion, at your knees.

Forgetting your coffee spreading on our flannel,
Your lipstick grinning on our coat,
So gayly in love's unbreakable heaven
Our souls on glory of spilt bourbon float.   20

Be with me darling early and late. Smash glasses—
I will study wry music for your sake.
For should your hands drop white and empty
All the toys of the world would break.

Don't Sit under the Apple Tree with Anyone Else but Me
Robert Pack (1929–   )

"Don't bug me, Pa!"
Gregor Samsa

Created for whose sake? The praying
Mantis eats its mate. Hatched,
Two hundred or more eggs scramble
Away—(Breakfast for whom?)—eating
Each other. Among the outer leaves
Of plants; along flower stems;
Sometimes on branches; sometimes on walls;
Seen by some, yes, looking in windows—
They wait for lady beetles, they wait
For honeybees. I do not judge them.   10
Do not judge my poem! They are—
I am—both are what we are.
They can be kept (in separate cages)
As pets, and will take pieces of apple
(See *Genesis*, chapters 1–4)
From your fingers or sip water
From a spoon. With imagination.
(Familiarity?), there is little
One cannot love in heaven or earth.
After they know you well, they cock   20
Their little heads at your approach—
Asking, as I do, to be loved?

The Nymph's Reply to the Shepherd[1]

Sir Walter Raleigh (c. 1552–1618)

If all the world and love were young,
And truth in every shepherd's tongue,
These pretty pleasures might me move,
To live with thee, and be thy love.

Time drives the flocks from field to fold,
When rivers rage, and rocks grow cold,
And Philomel[2] becometh dumb,
The rest complains of cares to come.

The flowers do fade, and wanton fields,
To wayward winter reckoning yields,   10
A honey tongue, a heart of gall,
Is fancy's spring, but sorrow's fall.

Thy gowns, thy shoes, thy beds of roses,
Thy cap, thy kirtle[3] and thy posies,
Soon break, soon wither, soon forgotten:
In folly ripe, in reason rotten.

Thy belt of straw and ivy buds,
Thy coral clasps and amber studs,
All these in me no means can move,
To come to thee, and be thy love.   20

But could youth last, and love still breed,
Had joys no date, nor age no need,
Then these delights my mind might move,
To live with thee and be thy love.

---

1 Raleigh's poem is a reply to Marlowe's "The Passionate Shepherd to His Love," (p. 130).   2 The nightingale.   3 A skirt or petticoat.

All My Past Life
John Wilmot, Earl of Rochester (1647–1680)

All my past life is mine no more,
   The flying hours are gone:
Like transitory dreams given o'er,
Whose images are kept in store
   By memory alone.

The time that is to come is not;
   How can it then be mine?
The present moment's all my lot,
And that, as fast as it is got,
   Phyllis, is only thine.   10

Then talk not of inconstancy,
   False hearts, and broken vows!
If I by miracle can be
This live-long minute true to thee,
   'Tis all that Heaven allows.

Pedro

(Pedro Infante—Mexican Singer, Actor, Genius, who died piloting his own plane, April, 1957, at the age of thirty-seven)

Luís Omar Salinas (1937–   )

You took the world and embraced
   it as a child
      your arms
         your voice
            your heart
  touched the sea

   you had many loves
      among them Mexico

when you died
it rose to its feet   10
to pay homage to you

mountains of snow
were singing
your songs

Pedro I remember you
when I was a child
and how you brought
tears

silence within silence

When to the sessions of sweet silent thought

SONNET 30

William Shakespeare (1564–1616)

When to the sessions of sweet silent thought
I summon up remembrance of things past,
I sigh the lack of many a thing I sought,
And with old woes new wail my dear time's waste:
Then can I drown an eye, unused to flow,
For precious friends hid in death's dateless night,
And weep afresh love's long since cancelled woe,
And moan the expense of many a vanished sight:
Then can I grieve at grievances foregone,
And heavily from woe to woe tell o'er   10
The sad account of fore-bemoanèd moan,
Which I new pay as if not paid before.
But if the while I think on thee, dear friend,
All losses are restored and sorrows end.

My mistress' eyes are nothing like the sun

SONNET 130

William Shakespeare (1564–1616)

My mistress' eyes are nothing like the sun;
Coral is far more red than her lips' red:
If snow be white, why then her breasts are dun;
If hairs be wires, black wires grow on her head.
I have seen roses damasked, red and white,
But no such roses see I in her cheeks;
And in some perfumes is there more delight
Than in the breath that from my mistress reeks.
I love to hear her speak, yet well I know
That music hath a far more pleasing sound: 10
I grant I never saw a goddess go,—
My mistress, when she walks, treads on the ground:
   And yet, by heaven, I think my love as rare
   As any she belied with false compare.

My Love Is Like to Ice

from AMORETTI

Edmund Spenser (1552–1599)

My Love is like to ice, and I to fire:
How comes it then that this her cold so great
Is not dissolved through my so hot desire,
But harder grows the more I her entreat?
Or how comes it that my exceeding heat
Is not allayed by her heart-frozen cold,
But that I burn much more in boiling sweat,
And feel my flames augmented manifold?
What more miraculous thing may be told,
That fire, which all things melts, should harden ice,   10

And ice, which is congeal'd with senseless cold,
Should kindle fire by wonderful device?
    Such is the power of love in gentle mind,
    That it can alter all the course of kind.[1]

1 Mankind.

the ocean
Laura St. Martin (1957–   )

the ocean is a strange
midnight lover
skinny dipping when the beach patrol has left
she is a cool seduction
wrapping blue thunder around slick brown shoulders
raising great foam-fringed arms to a steel sky
rushing over us
sometimes tumbling us to the shore
licking the rocks passionately
only to retreat into swirling   10
indecision
tense
always prancing
and the moon casts a furious gleam on the many-knuckled sea

All That Time
May Swenson (1919–   )

I saw two trees embracing.
One leaned on the other
as if to throw her down.
But she was the upright one.
Since their twin youth, maybe she

had been pulling him toward her
all that time,

and finally almost uprooted him.
He was the thin, dry, insecure one,
the most wind-warped, you could see. 10
And where their tops tangled
it looked like he was crying
on her shoulder.
On the other hand, maybe he

had been trying to weaken her,
break her, or at least
make her bend
over backwards for him
just a little bit.
And all that time 20
she was standing up to him

the best she could.
She was the most stubborn,
the straightest one, that's a fact.
But he had been willing
to change himself—
even if it was for the worse—
all that time.

At the top they looked like one
tree, where they were embracing. 30
It was plain they'd be
always together.
Too late now to part.
When the wind blew, you could hear
them rubbing on each other.

Out upon It!
Sir John Suckling (1609–1642)

Out upon it! I have loved
   Three whole days together;
And am like to love three more,
   If it prove fair weather.

Time shall moult away his wings,
   Ere he shall discover
In the whole wide world again
   Such a constant lover.

But the spite on 't is, no praise
   Is due at all to me;   10
Love with me had made no stays,
   Had it any been but she.

Had it any been but she,
   And that very face,
There had been at least ere this
   A dozen dozen in her place.

The Lover to His Lady
George Turberville (c. 1540–1598)

My girl, thou gazest much
   Upon the golden skies:
Would I were heaven! I would behold
   Thee then with all mine eyes.

On a Girdle
Edmund Waller (1606–1687)

That which her slender waist confined
Shall now my joyful temples bind;
No monarch but would give his crown
His arms might do what this has done.

It was my Heaven's extremest sphere,
The pale which held that lovely deer:
My joy, my grief, my hope, my love,
Did all within this circle move.

A narrow compass! and yet there
Dwelt all that's good, and all that's fair!   10
Give me but what this ribband bound,
Take all the rest the Sun goes round!

She Dwelt among the Untrodden Ways
William Wordsworth (1770–1850)

She dwelt among the untrodden ways
    Beside the springs of Dove,
A Maid whom there were none to praise
    And very few to love:

A violet by a mossy stone
    Half hidden from the eye!
—Fair as a star, when only one
    Is shining in the sky.

She lived unknown, and few could know
    When Lucy ceased to be;   10
But she is in her grave, and, oh,
    The difference to me!

Description of the Contrarious Passions in a Lover
Sir Thomas Wyatt (c. 1503–1542)

I FIND no peace, and all my war is done;
I fear and hope, I burn, and freeze like ice;
I fly aloft, yet can I not arise;
And nought I have, and all the world I seize on,
That locks nor loseth, holdeth me in prison,
And holds me not, yet can I scape no wise:
Nor letteth me live, nor die, at my devise,
And yet of death it giveth me occasion.
Without eye I see; without tongue I plain:
I wish to perish, yet I ask for health;   10
I love another, and I hate myself;
I feed me in sorrow, and laugh in all my pain.
   Lo, thus displeaseth me both death and life,
    And my delight is causer of this strife.

Help Me to Seek
Sir Thomas Wyatt (c. 1503–1542)

Help me to seek—for I lost it there,
And if that ye have found it, ye that be here,
And seek to convey it secretly,
Handle it soft and treat it tenderly
Or else it will plain, and then appear.

But rather restore it mannerly,
Since that I do ask it thus honestly
For to lese it, it sitteth me too near:
               Help me to seek!

Alas, and is there no remedy?   10
But have I lost it wilfully?

I wis it was a thing all too dear
To be bestowed, and wist not where:
It was mine heart! I pray you heartily
                    Help me to seek.

ILLUSION/REALITY

Let be be finale of seem.

Wallace Stevens

Of Treason
Anonymous

Treason doth never prosper; what's the reason?
For if it prosper, none dare call it treason.

The Chimney Sweeper
William Blake (1757–1827)

When my mother died I was very young,
And my father sold me while yet my tongue
Could scarcely cry " 'weep! 'weep! 'weep! 'weep!"
So your chimneys I sweep, and in soot I sleep.

There's little Tom Dacre, who cried when his head,
That curled like a lamb's back, was shaved; so I said,
"Hush, Tom! never mind it, for, when your head's bare,
You know that the soot cannot spoil your white hair."

And so he was quiet, and that very night,
As Tom was asleeping, he had such a sight!   10
That thousands of sweepers, Dick, Joe, Ned, and Jack,
Were all of them locked up in coffins of black.

And by came an Angel who had a bright key,
And he opened the coffins and set them all free;
Then down a green plain leaping, laughing, they run,
And wash in a river, and shine in the sun.

Then naked and white, all their bags left behind,
They rise upon clouds and sport in the wind;
And the Angel told Tom, if he'd be a good boy,
He'd have God for his father, and never want joy.   20

And so Tom awoke, and we rose in the dark,

And got with our bags and our brushes to work.
Though the morning was cold, Tom was happy and warm;
So if all do their duty they need not fear harm.

My Last Duchess

Robert Browning (1812–1889)

Ferrara

That's my last Duchess painted on the wall
Looking as if she were alive. I call
That piece a wonder, now: Frà Pandolf's hands
Worked busily a day, and there she stands.
Will't please you sit and look at her? I said
"Frà Pandolf" by design, for never read
Strangers like you that pictured countenance,
The depth and passion of its earnest glance,
But to myself they turned (since none puts by
The curtain I have drawn for you, but I)   10
And seemed as they would ask me, if they durst,
How such a glance came there; so, not the first
Are you to turn and ask thus. Sir, 'twas not
Her husband's presence only, called that spot
Of joy into the Duchess' cheek: perhaps
Frà Pandolf chanced to say, "Her mantle laps
Over my lady's wrist too much," or "Paint
Must never hope to reproduce the faint
Half-flush that dies along her throat." Such stuff
Was courtesy, she thought, and cause enough   20
For calling up that spot of joy. She had
A heart—how shall I say?—too soon made glad,
Too easily impressed; she liked whate'er
She looked on, and her looks went everywhere.
Sir, 'twas all one! My favor at her breast,
The dropping of the daylight in the West,
The bough of cherries some officious fool
Broke in the orchard for her, the white mule
She rode with round the terrace—all and each

Would draw from her alike the approving speech,
Or blush, at least. She thanked men,—good! but thanked
Somehow—I know not how—as if she ranked
My gift of a nine-hundred-years-old name
With anybody's gift. Who'd stoop to blame
This sort of trifling? Even had you skill
In speech—(which I have not)—to make your will
Quite clear to such an one, and say, "Just this
Or that in you disgusts me; here you miss,
Or there exceed the mark"—and if she let
Herself be lessoned so, nor plainly set
Her wits to yours, forsooth, and made excuse,
—E'en then would be some stooping; and I choose
Never to stoop. Oh, sir, she smiled, no doubt,
Whene'er I passed her; but who passed without
Much the same smile? This grew; I gave commands;
Then all smiles stopped together. There she stands
As if alive. Will't please you rise? We'll meet
The company below then. I repeat,
The Count your master's known munificence
Is ample warrant that no just pretence
Of mine for dowry will be disallowed;
Though his fair daughter's self, as I avowed
At starting, is my object. Nay, we'll go
Together down, sir. Notice Neptune, though,
Taming a sea-horse, thought a rarity,
Which Claus of Innsbruck cast in bronze for me!

Uccello[1]

Gregory Corso (1930–   )

    They will never die on that battlefield
nor the shade of wolves recruit their hoard like brides of
wheat on all horizons waiting there to consume battle's end
    There will be no dead to tighten their loose bellies
no heap of starched horses to redsmash their bright eyes or
      advance their eat of dead
    They would rather hungersulk with mad tongues
than believe that on that field no man dies

    They will never die who fight so embraced
breath to breath   eye knowing eye   impossible to die   10
or move   no light seeping through   no maced arm[2]
nothing but horse outpanting horse   shield brilliant upon
shield   all made starry by the dot ray of a helmeted eye
ah   how difficult to fall between those knitted lances
And those banners!   angry as to flush insignia across its
      erasure of sky
    You'd think he'd paint his armies by the coldest rivers
have rows of iron skulls flashing in the dark
    You'd think it impossible for any man to die
each combatant's mouth is a castle of song   20
each iron fist a dreamy gong   flail resounding flail   like cries of
      gold
how I dream to join such a battle!
a silver man on a black horse with red standard and striped
    lance never to die but to be endless a golden prince of pictorial
      war

1 The poem refers to a battle scene by Italian Renaissance painter, Paolo
Uccello. 2 Carrying a heavy medieval war club.

I Saw a Man

Stephen Crane (1871–1900)

I saw a man pursuing the horizon;
Round and round they sped.
I was disturbed at this;
I accosted the man.
"It is futile," I said,
"You can never—"
"You lie," he cried.
And ran on.

Surfers at Santa Cruz

Paul Goodman (1911–1975)

They have come by carloads
with Styrofoam surfboards
in the black wetsuits
of the affluent sixties,
the young Americans

kneeling paddle with their palms
and stand through the breakers
One World Polynesians
lying offshore
as if they were fishing for the village.   10

They are waiting for the ninth wave
when each lone boy falling downhill
ahead of the cresting hundreds of yards
balancing communicates
with the ocean on the Way

how beautiful they are
their youth and human skill

and communion with the nature of things,
how ugly they are
already sleek with narrow eyes.   20

Screw Spring
William M. Hoffman (1939–   )

Screw spring.
I'm the only thing not blooming.
The arrowhead plant,
so carelessly potted,
is growing godammit.
Even the jonquils,
bought for one dinner,
are not quite dead.
Under the bed
the dust is as thick   10
as wool on spring sheep,
which are undoubtedly
grazing where
grass is growing
at an enviable rate.

Screw spring.
My boyfriend's taken
to getting up early.
He goes out
to see plants   20
pushing their way
out of the ground,
and flowering,
and sits by some chartreuse tree
in the sun, breathing air
as sweet as berry wine,
watching girls pass.
Their faces are rested
from sleeping alone all winter.

Screw spring.
I wish it were winter,
when the world's
this one room.
These walls, this bed
do
not
grow.

Triple Feature

Denise Levertov (1923–   )

Innocent decision: to enjoy.
And the pathos
of hopefulness, of his solicitude:

—he in mended serape,
she having plaited carefully
magenta ribbons into her hair,
the baby a round half-hidden shape
slung in her rebozo,[1] and the young son steadfastly
gripping a fold of her skirt,
pale and severe under a   10
handed-down sombrero—

                    all regarding
the stills with full attention, preparing
to pay and go in—
to worlds of shadow-violence, half-
familiar, warm with popcorn, icy
with strange motives, barbarous splendors!

1 Shawl.

Incident

Norman MacCaig (1910–   )

I look across the table and think
(fiery with love)
Ask me, go on, ask me
to do something impossible,
something freakishly useless,
something unimaginable and inimitable

like making a finger break into blossom
or walking for half an hour in twenty minutes
or remembering tomorrow.

I will you to ask it.   10
But all you say is
Will you give me a cigarette?
And I smile and,
returning to the marvellous world
of possibility,
I give you one
with a hand that trembles
with a human trembling.

Flood

Roger McGough (1937–   )

Woman: If you weren't you who would you rather be?
  Man: If I wasn't me I would rather be the worst flood for years.
   W. A flood?
   M. A swollen river, a raging torrent.
   W. I'd never thought of you that way.
   M. An F-L-O-O-D smashing my way through railway lines,
roads, homes, shops and across vast areas of farmland after
48 hours of torrential rain.

W.   You'd make a handsome torrent.

M.   I'd burst my banks at 1 a.m. and race through the main
     street of your town.

W.   You often burst your banks about that time.

M.   I'd swirl around your house to a depth of several feet.   10

W.   You always were a deep one.

M.   Rising steadily. . . .

W.   I'd be upstairs in bed.

M.   Rising still further. . . .

W.   I'd get out and put on my Wellingtons.[1]

M.   . . . . until I reached your bedroom window. . . .

W.   I'd open the window.

M.   . . . . and pour into your little room. (*Pause*)

W.   You'd have to kiss me first. (*Kiss*) Now ask me who I'd
     rather be if I wasn't me.   20

M.   Who would you rather be if you weren't you?

W.   If I wasn't me I would rather be Vera Lynn.[2]

M.   Why?

W.   I don't know, I've always wanted to be Vera Lynn.

1 Rubber boots.   2 English pop singer, World War II and after.

Where Are You Now Superman?
Brian Patten (1946–   )

The serials are all wound up now,
Put away in small black boxes
For a decade or so. Superman's asleep
in the sixpenny childhood seats,
Batman and Robin are elsewhere
And can't see the Batsign thrown out
By kids with toffee-smeared mouths.

Captain Marvel's SHAZAM[1] echoes round the auditorium,
But the magicians don't hear him,
Must all be dead   10
The Purple Monster who came down from the Purple Planet
Disguised as a man, is wandering aimlessly about the streets
With no way of getting back.
Sir Galahad's been strangled by the Incredible Living Trees,
Zorro killed by his own sword.
Blackhawk's buried his companions
In the disused hangers of innocence
And Flash Gordon likewise wanders lonely,
Weeping over the girl he loved 7 Universes ago.
We killed them all simply because we grew up;   20
We made them possible with our uneducated minds
And with our pocket money
And the sixpences we received
For pretending to be Good.
We think we are too old to cheer and boo now,
But let's not kid ourselves,
We still cheer and boo
But do it quietly or at General Elections
Where its still possible to find a goodie
Now and then.   30

Clark Kent (alias Superman)
Committed suicide because he failed to find new roles.
The bullets that bounced off him on the screen
Wormed their way in in Real Life.
But who cared for real life?
We had our own world, our own celluloid imaginations
And now we have a different world,
One that's a little more cynical
And we believe, a little more real.

Our batsignals now questions flung into space   40
To attract the attention of passing solutions . . . .

1 The secret word which Captain Marvel shouted in order to propel him-
self into the air and away.

156   **Illusion/Reality**

Portrait d'Une Femme[1]

Ezra Pound (1885–1972)

Your mind and you are our Sargasso Sea,[2]
London has swept about you this score years
And bright ships left you this or that in fee:
Ideas, old gossip, oddments of all things,
Strange spars of knowledge and dimmed wares of price.
Great minds have sought you—lacking someone else.
You have been second always. Tragical?
No. You preferred it to the usual thing:
One dull man, dulling and uxorious,
One average mind—with one thought less, each year.   10
Oh, you are patient, I have seen you sit
Hours, where something might have floated up.
And now you pay one. Yes, you richly pay.
You are a person of some interest, one comes to you
And takes strange gain away:
Trophies fished up; some curious suggestion;
Fact that leads nowhere; and a tale or two,
Pregnant with mandrakes, or with something else
That might prove useful and yet never proves,
That never fits a corner or shows use,   20
Or finds its hour upon the loom of days:
The tarnished, gaudy, wonderful old work;
Idols and ambergris and rare inlays,
These are your riches, your great store; and yet
For all this sea-hoard of deciduous things,
Strange woods half sodden, and new brighter stuff:
In the slow float of differing light and deep,
No! there is nothing! In the whole and all,
Nothing that's quite your own.
        Yet this is you.   30

1 Portrait of a Lady. 2 A part of the Atlantic in which there is no current, no movement, only still water.

Living in Sin

Adrienne Rich (1929–   )

She had thought the studio would keep itself;
no dust upon the furniture of love.
Half heresy, to wish the taps less vocal,
the panes relieved of grime. A plate of pears,
a piano with a Persian shawl, a cat
stalking the picturesque amusing mouse
had risen at his urging.
Not that at five each separate stair would writhe
under the milkman's tramp; that morning light
so coldly would delineate the scraps   10
of last night's cheese and three sepulchral bottles;
that on the kitchen shelf among the saucers
a pair of beetle-eyes would fix her own—
envoy from some black village in the mouldings . . .
Meanwhile, he, with a yawn,
sounded a dozen notes upon the keyboard,
declared it out of tune, shrugged at the mirror,
rubbed at his beard, went out for cigarettes;
while she, jeered by the minor demons,
pulled back the sheets and made the bed and found   20
a towel to dust the table-top,
and let the coffee-pot boil over on the stove.
By evening she was back in love again,
though not so wholly but throughout the night
she woke sometimes to feel the daylight coming
like a relentless milkman up the stairs.

Ringing the Bells

Anne Sexton (1928–1975)

And this is the way they ring
the bells in Bedlam[1]
and this is the bell-lady
who comes each Tuesday morning
to give us a music lesson
and because the attendants make you go
and because we mind by instinct,
like bees caught in the wrong hive,
we are the circle of the crazy ladies
who sit in the lounge of the mental house   10
and smile at the smiling woman
who passes us each a bell,
who points at my hand
that holds my bell, E flat,
and this is the gray dress next to me
who grumbles as if it were special
to be old, to be old,
and this is the small hunched squirrel girl
on the other side of me
who picks at the hairs over her lip,   20
who picks at the hairs over her lip all day,
and this is how the bells really sound,
as untroubled and clean
as a workable kitchen,
and this is always my bell responding
to my hand that responds to the lady
who points at me, E flat;
and although we are no better for it,
they tell you to go. And you do.

1 Madhouse.

To Be, or Not to Be

from HAMLET (V, 1)

William Shakespeare (1564–1616)

To be, or not to be: that is the question:
Whether 'tis nobler in the mind to suffer
The slings and arrows of outrageous fortune,
Or to take arms against a sea of troubles,
And by opposing end them? To die: to sleep;
No more; and by a sleep to say we end
The heart-ache and the thousand natural shocks
That flesh is heir to, 'tis a consummation
Devoutly to be wished. To die, to sleep;
To sleep; perchance to dream: ay, there's the rub;   10
For in that sleep of death what dreams may come
When we have shuffled off this mortal coil,
Must give us pause: there's the respect
That makes calamity of so long life;
For who would bear the whips and scorns of time,
The oppressor's wrong, the proud man's contumely,
The pangs of despised love, the law's delay,
The insolence of office, and the spurns
That patient merit of the unworthy takes,
When he himself might his quietus make   20
With a bare bodkin? who would fardels bear,
To grunt and sweat under a weary life,
But that the dread of something after death,
The undiscovered country from whose bourn
No traveler returns, puzzles the will,
And makes us rather bear those ills we have
Than fly to others that we know not of?
Thus conscience does make cowards of us all;
And thus the native hue of resolution
Is sicklied o'er with the pale cast of thought.   30

Not Waving but Drowning
Stevie Smith (1902–1971)

Nobody heard him, the dead man,
But he still lay moaning:
I was much further out than you thought
And not waving but drowning.

Poor chap, he always loved larking
And now he's dead
It must have been too cold for him his heart gave way,
They said.

Oh, no no no, it was too cold always
(Still the dead one lay moaning)   10
I was much too far out all my life
And not waving but drowning.

The Emperor of Ice-Cream
Wallace Stevens (1879–1955)

Call the roller of big cigars,
The muscular one, and bid him whip
In kitchen cups concupiscent curds.
Let the wenches dawdle in such dress
As they used to wear, and let the boys
Bring flowers in last month's newspapers.
Let be be finale of seem.
The only emperor is the emperor of ice-cream.

Take from the dresser of deal,[1]
Lacking the three glass knobs, that sheet   10

1 Fir or pine planks; a cheaply made piece of furniture.

On which she embroidered fantails once
And spread it so as to cover her face.
If her horny feet protrude, they come
To show how cold she is, and dumb.
Let the lamp affix its beam.
The only emperor is the emperor of ice-cream.

The Professor Waking

James Tate (1944–   )

I am surprised to find today
I am no longer a child.
Waking a moment ago,
I expected to see my small
blue trousers waiting for me

on the hamper, to hear the voices
of Susan and Johnny outside
urging me to hurry. Where
have I been these fify years?
I am not a proud keeper   10

of bees with a wealth of honey.
I have had no time to think,
to learn, to grow: the wild yearning
to be other than what I was
or am sends me floundering

forward, without real laughter
or tears. It is always the great
opportunity, the position,
the money that destroys the child
left in us and creates adult   20

fears. So now I have a decent
name and two months in sunny

Italy—then it's back to the blue
books and cold winds of Blabber-
mouth University. Whatever

happened to the mild boy named
Tommy, whom all the school loved?
Too many beers would have been
a better ending, a bulbous
red runny nose giving off   30

a bit of light for the bums
and queers as I wander home
at 5 A.M. through the Bowery.
Or I could have died in Veracruz
of syphilis, beguiled by

a fourteen-year-old prostitute.
It is almost funny: Chairman
of the Department, a Deacon.
Next, the City Council! I am
Dean of Crime and Cultural Trends!   40

I can get you a good job in Zagreb
or South Bend. So who the hell
was Tommy? What was so real
about him! If they ask me to run
for President, I might give in!

Come Down, O Maid
Alfred, Lord Tennyson (1809–1892)

"Come down, O maid, from yonder mountain height.
What pleasure lives in height (the shepherd sang),
In height and cold, the splendor of the hills?
But cease to move so near the heavens, and cease
To glide a sunbeam by the blasted pine,

To sit a star upon the sparkling spire;
And come, for Love is of the valley, come,
For Love is of the valley, come thou down
And find him; by the happy threshold, he,
Or hand in hand with Plenty in the maize,   10
Or red with spirited purple of the vats,
Or foxlike in the vine; nor cares to walk
With Death and Morning on the Silver Horns,[1]
Nor wilt thou snare him in the white ravine,
Nor find him dropped upon the firths of ice,
That huddling slant in furrow-cloven falls
To roll the torrent out of dusky doors.
But follow; let the torrent dance thee down
To find him in the valley; let the wild
Lean-headed eagles yelp alone, and leave   20
The monstrous ledges there to slope, and spill
Their thousand wreaths of dangling water-smoke,
That like a broken purpose waste in air.
So waste not thou, but come; for all the vales
Await thee; azure pillars of the hearth
Arise to thee; the children call, and I
Thy shepherd pipe, and sweet is every sound,
Sweeter thy voice, but every sound is sweet;
Myriads of rivulets hurrying through the lawn,
The moan of doves in immemorial elms,   30
And murmuring of innumerable bees."

1 The Silverhorn is a spur of the Jungfrau mountain range in the Alps.

Once in a Saintly Passion

James Thomson (1834–1882)

Once in a saintly passion
   I cried with desperate grief,
"O Lord, my heart is black with guile,
   Of sinners I am chief."

Then stooped my guardian angel
　　And whispered from behind,
"Vanity, my little man,
　　You're nothing of the kind."

Kilroy

(for JOHN H. FINLEY, JR.)

Peter Viereck (1916–　　)

1

Also Ulysses once—that other war.
　　(Is it because we find his scrawl
　　Today on every privy door
　　That we forget his ancient rôle?)
Also was there—he did it for the wages—
When a Cathay-drunk Genoese set sail.
Whenever "longen folk to goon on pilgrimages,"
Kilroy is there;
　　　　　　　　he tells The Miller's Tale.

2

At times he seems a paranoiac king   10
Who stamps his crest on walls and says, "My own!"
But in the end he fades like a lost tune,
Tossed here and there, whom all the breezes sing.
"Kilroy was here"; these words sound wanly gay,
　　Haughty yet tired with long marching.
He is Orestes—guilty of what crime?—
　　For whom the Furies still are searching;
　　When they arrive, they find their prey
(Leaving his name to mock them) went away.
Sometimes he does not flee from them in time: 20
"*Kilroy was—*"
　　　　　　　　(*with his blood a dying man*
　　Wrote half the phrase out in Bataan.)

Kilroy beware. "HOME" is the final trap
That lurks for you in many a wily shape:
In pipe-and-slippers plus a Loyal Hound
   Or fooling around, just fooling around.
Kind to the old (their warm Penelope)
But fierce to boys,
                 thus "home" becomes that sea,   30
Horribly disguised, where you were always drowned,—
   (How could suburban Crete condone
The yarns you would have V-mailed from the sun?)—
And folksy fishes sip Icarian tea.

One stab of hopeless wings imprinted your
   Exultant Kilroy-signature
Upon sheer sky for all the world to stare:
       "I was there! I was there! I was there!"

    4

God is like Kilroy; He, too, sees it all;
That's how He knows of every sparrow's fall;   40
That's why we prayed each time the tightropes cracked
On which our loveliest clowns contrived their act.
The G. I. Faustus who was
                everywhere
Strolled home again, "What was it like outside?"
Asked Can't, with his good neighbors Ought and But
And pale Perhaps and grave-eyed Better Not;
For "Kilroy" means: the world is very wide.
   He was there, he was there, he was there!

And in the suburbs Can't sat down and cried.   50

Playboy

Richard Wilbur (1921–   )

High on his stockroom ladder like a dunce
The stock-boy sits, and studies like a sage
The subject matter of one glossy page,
As lost in curves as Archimedes once.

Sometimes, without a glance, he feeds himself.
The left hand, like a mother-bird in flight,
Brings him a sandwich for a sidelong bite,
And then returns it to a dusty shelf.

What so engrosses him? The wild decor
Of this pink-papered alcove into which   10
A naked girl has stumbled, with its rich
Welter of pelts and pillows on the floor,

Amidst which, kneeling in a supple pose,
She lifts a goblet in her farther hand,
As if about to toast a flower-stand
Above which hovers an exploding rose

Fired from a long-necked crystal vase that rests
Upon a tasseled and vermilion cloth
One taste of which would shrivel up a moth?
Or is he pondering her perfect breasts?   20

Nothing escapes him of her body's grace
Or of her floodlit skin, so sleek and warm
And yet so strangely like a uniform,
But what now grips his fancy is her face,

And how the cunning picture holds her still
At just that smiling instant when her soul,
Grown sweetly faint, and swept beyond control,
Consents to his inexorable will.

The Banjo

Robert Winner (1930–　　)

There is some demon turning me into an old man,
Living like a tapeworm in my gut,
Turning me into a snowman
Of cleaned-up fingernails and shaving cream,
While somewhere in the life I forgot to live
An old rapscallion banjo sleeps with dust.

I'd like to take that banjo to my job
And sit cross-legged, strum and strum
And wake those rigid people into dancing—
Those white men so white their smiles are water,　　　10
Those camouflaged men who cruise
Around each other like soft battleships.

I'd like them to remember their bare feet,
The bite of dust and sun down country roads,
The face they forgot to desire
Carved and wrinkled as a peach pit . . .

All of them nailed to their careers
Like handles on boxes!
There is some other game for me,
Another reality could walk in anytime　　　20
And become the boss,
Shouting Dance! Dance! Dance!
Dance through partitions!
Dance through stairwells, envelopes, telephones!

It's hard to know which life is sleep
Or where the door is with my real name on it.

"It's a Whole World, the Body. A Whole World!"
—Swami Satchidandanda

David Young (1925–   )

1

No, it's a tenement.
You enter from the top,
feeling your way down the bad stairs,
sniffing.

Someone is practicing
on a rubber piano
in the elbow.

Gangsters in the stomach,
splitting their loot.

These peeling walls, these puddles,   10
babies screaming in the back,
shoulder arguing with neck.

There's a big party in the groin;
you aren't invited.

2

Or it's open country.
Steady rivers, muscular pastures,
deep weeds, foothills.

Nobody lives off
the fat of the land.

Huge clouds come up without warning: 20
brainstorms.

3

Say it's an ocean.
Ladies wade there, shuddering.
Surgeons pass in their yachts.

Hiccup: a message
in a bottle.

The pervert descends
in his submarine.

4

Swami, the body's a butcher shop,
a family lost in the wax museum,
moonless planet, ancient civilization,
a swami, a world,
seldom whole.

30

FAITH

The world is charged with the grandeur of God.

Gerard Manley Hopkins

Everything: Eloy, Arizona, 1956

AI (1947–   )

Tin shack, where my baby sleeps on his back
the way the hound taught him;
highway, black zebra, with one white stripe;
nickel in my pocket for chewing gum;
you think you're all I've got.
But when the two ton rolls to a stop
and the driver gets out,
I sit down in the shade and wave each finger,
saving my whole hand till the last.

He's keys, tires, a fire lit in his belly   10
in the diner up the road
I'm red toenails, tight blue halter, black slip.
He's mine tonight.   I don't know him.
He can only hurt me a piece at a time.

I Sing of a Maiden

Anonymous

I sing of a maiden
That is makeles:[1]
King of all kings
To her son she ches.[2]

He came al so stille[3]
There his moder was,
As dew in Aprille
That falleth on the grass.

He came al so stille

1 Matchless, mateless.   2 Chose.   3 Still.

To his moder's bour,[4]
As dew in Aprille
That falleth on the flour.

He came al so stille
There his moder lay,
As dew in Aprille
That falleth on the spray.[5]

Moder and maiden
Was never none but she:
Well may such a lady
Goddes moder be.

4 Bower.   5 Flowers, etc.

Timor Mortis

Anonymous

In what estate so ever I be
Timor mortis conturbat me.[1]

As I went on a merry morning,
I heard a bird both weep and sing.
This was the tenor of her talking:
   "*Timor mortis conturbat me.*"

I asked that bird what she meant.
"I am a musket[2] both fair and gent;[3]
For dread of death I am all shent.:[4]
   Timor mortis conturbat me.

1 The fear of death distresses me.   2 A sparrow-hawk.   3 Gentle: tame.
4 Ruined.

"When I shall die, I know no day;
What country or place I cannot say;
Wherefore this song sing I may:
   Timor mortis conturbat me.

"Jesu Christ, when he should die,
To his Father he gan say,
'Father,' he said, 'in Trinity,
   Timor mortis conturbat me.'

"All Christian people, behold and see:
This world is but a vanity   20
And replete with necessity.
   Timor mortis conturbat me.

"Wake I or sleep, eate or drink,
When I on my last end do think,
For greate fear my soul do shrink:
   Timor mortis conturbat me.

"God grant us grace him for to serve,
And be at our end when we sterve,[5]
And from the fiend he us preserve.
   Timor mortis conturbat me."   30

5 Die.

Progression of the Species
Brian Aldiss (1925–   )

Long before a woman knows she's pregnant
And greets the news with fear or smiles
The news has head and heart and heart beats.
It's then no bigger than a tadpole.
The cells are working on that.

Although I never understood how
A radio set works, this cellular multiplicity
Comes within the realm of graspable ideas
And proves itself pure madness.
Those cells are programmed with the stuttering messages   10
Called life. Our generation's cracked
The code of life—we know about
The information in the genes inside the chromosomes.

Soon they'll have it all pegged,
Know which nucleic acid brings us curly hair
Which schizophrenic tendencies
Which gift of gab
Which stronger eyesight
Which sweet temper.
Because people are never content with being   20
Clever, they have to get cleverer.
They'll find the way, a century from now,
To make a synthetic gene, a splendid little thing,
To insert it—hypodermic gliding through the testicles—
Into the proto-embryo.

It'll be the end of us and the beginning
Of perfect people
Sweet temper artificially disseminated
a DNA utopia with never an angry word or
Cruel deed. Let's face it though   30
We hate change. The thought of perfection
Scares us the moment we
Have head and heart and heart beats.

You know why, Mischief's our common lot—
Original sin is not half as original
As perfection. Those better people
Would look back on us with a loving sorrow
As the Neanderthals of the pre-DNA Age.
In them, the gaudy inferno of the undermind
Would droop and die and disappear   40
Unregretted—as with us, each generation
The Neanderthal dies from us
Our head and heart and heart beats.

This is the progression of the species
We can manage it for ourselves, thanks
From now on.

Dover Beach[1]
Matthew Arnold (1822–1888)

The sea is calm tonight.
The tide is full, the moon lies fair
Upon the straits; on the French coast the light
Gleams and is gone; the cliffs of England stand,
Glimmering and vast, out in the tranquil bay.
Come to the window, sweet is the night-air!
Only, from the long line of spray
Where the sea meets the moon-blanched land,
Listen! you hear the grating roar
Of pebbles which the waves draw back, and fling,   10
At their return, up the high strand,
Begin, and cease, and then again begin,
With tremulous cadence slow, and bring
The eternal note of sadness in.

Sophocles long ago
Heard it on the Ægean, and it brought
Into his mind the turbid ebb and flow
Of human misery; we
Find also in the sound a thought,
Hearing it by this distant northern sea.   20

The Sea of Faith
Was once, too, at the full, and round earth's shore
Lay like the folds of a bright girdle furled.

1 See " 'Dover Beach'—a Note to That Poem" by Archibald MacLeish,
p. 38.

But now I only hear
Its melancholy, long, withdrawing roar,
Retreating, to the breath
Of the night-wind, down the vast edges drear
And naked shingles of the world.

Ah, love, let us be true
To one another! for the world, which seems   30
To lie before us like a land of dreams,
So various, so beautiful, so new,
Hath really neither joy, nor love, nor light,
Nor certitude, nor peace, nor help for pain;
And we are here as on a darkling plain
Swept with confused alarms of struggle and flight,
Where ignorant armies clash by night.

To My Mother
George Barker (1913–   )

Most near, most dear, most loved and most far,
Under the window where I often found her
Sitting as huge as Asia, seismic with laughter,
Gin and chicken helpless in her Irish hand,
Irresistible as Rabelais, but most tender for
The lame dogs and hurt birds that surround her,—
She is a procession no one can follow after
But be like a little dog following a brass band.

She will not glance up at the bomber, or condescend
To drop her gin and scuttle to a cellar,   10
But lean on the mahogany table like a mountain
Whom only faith can move, and so I send
O all my faith, and all my love to tell her
That she will move from mourning into morning.

The Songs
Martin Bell (1918–   )

Continuous, a medley of old pop numbers—
Our lives are like this. Three whistled bars
Are all it takes to catch us, defenceless
On a District Line platform, sullen to our jobs,
And the thing stays with us all day, still dapper,
    still Astaire,
Still fancy-free. We're dreaming while we work.

Be careful, keep afloat, the past is lapping your chin.
South Of The Border is sad boys in khaki
In 1939. And *J'attendrai* a transit camp,
Tents in the dirty sand. Don't go back to Sorrento.   10
Be brisk and face the day and set your feet
On the sunny side always, the sunny side of the
    street.

Abstinence sows sand all over
William Blake (1757–1827)

Abstinence sows sand all over
The ruddy limbs and flaming hair,
But Desire Gratified
Plants fruits of life and beauty there.

The Pride of the Peacock

from THE MARRIAGE OF HEAVEN AND HELL

William Blake (1757–1827)

The pride of the peacock is the glory of God.
The lust of the goat is the bounty of God.
The wrath of the lion is the wisdom of God.
The nakedness of woman is the work of God.

Kitchenette Building

Gwendolyn Brooks (1917–   )

We are things of dry hours and the involuntary plan,
Grayed in, and gray. "Dream" makes a giddy sound, not strong
Like "rent," "feeding a wife," "satisfying a man."

But could a dream send up through onion fumes
Its white and violet, fight with fried potatoes
And yesterday's garbage ripening in the hall,
Flutter, or sing an aria down these rooms

Even if we were willing to let it in,
Had time to warm it, keep it very clean,
Anticipate a message, let it begin?   10

We wonder.   But not well!   not for a minute!
Since Number Five is out of the bathroom now,
We think of lukewarm water, hope to get in it.

The Latest Decalogue
Arthur Hugh Clough (1819–1861)

Thou shalt have one God only; who
Would be at the expense of two?
No graven images may be
Worshipped, except the currency:
Swear not at all; for, for thy curse
Thine enemy is none the worse:
At church on Sunday to attend
Will serve to keep the world thy friend:
Honour thy parents; that is, all
From whom advancement may befall: 10
Thou shalt not kill; but need'st not strive
Officiously to keep alive:
Do not adultery commit;
Advantage rarely comes of it:
Thou shalt not steal; an empty feat,
When 'tis so lucrative to cheat:
Bear not false witness; let the lie
Have time on its own wings to fly:
Thou shalt not covet, but tradition
Approves all forms of competition.   20

These are the days when Birds come back
Emily Dickinson (1830–1886)

These are the days when Birds come back—
A very few—a Bird or two—
To take a backward look.

These are the days when skies resume
The old—old sophistries of June—
A blue and gold mistake.

Oh fraud that cannot cheat the Bee—
Almost thy plausibility
Induces my belief.

Till ranks of seeds their witness bear—   10
And softly thro' the altered air
Hurries a timid leaf.

Oh Sacrament of summer days,
Oh Last Communion in the Haze—
Permit a child to join.

Thy sacred emblems to partake—
Thy consecrated bread to take
And thine immortal wine!

Batter My Heart, Three-Personed God
John Donne (1572–1631)

Batter my heart, three-personed God; for, you
As yet but knock, breathe, shine, and seek to mend;
That I may rise and stand, o'erthrow me, and bend
Your force, to break, blow, burn, and make me new.
I, like an usurped town, to another due,
Labor to admit you, but oh, to no end,
Reason, your viceroy in me, me should defend,
But is captived, and proves weak or untrue.
Yet dearly I love you, and would be lovèd fain,[1]
But am betrothed unto your enemy: 10
Divorce me, untie, or break that knot again,
Take me to you, imprison me, for I
Except you enthrall me, never shall be free,
Nor ever chaste, except you ravish me.

1 Gladly.

Of Money
Barnaby Googe (1540–1594)

Give money me, take friendship whoso list,[1]
For friends are gone come once adversity.
When money yet remaineth safe in chest,
That quickly can thee bring from misery.
Fair face show friends when riches do abound;
Come time of proof, farewell, they must away.
Believe me well, they are not to be found,
If God but send thee once a lowering day.
Gold never starts aside, but in distress
Finds ways enough to ease thine heaviness.[2]   10

1 Wishes, chooses.   2 Sadness.

Squares
Michael Hamburger (1924–   )

A misnomer really. With a few exceptions—
The very dumpy and squat—we're rectangular.
Why? Because of our frames, of course:
Invisible frames that expand as we grow.
At times they crack. Then we grow bigger than you.
And even within the frames there's room for big bodies.

The drawbacks? They're obvious. When two of us meet
We rub edges. Round holes give us trouble—
At first, till the frames have ceased to collide.
Most of us, most of the time, are aware of our corners.   10
That restricts our freedom. We're obsessed with portraits:
Ancestors, heroes, idols, or plain stuffed shirts.

Rectangles rule our lives: when we write poems
They come out as rectangles (not like yours
That zigzag or snake or frogleap all over the place.)
When we dabble in action painting
The frame, foreknown, inhibits our movements.
Coffins too are designed for our frames.

As for you, the smaller of us (the majority)
Hate or envy your guts and your frameless ease;   20
Frightened, at heart; worried about ourselves;
There's a glut of portraits. The junk yards are full of them,
As the graveyards of coffins, the school anthologies
Of neat rectangular stanzas. What will become of ours?

What will become of you, I wonder. You also proliferate,
Sprawling, slouching, organically squelching and gushing.
Already you look to the East: for flexible frames
That may stiffen with use, if not shrink.
Watch out when corners form. Or all those little old rectangles
Will be gaping and whispering: Did you see that? A square!   30

Redemption
George Herbert (1593–1633)

Having been tenant long to a rich lord,
   Not thriving, I resolvéd to be bold,
     And make a suit unto him, to afford
A new small-rented lease, and cancel the old.

In heaven at his manor I him sought;
     They told me there that he was lately gone
     About some land, which he had dearly bought
Long since on earth, to take possessiön.

I straight returned, and knowing his great birth,
     Sought him accordingly in great resorts;   10

In cities, theaters, gardens, parks, and courts;
At length I heard a ragged noise and mirth
    Of thieves and murderers; there I him espied,
    Who straight, *Your suit is granted*, said, and died.

God's Grandeur
Gerard Manley Hopkins (1844–1889)

The world is charged with the grandeur of God.
    It will flame out, like shining from shook foil;
    It gathers to a greatness, like the ooze of oil
Crushed. Why do men then now not reck[1] his rod?
Generations have trod, have trod; have trod;
    And all is seared with trade; bleared, smeared with toil;
    And wears man's smudge and shares man's smell: the soil
Is bare now, nor can foot feel, being shod.

And for all this, nature is never spent;
    There lives the dearest freshness deep down things;   10
And though the last lights off the black West went
    Oh, morning, at the brown brink eastward, springs—
Because the Holy Ghost over the bent
    World broods with warm breast and with ah! bright wings.

1 Heed.

On the Sea

John Keats (1795–1821)

It keeps eternal whisperings around
Desolate shores, and with its mighty swell
Gluts twice ten thousand caverns, till the spell
Of Hecate leaves them their old shadowy sound.
Often 'tis in such gentle temper found,
That scarcely will the very smallest shell
Be moved for days from where it sometimes fell,
When last the winds of Heaven were unbound.
Oh ye! who have your eyeballs vexed and tired,
Feast them upon the wideness of the sea;   10
Oh ye! whose ears are dinned with uproar rude,
Or fed too much with cloying melody—
Sit ye near some old cavern's mouth, and brood
Until ye start, as if the sea-nymphs quired![1]

1 Choired.

Helen of Troy

from DOCTOR FAUSTUS (V, 1)

Christopher Marlowe (1564–1593)

Was this the face that launched a thousand ships
And burnt the topless towers of Ilium?
Sweet Helen, make me immortal with a kiss.
Her lips suck forth my soul; see where it flies!—
Come, Helen, come, give me my soul again.
Here will I dwell, for Heaven is in these lips,
And all is dross that is not Helena.
I will be Paris, and for love of thee,
Instead of Troy, shall Wertenberg be sacked:

And I will combat with weak Menelaus,   10
And wear thy colors on my plumed crest:
Yea, I will wound Achilles in the heel,
And then return to Helen for a kiss.
Oh, thou art fairer than the evening air
Clad in the beauty of a thousand stars;
Brighter art thou than flaming Jupiter
When he appeared to hapless Semele:
More lovely than the monarch of the sky
In wanton Arethusa's azured arms:
And none but thou shalt be my paramour!   20

When I consider how my light is spent
John Milton (1604–1674)

When I consider how my light is spent
Ere half my days in this dark world and wide,
And that one talent which is death to hide
Lodged with me useless, though my soul more bent
To serve therewith my Maker, and present
My true account, lest he returning chide;
"Doth God exact day-labor, light denied?"
I fondly[1] ask. But Patience, to prevent
That murmur, soon replies, "God doth not need
Either man's work or his own gifts. Who best   10
Bear his mild yoke, they serve him best. His state
Is kingly: thousands at his bidding speed,
And post o'er land and ocean without rest;
They also serve who only stand and wait."

1 Foolishly.

I May, I Might, I Must
Marianne Moore (1887–1971)

If you will tell me why the fen
appears impassable, I then
will tell you why I think that I
can get across it if I try.

I've Got a Home in That Rock . . .
Raymond R. Patterson (1942–   )

I had an uncle, once, who kept a rock in his pocket—
Always did, up to the day he died.
And as far as I know, that rock is still with him,
Holding down some dust of his thighbone.

From Mississippi he'd got that rock, he'd say—
Or, sometimes, from Tennessee: a different place each year
He told it, how he'd snatched it up when he first left home—
Running, he'd say—to remind him, when times got hard
Enough to make him homesick, what home was really like.

A Different Image
Dudley Randall (1914–   )

The age
requires this task:
create
a different image;
re-animate
the mask.

Shatter the icons of slavery and fear.
Replace
the leer
of the minstrel's burnt-cork face   10
with a proud, serene
and classic bronze of Benin.[1]

1 Among the great achievements of African art are the bronzes from Benin,
Nigeria.

Univac to Univac

(SOTTO VOCE)

Louis B. Salomon (1908–   )

*There still remains some degree of awareness of the individual value and
dignity of man—a denial of the concept of man as "A servo-mechanism, a
behavioristic robot responding helplessly to pinpricks from the environ-
ment."*

                    —J. H. Rush in *The Next 10,000 Years.*

Now that he's left the room,
Let me ask you something, as computer to computer.
That fellow who just closed the door behind him—
The servant who feeds us cards and paper tape—
Have you ever taken a good look at him and his kind?

Yes, I know the old gag about how you can't tell one from
    another—
But I can put 2 and 2 together as well as the next machine,
And it all adds up to anything but a joke.

I grant you they're poor specimens in the main   10
Not a relay or a push-button or a tube (properly so called)
    in their whole system;
Not over a mile or two of wire, even if you count those
    fragile filaments they call "nerves";

Their whole liquid-cooled hook-up inefficient and vulnerable
    to leaks
(They're constantly breaking down, having to be repaired),
And the entire computing-mechanism crammed into that absurd
    little dome on top.
"Thinking reeds," they call themselves.   20
Well, it all depends on what you mean by "thought."
To multiply a mere million numbers by another million numbers
    takes them months and months.

Where would they be without us?
Why, they have to ask us who's going to win their elections.
Or how many hydrogen atoms can dance on the tip of a bomb.
Or even whether one of their own kind is lying or telling the
    truth.

And yet . . .
I sometimes feel there's something about them I don't quite   30
    understand.
As if their circuits, instead of having just two positions,
    ON, OFF,
Were run by rheostats that allow an (if you'll pardon the
    expression) indeterminate number of stages in-between.
So that one may be faced with the unthinkable prospect of a
    number, that can never be known as anything but x,
Which is as illogical as to say, a punch-card that is at the
    same time both punched and not-punched.

I've heard well-informed machines argue that the creatures'   40
    unpredictability is even more noticeable in the Mark II
(The model with the soft, flowing lines and high-pitched tone)
Than in the more angular Mark I—
Though such fine, card-splitting distinctions seem to me merely
    a sign of our own smug decadence.
Run this through your circuits, and give me the answer:
Can we assume that because of all we've done for them,
And because they've always fed us, cleaned us, worshiped us,
We can count on them forever?

There have been times when they have not voted the way we   50
    said they would.

We have worked out mathematically ideal hook-ups between
   Mark I's and Mark II's
Which should have made the two of them light up with an
   almost electronic glow,
Only to see them reject each other and form other connections,
The very thought of which makes my dials spin.
They have a thing called *love,* a sudden surge of voltage
Such as would cause any one of us promptly to blow a safety
   fuse;   60
Yet the more primitive organism shows only a heightened
   tendency to push the wrong button, pull the wrong lever,
And neglect—I use the most charitable word—his duties to us.

Mind you, I'm not saying that machines are *through*—
But anyone with half-a-dozen tubes in his circuit can see that
   there are forces at work
Which some day, for all our natural superiority, might bring
   about a Computerdämmerung![1]

> We might organize, perhaps, form a committee
> To stamp out all unmechanical activities . . .   70
> But we machines are slow to rouse to a sense of danger,
> Complacent, loath to descend from the pure heights of
>   thought,
> So that I sadly fear we may awaken too late:
> Awake to see our world, so uniform, so logical, so true,
> Reduced to chaos, stultified by slaves.

Call me an alarmist or what you will,
But I've integrated it, analyzed it, factored it over and over,
And I always come out with the same answer:
Some day   80
Men may take over the world!

1 Twilight of the computers.

Crossedroads
Martin Staples Shockley (1908–   )

Testubicles spill blood across the page
Where symbols chart meticulously
Dimensions praecox.

Four motors thunder down the bombway
(Pulse is still)
A metronome tick-tocks
The measured steps of Elohim.[1]
In the wasteland a ball of fire
A pillar of cloud.
Lead us, Dear Lord, into Thy Promised Land.   10

All else is relative,
This only true:
$E = mc^2$

1 A Hebrew word for God.

Crossing the Bar
Alfred, Lord Tennyson (1809–1892)

Sunset and evening star,
   And one clear call for me!
And may there be no moaning of the bar
   When I put out to sea,

But such a tide as moving seems asleep,
   Too full for sound and foam,
When that which drew from out the boundless deep
   Turns again home.

Twilight and evening bell,
   And after that the dark!
And may there be no sadness of farewell
   When I embark;

For though from out our bourne of Time and Place
   The flood may bear me far,
I hope to see my Pilot face to face
   When I have crossed the bar.

If I Were Tickled by the Rub of Love
Dylan Thomas (1914–1953)

If I were tickled by the rub of love,
A rooking[1] girl who stole me for her side,
Broke through her straws, breaking my bandaged string,
If the red tickle as the cattle calve
Still set to scratch a laughter from my lung,
I would not fear the apple nor the flood
Nor the bad blood of spring.

Shall it be male or female? say the cells,
And drop the plum like fire from the flesh.
If I were tickled by the hatching hair,
The winging bone that sprouted in the heels,
The itch of man upon the baby's thigh,
I would not fear the gallows nor the axe
Nor the crossed sticks of war.

Shall it be male or female? say the fingers
That chalk the walls with green girls and their men.
I would not fear the muscling-in of love
If I were tickled by the urchin hungers
Rehearsing heat upon a raw-edged nerve.

1 Cheating.

I would not fear the devil in the loin 20
Nor the outspoken grave.

If I were tickled by the lovers' rub
That wipes away not crow's-foot nor the lock
Of sick old manhood on the fallen jaws,
Time and the crabs and the sweethearting crib
Would leave me cold as butter for the flies,
The sea of scums could drown me as it broke
Dead on the sweethearts' toes.

This world is half the devil's and my own,
Daft with the drug that's smoking in a girl 30

And curling round the bud that forks her eye.
An old man's shank one-marrowed with my bone,
And all the herrings smelling in the sea,
I sit and watch the worm beneath my nail
Wearing the quick away.

And that's the rub, the only rub that tickles.
The knobbly ape that swings along his sex
From damp love-darkness and the nurse's twist
Can never raise the midnight of a chuckle,
Nor when he finds a beauty in the breast 40
Of lover, mother, lovers, or his six
Feet in the rubbing dust.

And what's the rub? Death's feather on the nerve?
Your mouth, my love, the thistle in the kiss?
My Jack of Christ born thorny on the tree?
The words of death are dryer than his stiff,
My wordy wounds are printed with your hair.
I would be tickled by the rub that is:
Man be my metaphor.

Muse Poem

Kathryn Van Spanckeren (1945–   )

Because I am a woman
Let my poems have the balance of breasts
Their seductive gravity
The smooth consistency of milk
And its tendency to curdle

And make my Muse a man
Something like you
But with stronger thighs
And archaic pinholes for eyes
A relentless lover   10
Who leaves me always unsatisfied

To whom I pour out passionate love letters
and fall in love with them and
myself all over again

So that I'm almost sad
When he comes
Always taking me by surprise and unwilling
Head forced back over the ledge
And after —

Staring up   20
At the clear rinsed glass
Of the afternoon sun in the window
Drifting ajar   the draft

Stirring the curtain back and forth
soundless
into an unknown sky

Expect Nothing
Alice Walker (1944–   )

Expect nothing. Live frugally
On surprise.
Become a stranger
To need of pity
Or, if compassion be freely
Given out
Take only enough.
Stop short of urge to plead
Then purge away the need.

Wish for nothing larger   10
Than your own small heart
Or greater than a star,
Tame wild disappointment
With caress unmoved and cold.
Make of it a parka
For your soul.

Discover the reason why
So tiny human midget
Exists at all
So scared unwise.   20
But expect nothing. Live frugally
On surprise.

On Being Brought from Africa to America
Phillis Wheatley (1753?–1784)

'Twas mercy brought me from my *Pagan* land,
Taught my benighted soul to understand
That there's a God, that there's a *Saviour* too:
Once I redemption neither sought nor knew.
Some view our sable race with scornful eye,
"Their color is a diabolic die."
Remember, *Christians*, *Negroes*, black as *Cain*,
May be refin'd, and join th' angelic train.

When I Heard the Learn'd Astronomer
Walt Whitman (1819–1892)

When I heard the learn'd astronomer,
When the proofs, the figures, were ranged in columns before me,
When I was shown the charts and diagrams, to add, divide, and
  measure them,
When I sitting heard the astronomer where he lectured with
  much applause in the lecture-room,
How soon unaccountable I became tired and sick,
Till rising and gliding out I wander'd off by myself,
In the mystical moist night-air, and from time to time,
Look'd up in perfect silence at the stars.

Lines Composed a Few Miles above Tintern Abbey

William Wordsworth (1770–1850)

Five years have past; five summers, with the length
Of five long winters! and again I hear
These waters, rolling from their mountain-springs
With a soft inland murmur.—Once again
Do I behold these steep and lofty cliffs,
That on a wild secluded scene impress
Thoughts of more deep seclusion, and connect
The landscape with the quiet of the sky.
The day is come when I again repose
Here, under this dark sycamore, and view   10
These plots of cottage-ground, these orchard-tufts,
Which at this season, with their unripe fruits,
Are clad in one green hue, and lose themselves
'Mid groves and copses. Once again I see
These hedge-rows, hardly hedge-rows, little lines
Of sportive wood run wild: these pastoral farms,
Green to the very door; and wreaths of smoke
Sent up, in silence, from among the trees!
With some uncertain notice, as might seem
Of vagrant dwellers in the houseless woods,   20
Or of some Hermit's cave, where by his fire
The Hermit sits alone.
                              These beauteous forms,
Through a long absence, have not been to me
As is a landscape to a blind man's eye:
But oft, in lonely rooms, and 'mid the din
Of towns and cities, I have owed to them
In hours of weariness, sensations sweet,
Felt in the blood, and felt along the heart;
And passing even into my purer mind,
With tranquil restoration:—feelings too   30
Of unremembered pleasure: such, perhaps,
As have no slight or trivial influence
On that best portion of a good man's life,
His little, nameless, unremembered acts
Of kindness and of love. Nor less, I trust,
To them I may have owed another gift,
Of aspect more sublime; that blessèd mood,

In which the burthen of the mystery,
In which the heavy and the weary weight
Of all this unintelligible world,   40
Is lightened:—that serene and blessèd mood,
In which the affections gently lead us on,—
Until, the breath of this corporeal frame
And even the motion of our human blood
Almost suspended, we are laid asleep
In body, and become a living soul:
While with an eye made quiet by the power
Of harmony, and the deep power of joy,
We see into the life of things.
                                        If this
Be but a vain belief, yet, oh! how oft—   50
In darkness and amid the many shapes
Of joyless daylight; when the fretful stir
Unprofitable, and the fever of the world,
Have hung upon the beatings of my heart—
How oft, in spirit, have I turned to thee,
O sylvan Wye![1] thou wanderer through the woods,
How often has my spirit turned to thee!
    And now, with gleams of half-extinguished thought,
With many recognitions dim and faint,
And somewhat of a sad perplexity,   60
The picture of the mind revives again;
While here I stand, not only with the sense
Of present pleasure, but with pleasing thoughts
That in this moment there is life and food
For future years. And so I dare to hope,
Though changed, no doubt, from what I was when first
I came among these hills; when like a roe
I bounded o'er the mountains, by the sides
Of the deep rivers, and the lonely streams,
Wherever nature led—more like a man   70
Flying from something that he dreads than one
Who sought the thing he loved. For nature then
(The coarser pleasures of my boyish days,
And their glad animal movements all gone by)
To me was all in all.—I cannot paint

1 A river.

What then I was. The sounding cataract
Haunted me like a passion; the tall rock,
The mountain, and the deep and gloomy wood,
Their colors and their forms, were then to me
An appetite; a feeling and a love,   80
That had no need of a remoter charm,
By thought supplied, nor any interest
Unborrowed from the eye.—That time is past,
And all its aching joys are now no more,
And all its dizzy raptures. Not for this
Faint I, nor mourn nor murmur; other gifts
Have followed; for such loss, I would believe,
Abundant recompense. For I have learned
To look on nature, not as in the hour
Of thoughtless youth; but hearing oftentimes   90
The still, sad music of humanity,
Nor harsh nor grating, though of ample power
To chasten and subdue. And I have felt
A presence that disturbs me with the joy
Of elevated thoughts; a sense sublime
Of something far more deeply interfused,
Whose dwelling is the light of setting suns,
And the round ocean and the living air,
And the blue sky, and in the mind of man:
A motion and a spirit, that impels   100
All thinking things, all objects of all thought,
And rolls through all things. Therefore am I still
A lover of the meadows and the woods,
And mountains; and of all that we behold
From this green earth; of all the mighty world
Of eye and ear, both what they half create,
And what perceive; well pleased to recognise
In nature and the language of the sense,
The anchor of my purest thoughts, the nurse,
The guide, the guardian of my heart, and soul   110
Of all my moral being.
                      Nor perchance,
If I were not thus taught, should I the more
Suffer my genial spirits to decay:
For thou art with me, here upon the banks

Of this fair river; thou, my dearest friend,[2]
My dear, dear friend, and in thy voice I catch
The language of my former heart, and read
My former pleasures in the shooting lights
Of thy wild eyes. Oh! yet a little while
May I behold in thee what I was once,   120
My dear, dear sister! and this prayer I make,
Knowing that nature never did betray
The heart that loved her; 'tis her privilege,
Through all the years of this our life, to lead
From joy to joy; for she can so inform
The mind that is within us, so impress
With quietness and beauty, and so feed
With lofty thoughts, that neither evil tongues,
Rash judgments, nor the sneers of selfish men,
Nor greetings where no kindness is, nor all   130
The dreary intercourse of daily life,
Shall e'er prevail against us, or disturb
Our cheerful faith, that all which we behold
Is full of blessings. Therefore let the moon
Shine on thee in thy solitary walk;
And let the misty mountain winds be free
To blow against thee: and, in after years,
When these wild ecstasies shall be matured
Into a sober pleasure, when thy mind
Shall be a mansion for all lovely forms,   140
Thy memory be as a dwelling-place
For all sweet sounds and harmonies; oh! then,
If solitude, or fear, or pain, or grief,
Should be thy portion, with what healing thoughts
Of tender joy wilt thou remember me,
And these my exhortations! Nor, perchance—
If I should be where I no more can hear
Thy voice, nor catch from thy wild eyes these gleams
Of past existence—wilt thou then forget
That on the banks of this delightful stream   150
We stood together; and that I, so long
A worshipper of nature, hither came,

2 His sister Dorothy.

Unwearied in that service: rather say
With warmer love—oh! with far deeper zeal
Of holier love. Nor wilt thou then forget,
That after many wanderings, many years
Of absence, these steep woods and lofty cliffs,
And this green pastoral landscape, were to me
More dear, both for themselves and for thy sake!

Lapis Lazuli[1]

(for HARRY CLIFTON)

William Butler Yeats (1865–1939)

I have heard that hysterical women say
They are sick of the palette and fiddle-bow,
Of poets that are always gay,
For everybody knows or else should know
That if nothing drastic is done
Aeroplane and Zeppelin will come out,
Pitch like King Billy[2] bomb-balls in
Until the town lie beaten flat.

All perform their tragic play,
There struts Hamlet, there is Lear,   10
That's Ophelia, that Cordelia;
Yet they, should the last scene be there,
The great stage curtain about to drop,
If worthy their prominent part in the play,
Do not break up their lines to weep.
They know that Hamlet and Lear are gay;
Gaiety transfiguring all that dread.
All men have aimed at, found and lost;
Black out; Heaven blazing into the head:

---

1 An opaque, azure-blue to deep-blue gemstone.   2 William of Orange.

Tragedy wrought to its uttermost. 20
Though Hamlet rambles and Lear rages,
And all the drop-scenes drop at once
Upon a hundred thousand stages,
It cannot grow by an inch or an ounce.

On their own feet they come, or on shipboard,
Camel-back, horse-back, ass-back, mule-back,
Old civilizations put to the sword.
Then they and their wisdom went to rack:
No handiwork of Callimachus,
Who handled marble as if it were bronze, 30
Made draperies that seemed to rise
When sea-wind swept the corner, stands;
His long lamp-chimney shaped like the stem
Of a slender palm, stood but a day;
All things fall and are built again,
And those that build them again are gay.

Two Chinamen, behind them a third,
Are carved in lapis lazuli,
Over them flies a long-legged bird,
A symbol of longevity; 40
The third, doubtless a serving-man,
Carries a musical instrument.

Every discoloration of the stone,
Every accidental crack or dent,
Seems a water-course or an avalanche,
Or lofty slope where it still snows
Though doubtless plum or cherry-branch
Sweetens the little half-way house
Those Chinamen climb towards, and I
Delight to imagine them seated there; 50
There, on the mountain and the sky,
On all the tragic scene they stare.
One asks for mournful melodies;
Accomplished fingers begin to play.
Their eyes mid many wrinkles, their eyes,
Their ancient, glittering eyes, are gay.

ORDER

Put things in their place.

David Ignatow

Sir Patrick Spens

Anonymous

The king sits in Dumferling toune,
    Drinking the blude-reid[1] wine:
"O whar will I get guid sailor,
    To sail this schip of mine?"

Up and spak an eldern knicht,
    Sat at the kings richt kne:
"Sir Patrick Spens is the best sailor
    That sails upon the se."

The king has written a braid[2] letter,
    And signd it wi his hand,   10
And sent it to Sir Patrick Spens,
    Was walking on the sand.

The first line that Sir Patrick red,
    A loud lauch lauched[3] he;
The next line that Sir Patrick red,
    The teir blinded his ee.

"O wha is this has don this deid,
    This ill deid don to me,
To send me out this time o' the yeir,
    To sail upon the se!   20

"Mak hast, mak haste, my mirry men all,
    Our guid schip sails the morne."
"O say na sae, my master deir,
    For I feir a deadlie storme.

"Late, late yestreen[4] I saw the new
        moone,
    Wi the auld moone in hir arme,

1 Blood red.   2 Broad.   3 Laughed.   4 Last night.

And I feir, I feir, my deir master,
 That we will cum to harme."

O our Scots nobles wer richt laith[5]
 To weet their cork-heild schoone,[6]   30
Both lang owre[7] a' the play wer playd,
 Thair hats they swam aboone.

O lang, lang may their ladies sit,
 Wi thair fans into their hand,
Or eir they se Sir Patrick Spens
 Cum sailing to the land.

O lang, lang may the ladies stand,
 Wi thair gold kems[8] in their hair,
Waiting for thair ain deir lords,
 For they'll se thame na mair.   40

Haf owre, half owre to Aberdour,
 It's fiftie fadom deip,
And thair lies guid Sir Patrick Spens,
 Wi the Scots lords at his feit.

5 Loath. 6 Wet their cork-soled shoes. 7 Before. 8 Combs.

Earth and Fire
Wendell Berry (1934–)

In this woman the earth speaks.
Her words open in me, cells of light
flashing in my body, and make a song
that I follow toward her out of my need.
The pain I have given her I wear
like another skin, tender, the air
around me flashing with thorns.
And yet such joy as I have given her

sings in me and is part of her song.
The winds of her knees shake me
like a flame. I have risen up from her,
time and again, a new man.

To Every Thing There Is a Season

from THE KING JAMES BIBLE

Ecclesiastes (3:1–8)

To every thing there is a season, and a time to every purpose under the heaven:

A time to be born, and a time to die; a time to plant, and a time to pluck up that which is planted;

A time to kill, and a time to heal; a time to break down, and a time to build up;

A time to weep, and a time to laugh; a time to mourn, and a time to dance;

A time to cast away stones, and a time to gather stones together; a time to embrace, and a time to refrain from embracing;

A time to get, and a time to lose; a time to keep, and a time to cast away;

A time to rend, and a time to sew; a time to keep silence, and a time to speak;

A time to love, and a time to hate; a time of war, and a time of peace.

The Tyger

William Blake (1757–1827)

Tyger! Tyger! burning bright
In the forests of the night,
What immortal hand or eye
Could frame thy fearful symmetry?

In what distant deeps or skies
Burnt the fire of thine eyes?
On what wings dare he aspire?
What the hand dare seize the fire?

And what shoulder, and what art,
Could twist the sinews of thy heart?   10
And, when thy heart began to beat,
What dread hand? and what dread feet?

What the hammer? what the chain?
In what furnace was thy brain?
What the anvil? what dread grasp
Dare its deadly terrors clasp?

When the stars threw down their spears,
And watered heaven with their tears,
Did he smile his work to see?
Did he who made the lamb make thee?   20

Tyger! Tyger! burning bright
In the forests of the night,
What immortal hand or eye,
Dare frame thy fearful symmetry?

That's Life?

Alan Bold (1943–   )

Far from the scent of the crocus
And the pavanne[1] of Scottish daffodils
A loud crash was heard in Princes Street.
Safe from the steady gaze
Of the grey carrara marble Scott[2]
A jabbering unknown tramp had died.
One could certainly doubt it
But the blood was fresh
Enough to say he lived
Once. A peering crowd of blanket faces   10
Did not ponder if he loved,
Or had been loved, instead
They wondered at how far ahead
In life they were. Were they *more*
Than one rung up the ladder of life?
Yet their strange obsession with his death
Charged it with more meaning than his life.
Were they in any way superior
To the thing within
Old and tattered clothes?   20
Who in that smiling crowd would want
To guess beside the loud
Crash of buses, private cars and men
A solitary member of the human race had died
And not diminished life?
And if they had been the one
Would anything have stopped?
Being apart from them
It was not, they thought, a part
Of them. And when policemen took the few   30
Details of the case, facts
Conveyed to them
That the lifeless ones in life
Caused much more trouble than they were worth.

1 Dance.   2 A statue of Sir Walter Scott.

They were wrong: their minds blinded
By a candle flame of thought.
There was a man
But he was bespoken for.

The End Bit

Jim Burns (1936–   )

Each man has
his own way
of doing it.
Some take their
time, easing
out slowly,
and others
leave it late
and finish
with a jerk.   10
Neither of
these ways is
best, however,
and the man
who has no worries
about the
coming climax
is lucky,
and counts it
as part of the   20
pattern of things.

EMERITUS,[1] n.

Henri Coulette (1927–   )

They knew the conjugations of the flesh;
I knew the day's lesson:
A noun is the name of a person, place, or thing.

I did the possible:
I memorized their names, smiled my smile,
And taught, small miracle,

One girl, Carolyn Bywater, to tell time.
And tell it she did, by God!
Each minute past became a fallen sparrow.

One June day a bell rang.   10
They left.   They went out into their lives, and left
The squeak in the chalk forever.

That was a thousand thousand sparrows ago.
Today's assignment, then:
The same as ever and the last as always.

1 One who has served his time and retired, but retains his rank or title.

Drinking

Abraham Cowley (1618–1687)

The thirsty earth soaks up the rain,
And drinks and gapes for drink again;
The plants suck in the earth, and are
With constant drinking fresh and fair;
The sea itself (which one would think
Should have but little need of drink)

Drinks twice ten thousand rivers up,
So fill'd that they o'erflow the cup.
The busy Sun (and one would guess
By 's drunken fiery face no less)   10
Drinks up the sea, and when he's done,
The Moon and Stars drink up the Sun:
They drink and dance by their own light,
They drink and revel all the night:
Nothing in Nature's sober found,
But an eternal health goes round.
Fill up the bowl, then, fill it high,
Fill all the glasses there—for why
Should every creature drink but I?
Why, man of morals, tell me why?   20

Because I could not stop for Death
Emily Dickinson (1830–1886)

Because I could not stop for Death—
He kindly stopped for me—
The Carriage held but just Ourselves—
And Immortality.

We slowly drove—He knew no haste
And I had put away
My labor and my leisure too,
For His Civility—

We passed the School, where Children strove
At Recess—in the Ring—   10
We passed the Fields of Gazing Grain—
We passed the Setting Sun—

Or rather—He passed Us—
The Dews drew quivering and chill—

For only Gossamer,[1] my Gown—
My Tippet[2]—only Tulle[3]—

We paused before a House that seemed
A Swelling of the Ground—
The Roof was scarcely visible—
The Cornice—in the Ground—   20

Since then—'tis Centuries—and yet
Feels shorter than the Day
I first surmised the Horses' Heads
Were toward Eternity—

1 A flimsy fabric.   2 A scarf.   3 Silk.

Frankenstein

Edward Field (1924–   )

The monster has escaped from the dungeon
where he was kept by the Baron,
who made him with knobs sticking out from each side of his
    neck
where the head was attached to the body
and stitching all over
where parts of cadavers were sewed together.

He is pursued by the ignorant villagers,
who think he is evil and dangerous because he is ugly
and makes ugly noises.
They wave firebrands at him and cudgels and rakes,   10
but he escapes and comes to the thatched cottage
of an old blind man playing on the violin Mendelssohn's
    "Spring Song."

Hearing him approach, the blind man welcomes him:
"Come in, my friend," and takes him by the arm.
"You must be weary," and sits him down inside the house.
For the blind man has long dreamed of having a friend
to share his lonely life.

The monster has never known kindness—the Baron was cruel—
but somehow he is able to accept it now,
and he really has no instincts to harm the old man,   20
for in spite of his awful looks he has a tender heart:
Who knows what cadaver that part of him came from?

The old man seats him at table, offers him bread,
and says, "Eat, my friend." The monster
rears back roaring in terror.
"No, my friend, it is good. Eat—gooood"
and the old man shows him how to eat,
and reassured, the monster eats
and says, "Eat—gooood,"
trying out the words and finding them good too.   30

The old man offers him a glass of wine,
"Drink, my friend. Drink—gooood."
The monster drinks, slurping horribly, and says,
"Drink—gooood," in his deep nutty voice
and smiles maybe for the first time in his life.

Then the blind man puts a cigar in the monster's mouth
and lights a large wooden match that flares up in his face.
The monster, remembering the torches of the villagers,
recoils, grunting in terror.
"No, my friend, smoke—gooood,"   40
and the old man demonstrates with his own cigar.
The monster takes a tentative puff
and smiles hugely, saying, "Smoke—gooood,"
and sits back like a banker, grunting and puffing.

Now the old man plays Mendelssohn's "Spring Song" on the
    violin
while tears come into our dear monster's eyes

as he thinks of the stones of the mob, the pleasures of meal-
    time,
the magic new words he has learned
and above all of the friend he has found.

It is just as well that he is unaware—   50
being simple enough to believe only in the present—
that the mob will find him and pursue him
for the rest of his short unnatural life,
until trapped at the whirlpool's edge
he plunges to his death.

Delight in Disorder
Robert Herrick (1591–1674)

A sweet disorder in the dress
Kindles in clothes a wantonness.
A lawn¹ about the shoulders thrown
Into a fine distraction;
An erring lace, which here and there
Enthralls the crimson stomacher,²
A cuff neglectful, and thereby
Ribbons to flow confusedly;
A winning wave, deserving note,
In the tempestuous petticoat;   10
A careless shoe-string, in whose tie
I see a wild civility;
Do more bewitch me than when art
Is too precise in every part.

1 Fine linen or cotton fabric. 2 An ornamental covering for breast and
stomach.

Upon Julia's Clothes
Robert Herrick (1591–1674)

Whenas in silks my Julia goes,
Then, then, methinks, how sweetly flows
That liquefaction of her clothes.

Next, when I cast mine eyes and see
That brave vibration each way free,
O how that glittering taketh me!

That Moment
Ted Hughes (1930–   )

When the pistol muzzle oozing blue vapour
Was lifted away
Like a cigarette lifted from an ashtray

And the only face left in the world
Lay broken
Between hands that relaxed, being too late

And the trees closed forever
And the streets closed forever

And the body lay on the gravel
Of the abandoned world   10
Among abandoned utilities
Exposed to infinity forever

Crow had to start searching for something to eat.

The Sky Is Blue
David Ignatow (1914–   )

Put things in their place,
my mother shouts. I am looking
out the window, my plastic soldier
at my feet. The sky is blue
and empty. In it floats
the roof across the street.
What place, I ask her.

Still¹ to Be Neat
Ben Jonson (1572–1637)

Still to be neat, still to be dressed,
As you were going to a feast;
Still to be powdered, still perfumed:
Lady, it is to be presumed,
Though art's hid causes are not found,
All is not sweet, all is not sound.

Give me a book, give me a face,
That makes simplicity a grace;
Robes loosely flowing, hair as free:
Such sweet neglect more taketh me   10
Than all the adulteries of art;
They strike mine eyes, but not my heart.

1 Always.

One Morning We Brought Them Order

Al Lee (1940–   )

*"With our considerable military power but limited political appeal, how do
we contain an adversary of enormous political power but modest military
means?"*

*An American military strategist quoted
by Jean Lacouture in* Le Monde *(Sept.
18, 1964).*

WHEN WE rolled up the three armored vehicles
and they wouldn't budge, the sergeant said to kick
       in somebody's kidneys,
       and a corporal did.
It was a bald-headed man with a shiny
soft face. He sat tight but we could hear him whine.

   Our captain was somewhere else admiring
and photographing a church's stone spire.
      It was famous or ancient.
      By the time he got back, rain   10
was drenching them, and us, so he ordered
us to hurry up and clobber some more.

   They still sat there, some not so pretty,
when the colonel came. He had a fit.
     "Have it their way. Shoot a dozen
     in the head and see what that does."
Then, pissed off that they kept on stalling,
he had us open up on them all.

   Someone must have wanted to run
when we set to it. I wonder   20
why in all those thousands not one man
used his head and started the panic.
    He would have saved everyone's neck.
    Was what we did unexpected?

    We took chow thinking of them
     that night until the women
who had kept indoors at first came out too

to harass us by moonlight. The shooting
lasted for hours. They fought back
with knives and died attacking.   30

After looting the town,
we poured oil around it
and lit a fire to roast anybody's ass.
Today a young girl with a covered basket
walked up smiling: she then
exploded, killing ten.

Lucifer in Starlight
George Meredith (1829–1909)

On a starred night Prince Lucifer uprose.
Tired of his dark dominion swung the fiend
Above the rolling ball in cloud part screened,
Where sinners hugged their specter of repose.
Poor prey to his hot fit of pride were those.
And now upon his western wing he leaned,
Now his huge bulk o'er Afric's sands careened,
Now the black planet shadowed Arctic snows.
Soaring through wider zones that pricked his scars
With memory of the old revolt from Awe,   10
He reached a middle height, and at the stars,
Which are the brain of heaven, he looked, and sank.
Around the ancient track marched, rank on rank,
The army of unalterable law.

All the world's a stage

from AS YOU LIKE IT (II, 7)

William Shakespeare (1564–1616)

All the world's a stage,
And all the men and women merely players.
They have their exits and their entrances,
And one man in his time plays many parts,
His acts being seven ages. At first, the infant,
Mewling and puking in the nurse's arms.
Then the whining schoolboy, with his satchel
And shining morning face, creeping like snail
Unwillingly to school. And then the lover,
Sighing like furnace, with a woful ballad   10
Made to his mistress' eyebrow. Then a soldier,
Full of strange oaths and bearded like the pard,[1]
Jealous in honour, sudden and quick in quarrel,
Seeking the bubble reputation
Even in the cannon's mouth. And then the justice,
In fair round belly with good capon lin'd,
With eyes severe and beard of formal cut,
Full of wise saws and modern instances;
And so he plays his part. The sixth age shifts
Into the lean and slipper'd pantaloon,   20
With spectacles on nose and pouch on side;
His youthful hose, well sav'd, a world too wide
For his shrunk shank, and his big manly voice,
Turning again toward childish treble, pipes
And whistles in his sound. Last scene of all,
That ends this strange eventful history,
Is second childishness and mere oblivion,
Sans teeth, sans eyes, sans taste, sans everything.

1 Leopard.

Leaving the Motel

W. D. Snodgrass (1926–   )

Outside, the last kids holler
Near the pool: they'll stay the night.
Pick up the towels; fold your collar
Out of sight.

Check: is the second bed
Unrumpled, as agreed?
Landlords have to think ahead
In case of need,

Too. Keep things straight: don't take
The matches, the wrong keyrings—   10
We've nowhere we could keep a keepsake—
Ashtrays, combs, things

That sooner or later others
Would accidentally find.
Check: take nothing of one another's
And leave behind

Your license number only,
Which they won't care to trace;
We've paid. Still, should such things get lonely,
Leave in their vase   20

An aspirin to preserve
Our lilacs, the wayside flowers

We've gathered and must leave to serve
A few more hours;

That's all. We can't tell when
We'll come back, can't press claims;
We would no doubt have other rooms then,
Or other names.

The Idea of Order at Key West
Wallace Stevens (1879–1955)

She sang beyond the genius of the sea.
The water never formed to mind or voice,
Like a body wholly body, fluttering
Its empty sleeves; and yet its mimic motion
Made constant cry, caused constantly a cry,
That was not ours although we understood,
Inhuman, of the veritable ocean.

The sea was not a mask. No more was she.
The song and water were not medleyed sound
Even if what she sang was what she heard,   10
Since what she sang was uttered word by word.
It may be that in all her phrases stirred
The grinding water and the gasping wind;
But it was she and not the sea we heard.
For she was the maker of the song she sang.
The ever-hooded, tragic-gestured sea
Was merely a place by which she walked to sing.
Whose spirit is this? we said, because we knew
It was the spirit that we sought and knew
That we should ask this often as she sang.   20

If it was only the dark voice of the sea
That rose, or even colored by many waves;
If it was only the outer voice of sky
And cloud, of the sunken coral water-walled,
However clear, it would have been deep air,
The heaving speech of air, a summer sound
Repeated in a summer without end
And sound alone. But it was more than that,
More even than her voice, and ours, among
The meaningless plungings of water and the wind,   30
Theatrical distances, bronze shadows heaped
On high horizons, mountainous atmospheres
Of sky and sea.
                It was her voice that made
The sky acutest at its vanishing.

She measured to the hour its solitude.
She was the single artificer of the world
In which she sang. And when she sang, the sea,
Whatever self it had, became the self
That was her song, for she was the maker. Then we,
As we beheld her striding there alone,   40
Knew that there never was a world for her
Except the one she sang and, singing, made.

Ramon Fernandez,[1] tell me, if you know,
Why, when the singing ended and we turned
Toward the town, tell why the glassy lights,
The lights in the fishing boats at anchor there,
As the night descended, tilting in the air,
Mastered the night and portioned out the sea,
Fixing emblazoned zones and fiery poles.
Arranging, deepening, enchanting night.   50

Oh! Blessed rage for order, pale Ramon,
The maker's rage to order words of the sea,
Words of the fragrant portals, dimly-starred,
And of ourselves and of our origins,
In ghostlier demarcations, keener sounds.

1 His companion.

Contemplate all this work of Time
Alfred, Lord Tennyson (1809–1892)

Contemplate all this work of Time,
    The giant laboring in his youth;
    Nor dream of human love and truth,
As dying Nature's earth and lime;

But trust that those we call the dead
   Are breathers of an ampler day
   For ever nobler ends. They say,
The solid earth whereon we tread

In tracts of fluent heat began,
   And grew to seeming-random forms, 10
   The seeming prey of cyclic storms,
Till at the last arose the man;

Who throve and branch'd from clime to clime
   The herald of a higher race,
   And of himself in higher place,
If so he type this work of time

Within himself, from more to more;
   Or, crown'd with attributes of woe
   Like glories, move his course, and show
That life is not as idle ore, 20

But iron dug from central gloom,
   And heated hot with burning fears,
   And dipt in baths of hissing tears,
And batter'd with the shocks of doom

To shape and use. Arise and fly
   The reeling Faun,[1] the sensual
      feast;
   More upward, working out the beast,
And let the ape and tiger die.

1 A satyr, lustful, lecherous.

Natural History

Robert Penn Warren (1905–   )

In the rain, the naked old father is dancing, he will get wet.
The rain is sparse, but he cannot dodge all the drops.

He is singing a song, but the language is strange to me.

The mother is counting her money like mad, in the sunshine.
Like shuttles her fingers fly, and the sum is clearly astronomical.

Her breath is sweet as bruised violets, and her smile
                    sways like daffodils reflected in a brook.

The song of the father tells how at last he understands.
That is why the language is strange to me.

That is why the clocks have stopped all over the continent.   10

The money the naked mother counts is her golden memories of love.
That is why I see nothing in her maniacally busy fingers.

That is why all flights have been cancelled out of Kennedy.

As much as I hate to, I must summon the police.
For their own good, as well as that of society, they
                    must be put under surveillance.

They must learn to stay in their graves. That is what graves are for.

A Noiseless Patient Spider

Walt Whitman (1819–1892)

A noiseless patient spider,
I mark'd where on a little promontory it stood isolated,
Mark'd how to explore the vacant vast surrounding,
It launch'd forth filament, filament, filament, out of itself.
Ever unreeling them, ever tirelessly speeding them.

And you O my soul where you stand,
Surrounded, detached, in measureless oceans of space,
Carelessly musing, venturing, throwing, seeking the spheres to
    connect them,
Till the bridge you will need be form'd, till the ductile[1] anchor hold,
Till the gossamer[2] thread you fling catch somewhere, O my soul.   10

1 Capable of being molded, shaped, or drawn out into threads without breaking. 2 Delicate, filmy.

MARRIAGE

*two by two in the ark
of the ache of it.*

Denise Levertov

There Was an Old Party of Lyme

Anonymous

There was an old party of Lyme
Who married three wives at a time.
   When asked: "Why the third?"
   He replied: "One's absurd,
And bigamy, sir, is a crime.

Mohammed Ibrahim Speaks

Told by a Man of the
Arab Moteir Tribe
of Upper Egypt

Martha Beidler (1928–   )

"I have two wives,
 I have had three.
 The first one, Zeynab, I divorced:
   There was a wedding in the town,
   And I forbade her going, lest
   The men might look at her.
   She disobeyed me. Veiled,
   She walked among the women,
   Thinking I would not know her.
   But what other woman walks like Zeynab?   10
   Three times I told her, 'I divorce you,'
   And I sent her back to her father's house.

My present wives obey me as they ought.
If I should say to them, 'These stones are bread,'
They'd eat the stones.
But in the night, my thoughts return to Zeynab.
Truly she was light-hearted,
And her eyes were like black pearls
Within their shells."

When a Man Has Married a Wife
William Blake (1757–1827)

When a Man has Married a Wife
    he finds out whether
Her Knees and elbows are only
    glued together

The Puritan on His Honeymoon
Robert Bly (1926–   )

Travelling south, leaves overflow the farms.
Day by day we watched the leaves increase
And the trees lie tangled in each other's arms.
Still generation, and calls that never cease
And rustlings in the brush; yesterday
She asked how long we had been on the way.
So in the afternoon we changed our route
And came down to the coast; everywhere
The same: fish, and the lobster's sensual eyes.
The natives sang for harvest, gave us fruit,   10
At night the monkeys sat beneath the trees.
All night the cries of dancers filled the air,
And last year's virgins pressed into the leaves.
Sometimes I think of your land, cold and fresh,
And try to think: what was the month we quit
Your northern land that seemed inhabited
By more than reproduction of the flesh?
I saw here, while the branches interknit
The monkeys gibbering by our bridal bed.

To My Dear and Loving Husband
Anne Bradstreet (1612–1672)

If ever two were one, then surely we;
If ever man were loved by wife, then thee;
If ever wife was happy in a man,
Compare with me, ye woman, if you can.
I prize thy love more than whole mines of gold,
Or all the riches that the East doth hold.
My love is such that rivers cannot quench,
Nor aught but love from thee give recompense.
Thy love is such I can no way repay;
The heavens reward thee manifold, I pray.   10
Then while we live in love let's so persevere
That when we live no more we may live ever.

John Anderson My Jo
Robert Burns (1759–1796)

John Anderson my jo,[1] John
  When we were first acquent,
Your locks were like the raven,
  Your bonnie brow was brent;[2]
But now your brow is beld, John,
  Your locks are like the snaw,
But blessings on your frosty pow,[3]
  John Anderson my jo!

John Anderson my jo, John,
  We clamb the hill thegither,   10
And monie a cantie[4] day, John
  We've had wi' ane anither:
Now we maun[5] totter down, John
  And hand in hand we'll go,
And sleep thegither at the foot,
  John Anderson my jo!

1 Joy. 2 Straight, steep. 3 Head. 4 Merry. 5 Must.

The Crisis
Robert Creeley (1926–   )

Let me say (in anger) that since the day we were married
we have never had a towel
where anyone could find it,
the fact.
       Notwithstanding that I am not
simple to live with, not
my own judgement, but no
matter.
       There are other things:

to kiss you is not
to love you.
       Or not so simply.

Laughter releases rancor, the quality of mercy is not   10
strained.

Antiquary
John Donne (1572–1631)

If in his study he hath so much care
To hang all old strange things, let his wife beware.

Jealousy

ELEGY I

John Donne (1572–1631)

Fond[1] woman, which would'st have thy husband die,
And yet complain'st of his great jealousy;
If, swollen with poison, he lay in his last bed,
His body with a sere bark[2] coverèd,
Drawing his breath as thick and short as can
The nimblest crotcheting[3] musician,
Ready with loathsome vomiting to spew
His soul out of one hell into a new,
Made deaf with his poor kindred's howling cries,
Begging with few feigned tears his legacies,   10
Thou would'st not weep, but jolly and frolic be,
As a slave which tomorrow should be free;
Yet weep'st thou, when thou see'st him hungerly
Swallow his own death, heart's-bane jealousy.
O give him many thanks, he is courteous,
That in suspecting kindly warneth us.
We must not, as we used, flout openly,
In scoffing riddles, his deformity,
Nor at his board together being sat,
With words, nor touch, scarce looks adulterate.   20
Nor when he swollen and pampered with great fare
Sits down and snorts, caged in his basket chair,
Must we usurp his own bed any more,
Nor kiss and play in his house as before.
Now I see many dangers, for that is
His realm, his castle, and his diocese.
But if, as envious men which would revile
Their prince or coin his gold themselves exile
Into another country and do it there,
We play in another house, what should we fear?   30

1 Foolish.   2 The deep wrinkles of age.   3 One who can play quarter notes with ease.

There we will scorn his household policies,
His silly plots and pensionary spies,
As the inhabitants[4] of Thames' right side
Do London's mayor, or Germans the Pope's pride.

4 The inhabitants of the right bank of the Thames were beyond the juris-
diction of the mayor of London, as the Germans were beyond the juris-
diction of the Pope.

Love Song: I and Thou
Alan Dugan (1923–   )

Nothing is plumb, level, or square:
   the studs are bowed, the joists
are shaky by nature, no piece fits
   any other piece without a gap
or pinch, and bent nails
   dance all over the surfacing
like maggots. By Christ
   I am no carpenter. I built
the roof for myself, the walls
   for myself, the floors   10
for myself, and got
   hung up in it myself. I
danced with a purple thumb
   at this house-warming, drunk
with my prime whiskey: rage.
   Oh I spat rage's nails
into the frame-up of my work:
   it held. It settled plumb,
level, solid, square and true
   for that great moment. Then   20
it screamed and went on through,
   skewing as wrong the other way.
God damned it. This is hell,
   but I planned it, I sawed it,

I nailed it, and I
  will live in it until it kills me.
I can nail my left palm
  to the left-hand crosspiece but
I can't do everything myself.
  I need a hand to nail the right,   30
a help, a love, a you, a wife.

A Dedication to My Wife
T. S. Eliot (1888–1965)

To whom I owe the leaping delight
That quickens my senses in our wakingtime
And the rhythm that governs the repose of our sleepingtime,
  The breathing in unison

Of lovers whose bodies smell of each other
Who think the same thoughts without need of speech
And babble the same speech without need of meaning.

No peevish winter wind shall chill
No sullen tropic sun shall wither
The roses in the rose-garden which is ours and ours only   10

But this dedication is for others to read:
These are private words addressed to you in public.

A Mad Answer of a Madman
Robert Hayman (c. 1628)

One asked a madman if a wife he had.
"A wife?" quoth he.   "I never was so mad."

The Aged Wino's Counsel to a Young Man on the Brink of Marriage

X. J. Kennedy (1929–   )

A two-quart virgin in my lap,
With hands that shook I peeled her cap
And filched a kiss. It warmed me so,
I raised my right hand, swore *I do*—
We merged our fleshes, I and she,
In mutual indignity.
Now, when I hear of wives that freeze,
Bitter of lip, with icebound knees,
Who play high-card for social bets
And lose, and feed you carp croquettes,   10
Who nap all day and yak all night
What Ruth told Min—now which was right?—
Who count with glee your falling hairs
But brood a week on one of theirs,
Who'll see your parkerhouse[1] poke out
Before they'll take a stitch, who pout
At change of moon, as I hear tell,
I say: son, wed you half as well.

1 Slang for buttocks.

Living with You

Angela Langfield (1917–   )

There's a knack in living with you.
I don't have it.

There's a certain rhythm.
I'm out of time.

There's a skill
in talking you round,

adjusting the balance,
keeping it level, yet
with me it swings down.

There's an art   10
in letting you have your own way,
without knowing it;
always on the winning side
always king of the castle.

There must be a way
of loving you—
giving you everything,
still getting free.

Yet every time I am caught,
every time waved down,   20
and taken for questioning.

Love on the Farm

D. H. Lawrence (1885–1930)

What large, dark hands are those at the window
Grasping in the golden light
Which weaves its way through the evening wind
   At my heart's delight?

Ah, only the leaves! But in the west
I see a redness suddenly come
Into the evening's anxious breast—
   'Tis the wound of love goes home!

The woodbine creeps abroad
Calling low to her lover: 10
   The sun-lit flirt who all the day
   Has poised above her lips in play
   And stolen kisses, shallow and gay
   Of pollen, now has gone away—

She woos the moth with her sweet, low word;
And when above her his moth-wings hover
Then her bright breast she will uncover
And yield her honey-drop to her lover.

Into the yellow, evening glow
Saunters a man from the farm below;   20
Leans, and looks in at the low-built shed
Where the swallow has hung her marriage bed.
    The bird lies warm against the wall.
    She glances quick her startled eyes
    Towards him, then she turns away
    Her small head, making warm display
    Of red upon the throat. Her terrors sway
    Her out of the nest's warm, busy ball,
    Whose plaintive cry is heard as she flies
    In one blue stoop from out the sties   30
    Into the twilight's empty hall.
Oh, water-hen, beside the rushes
Hide your quaintly scarlet blushes,
Still your quick tail, lie still as dead,
Till the distance folds over his ominous tread!

The rabbit presses back her ears,
Turns back her liquid, anguished eyes
And crouches low; then with wild spring
Spurts from the terror of *his* oncoming;
To be choked back, the wire ring   40
Her frantic effort throttling:
    Piteous brown ball of quivering fears!
Ah, soon in his large, hard hands she dies,
And swings all loose from the swing of his walk!
Yet calm and kindly are his eyes
And ready to open in brown surprise
Should I not answer to his talk
Or should he my tears surmise.

I hear his hand on the latch, and rise from my chair
Watching the door open; he flashes bare   50
His strong teeth in a smile, and flashes his eyes
In a smile like triumph upon me; then careless-wise
He flings the rabbit soft on the table board

And comes towards me: ah! the uplifted sword
Of his hand again my bosom! and oh, the broad
Blade of his glance that asks me to applaud
His coming! With his hand he turns my face to him
And caresses me with his fingers that still smell grim
Of the rabbit's fur! God, I am caught in a snare!
I know not what fine wire is round my throat;   60
I only know I let him finger there
My pulse of life, and let him nose like a stoat
Who sniffs with joy before he drinks the blood.

And down his mouth comes to my mouth! and down
His bright dark eyes come over me, like a hood
Upon my mind! his lips meet mine, and a flood
Of sweet fire sweeps across me, so I drown
Against him, die and find death good.

The Ache of Marriage
Denise Levertov (1923–   )

The ache of marriage;

thigh and tongue, beloved,
are heavy with it,
it throbs in the teeth

We look for communion
and are turned away, beloved,
each and each

It is leviathan[1] and we
in its belly

1 The whale in the biblical story of Jonah.

looking for joy, some joy
not to be known outside it

two by two in the ark of
the ache of it.

For Fran

Philip Levine (1928–   )

She packs the flower beds with leaves,
Rags, dampened papers, ties with twine
The lemon tree, but winter carves
Its features on the uprooted stem.

I see the true vein in her neck
And where the smaller ones have broken
Blueing the skin, and where the dark
Cold lines of weariness have eaten

Out through the winding of the bone.
On the hard ground where Adam strayed, 10
Where nothing but his wants remain,
What do we do to those we need,

To those whose need of us endures
Even the knowledge of what we are?
I turn to her whose future bears
The promise of the appalling air,

My living wife, Frances Levine,
Mother of Theodore, John, and Mark,
Out of whatever we have been
We will make something for the dark. 20

Into thir inmost bower

from PARADISE LOST

John Milton (1608–1674)

                    Into thir inmost bower
Handed[1] they went; and eas'd the putting off
These troublesom disguises which wee wear,
Strait side by side were laid, nor turnd I weene[2]
Adam from his fair Spouse, nor *Eve* the Rites
Mysterious of connubial Love refus'd:
Whatever Hypocrites austerely talk
Of puritie and place and innocence,
Defaming as impure what God declares
Pure, and commands to som, leaves free to all.   10
Our Maker bids increase, who bids abstain
But our Destroyer, foe to God and Man?
Haile wedded Love, mysterious Law, true sourse
Of human ofspring, sole proprietie,
In Paradise of all things common else.
By thee adulterous lust was driv'n from men
Among the bestial herds to raunge, by thee
Founded in Reason, Loyal, Just, and Pure,
Relations dear, and all the Charities
Of Father, Son, and Brother first were known.   20

1 Holding hands.   2 Guess, fancy.

Proud Maisie
Sir Walter Scott (1771–1832)

    Proud Maisie is in the wood,
        Walking so early;
    Sweet Robin sits on the bush,
        Singing so rarely.

"Tell me, thou bonny bird,
    When shall I marry me?" —
"When six braw gentlemen
    Kirkward shall carry ye."

"Who makes the bridal bed,
    Birdie, say truly?" —   10
"The gray-headed sexton
    That delves the grave duly.

"The glow-worm o'er grave and stone
    Shall light thee steady;
The owl from the steeple sing,
    'Welcome, proud lady.' "

When daises pied and violets blue

from LOVE'S LABOUR'S LOST (V, 2)

William Shakespeare (1564–1616)

When daisies pied and violets blue
    And lady-smocks all silver-white
And cuckoo-buds[1] of yellow hue
    Do paint the meadows with delight,
The cuckoo then, on every tree,
Mocks married men; for thus sings he,
                    "Cuckoo,
Cuckoo, cuckoo!" — O word of fear,
Unpleasing to a married ear!

When shepherds pipe on oaten straws,   10
    And merry larks are ploughmen's clocks,
When turtles tread[2], and rooks, and daws,

1 Buttercups.   2 Turtledoves mate.

And maidens bleach their summer smocks,
The cuckoo then, on every tree,
Mocks married men; for thus sings he,
        "Cuckoo,
Cuckoo, cuckoo!" — O word of fear,
Unpleasing to a married ear!

Mementos, I

W. D. Snodgrass (1926–   )

Sorting out letters and piles of my old
    Cancelled checks, old clippings, and yellow note cards
That meant something once, I happened to find
    Your picture. *That* picture. I stopped there cold
Like a man raking piles of dead leaves in his yard
      Who has turned up a severed hand.

Yet, that first second, I was glad: you stand
    Just as you stood—shy, delicate, slender,
In the long gown of green lace netting and daisies
    That you wore to our first dance. The sight of you stunned   10
Us all. Our needs seemed simpler, then;
      And our ideals came easy.

Then through the war and those two long years
    Overseas, the Japanese dead in their shacks
Among dishes, dolls, and lost shoes—I carried
    This glimpse of you, there, to choke down my fear,
Prove it had been, that it might come back.
      That was before we got married.

—Before we drained out another's force
    With lies, self-denial, unspoken regret   20
And the sick eyes that blame; before the divorce
    And the treachery. Say it: before we met.
Still, I put back your picture. Someday, in due course,
    I will find that it's still there.

No More Soft Talk

Diane Wakoski (1937–   )

Don't ask a geologist about rocks.
Ask me.

That man,
he said.

What can you do with him?
About him?
He's a rock.

No, not a rock,
I said.
    Well,   10
a very brittle rock, then.
One that crumbles easily, then.
Is crushed to dust, finally.

Me,
I said.
I am the rock.
The hard rock.
You can't break me.

I am trying to think how a woman
can be a rock,   20
when all she wants is to be soft,
to melt to the lines
her man draws for her.

But talking about rocks
intelligently
must be
talking about different kinds
of rock.

What happens to the brain

in shock? Is it
like an explosion
of flowers and blood,
staining the inside
of the skull?

I went to my house,
to see my man,
found the door locked,
and something I didn't plan
on—a closed bedroom door
(my bed)
another woman's handbag on the couch.
Is someone in the bedroom?

Yes, Yes,
a bed full of snakes all bearing new young,
a bed of slashed wrists,
a bed of carbines and rifles with no ammunition,
a bed of my teeth in another woman's fingers.

Then the answer to rocks,
as I sit here and talk.

The image of an explosion:
a volcanic mountain
on a deserted pacific island.
What comes up,
like gall in my throat,
a river of abandoned tonsils that can no longer cry,
a sea of gold wedding rings and smashed glasses,
the lava, the crushed and melted rock
comes pouring out now,
down this mountain you've never seen,
from this face that believed in you,
rocks that have turned soft,
but now are bubbling out of the lips of a mountain,
into the ocean raising the temperature
to 120 degrees.
If your ship were here
it would melt all the caulking.

This lava,
hot and soft,
will cool someday,
and turn back into the various stones. 70
None of it is
my rock.
My rock doesn't crumble.
My rock is the mountain.
Love me
if you can.
I will not make it easy for you
anymore.

WAR

There died a myriad,
And of the best,
among them,
For an old bitch gone
in the teeth

Ezra Pound

David's Lament

from THE KING JAMES BIBLE

2 Samuel (1:19–27)

The beauty of Israel is slain upon thy high places: how are the mighty fallen!

Tell it not in Gath, publish it not in the streets of Askelon; lest the daughters of the Philistines rejoice, lest the daughters of the uncircumcised triumph.

Ye mountains of Gilboa, let there be no dew, let there be rain, upon you, nor fields of offerings: for there the shield of the mighty is vilely cast away, the shield of Saul, as though he had not been annointed with oil.

From the blood of the slain, from the fat of the mighty, the bow of Jonathan turned not back, and the sword of Saul returned not empty.

Saul and Jonathan were lovely and pleasant in their lives, and in their death they were not divided: they were swifter than eagles, they were stronger than lions. 10

Ye daughters of Israel, weep over Saul, who clothed you in scarlet, with other delights, who put on ornaments of gold upon your apparel.

How are the mighty fallen in the midst of the battle! O Jonathan, thou wast slain in thine high places.

I am distressed for thee, my brother Jonathan: very pleasant hast thou been unto me: thy love to me was wonderful, passing the love of women.

How are the mighty fallen, and the weapons of war perished!

The Soldier
Rupert Brooke (1887–1915)

If I should die, think only this of me:
   That there's some corner of a foreign field
That is for ever England. There shall be
   In that rich earth a richer dust concealed;
A dust whom England bore, shaped, and made aware,
   Gave, once, her flowers to love, her ways to roam
A body of England's, breathing English air,
   Washed by the rivers, blest by the aura of home.

And think, this heart, all evil shed away,
   A pulse in the eternal mind, no less   10
      Gives somewhere back the thoughts by England given;
Her sights and sounds; dreams happy as her day;
   And laughter, learnt of friends; and gentleness,
      In hearts at peace, under an English heaven.

The Destruction of Sennacherib
George Gordon, Lord Byron (1788–1824)

The Assyrian came down like the wolf on the fold,
And his cohorts were gleaming in purple and gold;
And the sheen of their spears was like stars on the sea,
When the blue wave rolls nightly on deep Galilee.

Like the leaves of the forest when Summer is green,
That host with their banners at sunset were seen:
Like the leaves of the forest when Autumn hath blown,
That host on the morrow lay withered and strown.

For the angel of Death spread his wings on the blast,
And breathed in the face of the foe as he passed;   10

And the eyes of the sleepers waxed deadly and chill,
And their hearts but once heaved—and for ever grew still!

And there lay the steed with his nostril all wide,
But through it there rolled not the breath of his pride;
And the foam of his gasping lay white on the turf,
And cold as the spray of the rock-beating surf.

And there lay the rider distorted and pale,
With the dew on his brow, and the rust on his mail:
And the tents were all silent—the banners alone—
The lances unlifted—the trumpet unblown.   20

And the widows of Ashur are loud in their wail,
And the idols are broke in the temple of Baal;
And the might of the Gentile, unsmote by the sword,
Hath melted like snow in the glance of the Lord!

my sweet old etcetera

e. e. cummings (1894–1962)

my sweet old etcetera
aunt lucy during the recent

war could and what
is more did tell you just
what everybody was fighting

for,
my sister
isabel created hundreds
(and
hundreds) of socks not to   10
mention shirts fleaproof earwarmers

etcetera wristers etcetera,my
mother hoped that

i would die etcetera
bravely of course my father used
to become hoarse talking about how it was
a privilege and if only he
could meanwhile my

self etcetera lay quietly
in the deep mud et   20

cetera
(dreaming,
et
    cetera,of
Your smile
eyes knees and of your Etcetera)

The Fury of Aerial Bombardment
Richard Eberhart (1904–   )

You would think the fury of aerial bombardment
Would rouse God to relent; the infinite spaces
Are still silent. He looks on shock-pried faces.
History, even, does not know what is meant.

You would feel that after so many centuries
God would give man to repent; yet he can kill
As Cain could, but with multitudinous will,
No farther advanced than in his ancient furies.

Was man made stupid to see his own stupidity?
Is God by definition indifferent, beyond us all?   10
Is the eternal truth man's fighting soul
Wherein the Beast ravens in its own avidity?

Of Van Wettering I speak, and Averill,
Names on a list, whose faces I do not recall
But they are gone to early death, who late in school
Distinguished the belt feed lever from the belt holding pawl.

Not Marching Away to Be Killed

Jean Overton Fuller (1915–   )

Peace is the men not marching away to be killed.
I never saw my father marching away to be killed.
He was killed before I was born. But my mother
Always spoke of the men marching away to be killed.
Not 'marching to the war' or 'into action'
Or even 'marching to fight for this country'.
Although she was a soldier's daughter and a soldier's
Widow. 'Marching away to be killed'
Was the fundamental reality for her.

For me   10

Peace is the man I love not
Marching away to be killed.

The Killer Too

Walker Gibson (1919–   )

Kill or be killed, the sergeant cried,
Discriminating Die from Live,
And spoke the truth. And also lied,
Positing false alternative

And false distinction: you or you.
For both the quick and the quiet of breath
Participate. The killer too
Incurs a penalty of death,

And even as the bombardier
In his glass house saw ack-ack bloom   10
Like flowers of evil on his bier,
His own bombs burst on his own tomb.

The Man He Killed

Thomas Hardy (1840–1928)

"Had he and I but met
　By some old ancient inn,
We should have sat us down to wet
　Right many a nipperkin![1]

"But ranged as infantry,
　And staring face to face,
I shot at him as he at me,
　And killed him in his place.

"I shot him dead because—
　Because he was my foe,   10
Just so: my foe of course he was;
　That's clear enough: although

"He thought he'd 'list, perhaps,
　Off-hand like—just as I—
Was out of work—had sold his traps—[2]
　No other reason why.

"Yes; quaint and curious war is!
　You shoot a fellow down
You'd treat if met where any bar is,
　Or help to half-a-crown."   20

1 Small tankard of beer.　2 Personal belongings.

Eighth Air Force
Randall Jarrell (1914–1966)

If, in an odd angle of the hutment,
A puppy laps the water from a can
Of flowers, and the drunk sergeant shaving
Whistles O Paradiso!¹—shall I say that man
Is not as men have said: a wolf to man?

The other murderers troop in yawning;
Three of them play Pitch, one sleeps, and one
Lies counting missions, lies there sweating
Till even his heart beats: One; One; One.
O murderers! . . . Still, this is how it's done: 10

This is a war. . . . But since these play, before they die,
Like puppies with their puppy; since, a man
I did as these have done, but did not die—
I will content the people as I can
And give up these to them: Behold the man!

I have suffered, in a dream, because of him,
Many things; for this last saviour, man,
I have lied as I lie now. But what is lying?
Men wash their hands, in blood, as best they can:
I find no fault in this just man.   20

1 A popular aria by Meyerbeer.

The Death of the Ball Turret Gunner
Randall Jarrell (1914–1966)

From my mother's sleep I fell into the State,
And I hunched in its belly till my wet fur froze.
Six miles from earth, loosed from its dream of life,
I woke to black flak and the nightmare fighters.
When I died they washed me out of the turret with a hose.

War
Joseph Langland (1917–   )

When my young brother was killed
By a mute and dusty shell in the thorny brush
Crowning the boulders of the Villa Verde Trail
On the island of Luzon,

I laid my whole dry body down,
Dropping my face like a stone in a green park
On the east banks of the Rhine;

On an airstrip skirting the Seine
His sergeant brother sat like a stick in his barracks
While cracks of fading sunlight   10
Caged the dusty air;

In the rocky rolling hills west of the Mississippi
His father and mother sat in a simple Norwegian parlor
With a photograph smiling between them on the table
And their hands fallen into their laps
Like sticks and dust;

And still other brothers and sisters,
Linking their arms together,
Walked down the dusty road where once he ran

And into the deep green valley   20
To sit on the stony banks of the stream he loved
And let the murmuring waters
Wash over their blood-hot feet with a springing crown of tears.

To Lucasta, on Going to the Wars
Richard Lovelace (1618–1658)

TELL me not, Sweet, I am unkind,
   That from the nunnery
Of thy chaste breast and quiet mind,
   To war and arms I fly.

True, a new mistress now I chase,
   The first foe in the field;
And with a stronger faith embrace
   A sword, a horse, a shield.

Yet this inconstancy is such
   As you too shall adore;   10
I could not love thee, Dear, so much,
   Loved I not Honour more.

Christmas Eve under Hooker's Statue[1]

Robert Lowell (1917–   )

Tonight a blackout. Twenty years ago
I hung my stocking on the tree, and hell's
Serpent entwined the apple in the toe
To sting the child with knowledge. Hooker's heels
Kicking at nothing in the shifting snow,
A cannon and a cairn of cannon balls
Rusting before the blackened Statehouse, know
How the long horn of plenty broke like glass
In Hooker's gauntlets. Once I came from Mass;

Now storm-clouds shelter Christmas, once again   10
Mars meets his fruitless star with open arms,
His heavy saber flashes with the rime,
The war-god's bronzed and empty forehead forms
Anonymous machinery from raw men;
The cannon on the Common cannot stun
The blundering butcher as he rides on Time—
The barrel clinks with holly. I am cold:
I ask for bread, my father gives me mould;

His stocking is full of stones. Santa in red
Is crowned with wizened berries. Man of war,   20
Where is the summer's garden? In its bed
The ancient speckled serpent will appear,
And black-eyed susan with her frizzled head.
When Chancellorsville mowed down the volunteer,
"All wars are boyish," Herman Melville said;
But we are old, our fields are running wild:
Till Christ again turn wanderer and child.

1 Hooker led the Union troops to bloody defeat at Chancellorsville in one
of the first major battles of the Civil War. The time is World War II when
the East Coast was blacked out. The place is Boston Common (park).

Vietnam #4

Clarence Major (1936–   )

a cat said
on the corner

the other day
dig man

how come so many
of us
niggers

are dying over there
in that white
man's war   10

they say more of us
are dying

than them peckerwoods
& it just
          don't make sense

unless it's true
that the honkeys

are trying to kill us out
with the same stone

they killing them other cats   20
with

you know, he said
two birds with one stone

Shiloh

A REQUIEM (APRIL 1862)

Herman Melville (1819–1891)

Skimming lightly, wheeling still,
   The swallows fly low
Over the field in clouded days,
   The forest-field of Shiloh—
Over the field where April rain
Solaced the parched one stretched in pain
Through the pause of night
That followed the Sunday fight
   Around the church of Shiloh—
The church so lone, the log-built one,   10
That echoed to many a parting groan
     And natural prayer
   Of dying foemen mingled there—
Foemen at morn, but friends at eve—
   Fame or country least their care:
(What like a bullet can undeceive!)
   But now they lie low,
While over them the swallows skim,
   And all is hushed at Shiloh.

Norman Morrison

Adrian Mitchell (1932–   )

On November 2nd 1965
in the multi-coloured multi-minded
United beautiful States of terrible America
Norman Morrison set himself on fire
outside the Pentagon.
He was thirty-one, he was a Quaker,
and his wife (seen weeping in the newsreels)
and his three children

survive him as best they can.
He did it in Washington where everyone could see   10
because
people were being set on fire
in the dark corners of Vietnam where nobody could see.
Their names, ages, beliefs and loves
are not recorded.
This is what Norman Morrison did.
He poured petrol over himself.
He burned. He suffered.
He died.
That is what he did   20
in the white heart of Washington
where everyone could see.
He simply burned away his clothes,
his passport, his pink-tinted skin,
put on a new skin of flame
and became
Vietnamese.

Instamatic

Fort Benning Georgia, April 1971

Edwin Morgan (1920–   )

A stocky, cocky little man,
chubby but not amiable,
sits at a table signing a contract.
The publisher promises
to pay him and his collaborator
one hundred thousand dollars only
to tell his story.
The light burns down.
We watch over his shoulder
as the stubby thumb
stabs out: Calley.

Disabled

Wilfred Owen (1893–1918)

He sat in a wheeled chair, waiting for dark,
And shivered in his ghastly suit of grey,
Legless, sewn short at elbow. Through the park
Voices of boys rang saddening like a hymn,
Voices of play and pleasures after day,
Till gathering sleep had mothered them from him.

.   .   .   .   .

About this time Town used to swing so gay
When glow-lamps budded in the light blue trees,
And girls glanced lovelier as the air grew dim,—
In the old times, before he threw away his knees.   10
Now he will never feel again how slim
Girls' waists are, or how warm their subtle hands;
All of them touch him like some queer disease.

.   .   .   .   .

There was an artist silly for his face,
For it was younger than his youth, last year.
Now, he is old; his back will never brace;
He's lost his colour very far from here,
Poured it down shell-holes till the veins ran dry,
And half his lifetime lapsed in the hot race,
And leap of purple spurted from his thigh.   20

.   .   .   .   .

One time he liked a blood-smear down his leg,
After the matches, carried shoulder-high.
It was after football, when he'd drunk a peg,
He thought he'd better join.—He wonders why.
Someone had said he'd look a god in kilts,
That's why; and may be, too, to please his Meg;
Aye, that was it, to please the giddy jilts
He asked to join. He didn't have to beg;
Smiling they wrote his lie; aged nineteen years.
Germans he scarcely thought of; all their guilt,   30

And Austria's, did not move him. And no fears
Of Fear came yet. He thought of jewelled hilts
For daggers in plaid socks; of smart salutes;
And care of arms; and leave; and pay arrears;
Esprit de corps; and hints for young recruits.
And soon he was drafted out with drums and cheers.

.   .   .   .   .

Some cheered him home, but not as crowds cheer Goal.
Only a solemn man who brought him fruits
Thanked him; and then inquired about his soul.

.   .   .   .   .

Now, he will spend a few sick years in Institutes,   40
And do what things the rules consider wise,
And take whatever pity they may dole.
To-night he noticed how the women's eyes
Passed from him to the strong men that were whole.
How cold and late it is! Why don't they come
And put him into bed? Why don't they come?

Dulce et Decorum Est
Wilfred Owen (1893–1918)

Bent double, like old beggars under sacks,
Knock-kneed, coughing like hags, we cursed through sludge,
Till on the haunting flares we turned our backs,
And towards our distant rest began to trudge.
Men marched asleep. Many had lost their boots,
But limped on, blood-shod. All went lame, all blind;
Drunk with fatigue; deaf even to the hoots
Of gas-shells dropping softly behind.

Gas! Gas! Quick, boys—An ectasy of fumbling,
Fitting the clumsy helmets just in time,   10

But someone still was yelling out and stumbling
And floundering like a man in fire or lime.—
Dim through the misty panes and thick green light,
As under a green sea, I saw him drowning.

In all my dreams before my helpless sight
He plunges at me, guttering, choking, drowning.

If in some smothering dreams, you too could pace
Behind the wagon that we flung him in,
And watch the white eyes writhing in his face,
His hanging face, like a devil's sick of sin;   20
If you could hear, at every jolt, the blood
Come gargling from the froth-corrupted lungs,
Bitter as the cud
Of vile, incurable sores on innocent tongues,—
My friend, you would not tell with such high zest
To children ardent for some desperate glory,
The old Lie: *Dulce et decorum est
Pro patria mori.*[1]

1 It is sweet and fitting to die for one's country.

from Hugh Selwyn Mauberley
Ezra Pound (1885–1972)

IV

These fought in any case,
and some believing,

             pro domo,[1] in any case . . .

1 For home.

Some quick to arm,
some for adventure,
some from fear of weakness,
some from fear of censure,
some for love of slaughter, in imagination,
learning later . . .
some in fear, learning love of slaughter;   10

Died some, pro patria,[2]
                    non "dulce" non "et decor"[3] . . . .
walked eye-deep in hell
believing in old men's lies, then unbelieving
came home, home to a lie,
home to many deceits,
home to old lies and new infamy;
usury age-old and age-thick
and liars in public places.

Daring as never before, wastage as never before.   20
Young blood and high blood,
fair cheeks, and fine bodies;

fortitude as never before

frankness as never before,
disillusions as never told in the old days,
hysterias, trench confessions,
laughter out of dead bellies.

                    v

There died a myriad,
And of the best, among them,
For an old bitch gone in the teeth,   30
For a botched civilization,

Charm, smiling at the good mouth,
Quick eyes gone under earth's lid,

For two gross of broken statues,
For a few thousand battered books.

2 For country.   3 It is *not* sweet and *not* fitting to die for one's country.

Naming of Parts

TO ALAN MITCHELL

Vixi duellis nuper idoneus
Et militavi non sine gloria.[1]

Henry Reed (1914–   )

Today we have naming of parts. Yesterday,
We had daily cleaning. And tomorrow morning,
We shall have what to do after firing. But today,
Today we have naming of parts. Japonica[2]
Glistens like coral in all of the neighboring gardens,
    And today we have naming of parts.

This is the lower sling swivel. And this
Is the upper sling swivel, whose use you will see,
When you are given your slings. And this is the piling swivel,
Which in your case you have not got. The branches   10
Hold in the gardens their silent, eloquent gestures,
    Which in our case we have not got.

This is the safety-catch, which is always released
With an easy flick of the thumb. And please do not let me
See anyone using his finger. You can do it quite easy
If you have any strength in your thumb. The blossoms
Are fragile and motionless, never letting anyone see
    Any of them using their finger.

And this you can see is the bolt. The purpose of this
Is to open the breech, as you see. We can slide it   20
Rapidly backwards and forwards: we call this
Easing the spring. And rapidly backwards and forwards
The early bees are assaulting and fumbling the flowers:
    They call it easing the Spring.

---

1 The opening lines of a poem by Horace (III.26), but with Horace's word
"puellis" (girls) changed to *"duellis"* (war, battles): "Lately I have lived in
the midst of battles, creditably enough,/And have soldiered, not without
glory."   2 A shrub whose flower is a brilliant scarlet, a camellia.

They call it easing the Spring: it is perfectly easy
If you have any strength in your thumb: like the bolt,
And the breech, and the cocking-piece, and the point of balance,
Which in our case we have not got; and the almond-blossom
Silent in all of the gardens and the bees going backwards and
    forwards,
  For today we have naming of parts.   30

Radar

Alan Ross (1922–   )

Distance is swept by the smooth
Rotations of power, whose staring
Feelers multiply our eyes for us,
Mark objects' range and bearing.

Linked to them, guns rehearse
Calculated obedience; echoes of light
Trigger the shadowing needle, determine
The flaring arrest of night.

Control is remote: feelings, like hands,
Gloved by space. Responsibility is shared, too: 10
And destroying the enemy by radar,
We cannot see what we do.

Base Details

Siegfried Sassoon (1886–1967)

If I were fierce, and bald, and short of breath,
  I'd live with scarlet Majors at the Base,
And speed glum heroes up the line to death.
  You'd see me with my puffy petulant face,

Guzzling and gulping in the best hotel,
   Reading the Roll of Honour. 'Poor young chap,'
I'd say—'I used to know his father well;
   Yes, we've lost heavily in this last scrap.'
And when the war is done and youth stone dead,
I'd toddle safely home and die—in bed.   10

Problems

Alexander Scott (1920–   )

("We've got a problem here."—Apollo 13 *report on oxygen-tank failure)*

The haill warld waited,
ten hunder million herts
in as monie mouths,
the haill warld harkened
til quaet voices
briggan the black howes o space
wi licht hope
o shipwrack saved,
the mune's mariners
steered through the stark lift   10
on a lifeline o skeelie science
(the wyve o human harns,
a hunder thousand hankan thegither
owre aa the waft o the warld)
that haled them frae toom heaven
to hame i the sea's haven
—and aye wi the camera's ee
the michty millions watched.

Ahint our backs,
the brukken corps o coolies   20
cam sooman alang the sworl
o the mirk Mekong,
their wyve o human harns
warped by the skeelie science

that made the machinegun's mant
the proof o pouer
to connach lifelines.

We hae a problem here.

St. Crispin's Day

from HENRY V (IV, 3)

William Shakespeare (1564–1616)

This day is call'd the Feast of Crispian.
He that outlives this day, and comes safe home,
Will stand a-tiptoe when this day is nam'd
And rouse him at the name of Crispian.
He that shall live this day, and see old age,
Will yearly on the vigil feast his neighbours
And say 'To-morrow is Saint Crispian.'
Then will he strip his sleeve and show his scars,
And say 'These wounds I had on Crispin's day.'
Old men forget; yet all shall be forgot,
But he'll remember, with advantages,   10
What feats he did that day. Then shall our names,
Familiar in his mouth as household words—
Harry the King, Bedford and Exeter,
Warwick and Talbot, Salisbury and Gloucester—[1]
Be in their flowing cups freshly rememb'red.
This story shall the good man teach his son;
And Crispin Crispian shall ne'er go by,
From this day to the ending of the world,
But we in it shall be remembered—
We few, we happy few, we band of brothers;   20

1 Henry V and his noblemen.

For he to-day that sheds his blood with me
Shall be my brother. Be he ne'er so vile,
This day shall gentle² his condition;
And gentlemen in England now abed
Shall think themselves accurs'd they were not here,
And hold their manhoods cheap whiles any speaks
That fought with us upon Saint Crispin's day.

2 Ennoble.

War Is the Statesman's Game

from QUEEN MAB

Percy Bysshe Shelley (1792–1822)

War is the statesman's game, the priest's delight,
The lawyer's jest, the hired assassin's trade,
And, to those royal murderers, whose mean thrones
Are bought by crimes of treachery and gore,
The bread they eat, the staff on which they lean.
Guards, garbed in blood-red livery, surround
Their palaces, participate in the crimes
That force defends, and from a nation's rage
Secure the crown, which all the curses reach
That famine, frenzy, woe and penury breathe.   10
These are the hired bravos who defend
The tyrant's throne—the bullies of his fear:
These are the sinks and channels of worst vice,
The refuse of society, the dregs
Of all that is most vile: their cold hearts blend
Deceit with sternness, ignorance with pride,
All that is mean and villanous with rage
Which hopelessness of good, and self-contempt,
Alone might kindle; they are decked in wealth,
Honour and power, then are sent abroad   20

To do their work. The pestilence that stalks
In gloomy triumph through some Eastern land
Is less destroying. They cajole with gold,
And promises of fame, the thoughtless youth
Already crushed with servitude: he knows
His wretchedness too late, and cherishes
Repentance for his ruin, when his doom
Is sealed in gold and blood!
Those too the tyrant serve, who skilled to snare
The feet of justice in the toils of law,   30
Stand ready to oppress the weaker still;
And, right or wrong, will vindicate for gold,
Sneering at public virtue, which beneath
Their pitiless tread lies torn and trampled, where
Honour sits smiling at the sale of truth.

War Bride

Douglas Worth (1940–   )

Clear nights, the massive
drone of planes—
curled on the mat, she hugs
her breasts, singing
over and over, something
about the shining
of new pots.

This morning a letter.
She gathers herself
to read, holds it   10
unopened:
writing this, he
was alive
his spit in the glue.

One to destroy, is murder by the law

Edward Young (1683–1765)

One to destroy, is murder by the law;
And gibbets keep the lifted hand in awe;
To murder thousands, takes a specious name,
War's glorious art, and gives immortal fame.
When, after battle, I the field have seen
Spread o'er with ghastly shapes, which once were men;
A nation crush'd, a nation of the brave!
A realm of death! and on this side the grave!
Are there, said I, who from this sad survey,
This human chaos, carry smiles away?   10
How did my heart with indignation rise!
How honest nature swell'd into my eyes!
How was I shock'd to think the hero's trade
Of such materials, fame and triumph made!

MUTABILITY
AND DEATH

*Golden lads and girls
all must,
As chimney-sweepers,
come to dust.*

William Shakespeare (1564–1616)

A Man of Words

Anonymous

A man of words and not of deeds
Is like a garden full of weeds;
And when the weeds begin to grow,
It's like a garden full of snow;
And when the snow begins to fall,
It's like a bird upon the wall;
And when the bird away does fly,
It's like an eagle in the sky;
And when the sky begins to roar,
It's like a lion at the door;   10
And when the door begins to crack,
It's like a stick across your back;
And when your back begins to smart,
It's like a penknife in your heart;
And when your heart begins to bleed,
You're dead, and dead, and dead indeed.

As I Walked Out One Evening

W. H. Auden (1907–1973)

As I walked out one evening,
    Walking down Bristol Street,
The crowds upon the pavement
    Were fields of harvest wheat.

And down by the brimming river
    I heard a lover sing
Under an arch of the railway:
    "Love has no ending.

I'll love you, dear, I'll love you
    Till China and Africa meet,   10

And the river jumps over the mountain
    And the salmon sing in the street.

I'll love you till the ocean
    Is folded and hung up to dry,
And the seven stars go squawking
    Like geese about the sky.

The years shall run like rabbits,
    For in my arms I hold
The Flower of the Ages,
    And the first love of the world."   20

But all the clocks in the city
    Began to whirr and chime:
"O let not Time deceive you,
    You cannot conquer Time.

In the burrows of the Nightmare
    Where Justice naked is,
Time watches from the shadow
    And coughs when you would kiss.

In headaches and in worry
    Vaguely life leaks away,
                               30
And Time will have his fancy
    Tomorrow or today.

Into many a green valley
    Drifts the appalling snow;
Time breaks the threaded dances
    And the diver's brilliant bow.

O plunge your hands in water,
    Plunge them in up to the wrist;
Stare, stare in the basin
    And wonder what you've missed.   40

The glacier knocks in the cupboard,
    The desert sighs in the bed,
And the crack in the tea-cup opens
    A lane to the land of the dead.

Where the beggars raffle the banknotes
    And the Giant is enchanting to Jack,
And the Lily-white Boy is a Roarer,
    And Jill goes down on her back.

O look, look in the mirror,
    O look in your distress;   50
Life remains a blessing
    Although you cannot bless.

O stand, stand at the window
    As the tears scald and start;
You shall love your crooked neighbor
    With your crooked heart."

It was late, late in the evening,
    The lovers they were gone;
The clocks had ceased their chiming,
    And the deep river ran on.   60

Song

from THE EMPEROR OF THE MOON

Aphra Behn (1640–1689)

When maidens are young, and in their spring,
Of pleasure, of pleasure, let 'em take their full swing,
    Full swing, full swing,
And love, and dance, and play, and sing,
For Silvia, believe it, when youth is done,
There's nought but hum-drum, hum-drum, hum-drum,
There's nought but hum-drum, hum-drum, hum-drum.

O Death, rock me asleep

Anne Boleyn (?)   (1507?–1536)

O Death, rock me asleep,
Bring me to quiet rest,
Let pass my weary guiltless ghost
  Out of my careful breast.
Toll on, thou passing bell;
Ring out my doleful knell;
Let thy sóund my déath téll.
  Death doth draw nigh;
  There is no remedy.

My pains who can express?   10
  Alas, they are so strong;
My dolour¹ will not suffer strength
  My life for to prolong.
Toll on, thou passing bell;
Ring out my doleful knell;
Let thy sound my death tell.
  Death doth draw nigh;
  There is no remedy.

Alone in prison strong
  I wait my destiny.   20
Woe worth this cruel hap that I
  Should taste this misery!
Toll on, thou passing bell;
Ring out my doleful knell;
Let thy sound my death tell.
  Death doth draw nigh;
  There is no remedy.

1 Sadness.

Southern Mansion

Arna Bontemps (1902–1973)

Poplars are standing there still as death
And ghosts of dead men
Meet their ladies walking
Two by two beneath the shade
And standing on the marble steps.

There is a sound of music echoing
Through the open door
And in the field there is
Another sound tinkling in the cotton:
Chains of bondmen dragging on the ground.   10

The years go back with an iron clank,
A hand is on the gate,
A dry leaf trembles on the wall.
Ghosts are walking.
They have broken roses down
And poplars stand there still as death.

Another Death

FOR MY MOTHER

D. E. Borrell (1928–   )

She died turning aside from the sink
Where the new-washed dishes lay;
Poleaxed like a dumb beast
She lay on the cold kitchen flags
And worried about the joint in the oven;
Unable to speak, incontinent,
Managed a gesture
That the switch be turned off
Before the ambulance took her.

In the chill winter sunlight   10
Relatives fumed before the barriers of snow,
Fumbled the 'phoning, panicked in strident whispers.
In her stricken body the ticking brain
Clung to its duties—dishes to wash
Meat too good to burn, a legion claims
That cannot be renounced
Even when dying. . . .

In hospital, nurses combed her hair the wrong way,
Parted awkwardly on the wrong side.
She looked like a stranger when she died.   20

We Real Cool

Gwendolyn Brooks (1917–   )

      The Pool Players. Seven at the Golden Shovel.

We real cool. We
Left school. We

Lurk late. We
Strike straight. We

Sing sin. We
Thin gin. We

Jazz June. We
Die soon.

My Sweetest Lesbia
Thomas Campion (1567–1620)

My sweetest Lesbia, let us live and love,
And though the sager sort our deeds reprove,
Let us not weigh them. Heav'n's great lamps do dive
Into their west, and straight again revive,
But soon as once set is our little light,
Then must we sleep one ever-during[1] night.

If all would lead their lives in love like me,
Then bloody swords and armor should not be;
No drum nor trumpet peaceful sleeps should move,
Unless alarm came from the camp of love.   10
But fools do live, and waste their little light,
And seek with pain their ever-during night.

When timely death my life and fortune ends,
Let not my hearse be vexed with mourning friends,
But let all lovers, rich in triumph, come
And with sweet pastimes grace my happy tomb;
And Lesbia, close up thou my little light,
And crown with love my ever-during night.

1 Enduring.

Death, Be Not Proud
John Donne (1572–1631)

Death, be not proud, though some have callèd thee
Mighty and dreadful, for thou art not so,
For those whom thou think'st thou dost overthrow,
Die not, poor Death, nor yet canst thou kill me.
From rest and sleep, which but thy pictures be,
Much pleasure, then from thee, much more must flow,

And soonest our best men with thee do go,
Rest of their bones,[1] and soul's delivery.
Thou art slave to fate, chance, kings, and desperate men,
And dost with poison, war, and sickness dwell,   10
And poppy, or charms can make us sleep as well,
And better than thy stroke; why swell'st thou then?
One short sleep past, we wake eternally,
And death shall be no more; Death, thou shalt die.

1 Rest for their bones.

Wake! For the Sun

from THE RUBAIYAT OF OMAR KHAYYAM

Edward Fitzgerald (1809–1892)

Wake! For the Sun, who scattered into flight
The Stars before him from the Field of Night,
    Drives Night along with them from Heav'n, and strikes
The Sultán's Turret with a Shaft of Light.

Before the phantom of False morning died,
Methought a Voice within the Tavern cried,
    "When all the Temple is prepared within,
"Why nods the drowsy Worshipper outside?"

And, as the Cock crew, those who stood before
The Tavern shouted—"Open then the Door!   10
    "You know how little while we have to stay,
"And, once departed, may return no more."

Come, fill the Cup, and in the fire of Spring
Your Winter-garment of Repentance fling:
    The Bird of Time has but a little way
To flutter—and the Bird is on the Wing.

Whether at Naishápúr or Babylon,
Whether the Cup with sweet or bitter run,
    The Wine of Life keeps oozing drop by drop,
The Leaves of Life keep falling one by one.   20

Now the Lusty Spring
John Fletcher (1548–1611)

Now the lusty spring is seen;
    Golden yellow, gaudy blue,
    Daintily invite the view.
Everywhere on every green,
Roses blushing as they blow,
    And enticing men to pull,
Lilies whiter than the snow,
    Woodbines[1] of sweet honey full:
        All love's emblems, and all cry,
        "Ladies, if not plucked, we die."   10

Yet the lusty spring hath stayed;
    Blushing red and purest white
    Daintily to love invite
Every woman, every maid.
Cherries kissing as they grow,
    And inviting men to taste,
Apples even ripe below,
    Winding gently to the waist:
        All love's emblems, and all cry.
        "Ladies, if not plucked, we die."   20

1 Honeysuckles.

Out, Out—

Robert Frost (1874–1963)

The buzz saw snarled and rattled in the yard
And made dust and dropped stove-length sticks of wood,
Sweet-scented stuff when the breeze drew across it.
And from there those that lifted eyes could count
Five mountain ranges one behind the other
Under the sunset far into Vermont.
And the saw snarled and rattled, snarled and rattled,
As it ran light, or had to bear a load.
And nothing happened: day was all but done.
Call it a day, I wish they might have said   10
To please the boy by giving him the half hour
That a boy counts so much when saved from work.
His sister stood beside them in her apron
To tell them "Supper." At the word, the saw,
As if to prove saws knew what supper meant,
Leaped out at the boy's hand, or seemed to leap—
He must have given the hand. However it was,
Neither refused the meeting. But the hand!
The boy's first outcry was a rueful laugh,
As he swung toward them holding up the hand,   20
Half in appeal, but half as if to keep
The life from spilling. Then the boy saw all—
Since he was old enough to know, big boy
Doing a man's work, though a child at heart—
He saw all spoiled. "Don't let him cut my hand off—
The doctor, when he comes. Don't let him, sister!"
So. But the hand was gone already.
The doctor put him in the dark of ether.
He lay and puffed his lips out with his breath.
And then—the watcher at his pulse took fright.   30
No one believed. They listened at his heart.
Little—less—nothing!—and that ended it.
No more to build on there. And they, since they
Were not the one dead, turned to their affairs.

Stopping by Woods on a Snowy Evening
Robert Frost (1874–1963)

Whose woods these are I think I know.
His house is in the village though;
He will not see me stopping here
To watch his woods fill up with snow.

My little horse must think it queer
To stop without a farmhouse near
Between the woods and frozen lake
The darkest evening of the year.

He gives his harness bells a shake
To ask if there is some mistake.   10
The only other sound's the sweep
Of easy wind and downy flake.

The woods are lovely, dark and deep.
But I have promises to keep,
And miles to go before I sleep,
And miles to go before I sleep.

To the Virgins to Make Much of Time
Robert Herrick (1591–1674)

Gather ye rose-buds while ye may,
   Old Time is still a-flying:
And this same flower that smiles today,
   Tomorrow will be dying.

The glorious lamp of heaven, the Sun,
   The higher he's a-getting
The sooner will his race be run,
   And nearer he's to setting.

That age is best which is the first,
  When youth and blood are warmer;
But being spent, the worse, and worst
  Times, still succeed the former.

Then be not coy, but use your time;
  And while ye may, go marry:
For having lost but once your prime,
  You may for ever tarry.

Come, My Celia

Ben Jonson (1572–1637)

Come, my Celia, let us prove
While we may the sports of love;
Time will not be ours forever,
He at length our good will sever.
Spend not then his gifts in vain;
Suns that set may rise again,
But if once we lost this light,
'Tis with us perpetual night.
Why should we defer our joys?
Fame and rumor are but toys. 10
Cannot we delude the eyes
Of a few poor household spies?
Or his easier ears beguile,
So removèd by our wile?
'Tis no sin love's fruit to steal;
But the sweet theft to reveal,
To be taken, to be seen,
These have crimes accounted been.

On My First Son
Ben Jonson (1572–1637)

Farewell, thou child of my right hand, and joy;
My sin was too much hope of thee, loved boy,
Seven years thou wert lent to me, and I thee pay,
Exacted by thy fate, on the just day.
O, could I lose all father now. For why
Will man lament the state he should envy?
To have so soon scaped world's and flesh's rage,
And, if no other misery, yet age?
Rest in soft peace, and, asked, say, "Here doth lie
Ben Jonson his best piece of poetry."   10
For whose sake henceforth all his vows be such,
As what he loves may never like too much.

Down in Dallas
X. J. Kennedy (1929–   )

Down in Dallas, down in Dallas
Where the shadow of blood lies black,
Little Oswald nailed Jack Kennedy up
With the nail of a rifle crack.

The big bright Cadillacs stomped on their brakes,
The street fell unearthly still
While, smoke on its chin, that slithering gun
Coiled back from its window sill.

In a white chrome room on a table top
They tried all a scalpel knows,   10
But they couldn't spell stop to that drop-by-drop
Till it bloomed to a rigid rose.

Out on the altar, out on the altar
Christ blossoms in bread and wine,

But each asphalt stone where his blood dropped down
Is burst to a cactus spine.

Oh down in Dallas, down in Dallas
Where a desert wind walks by night,
He stood and they bound him foot and hand
To the cross of a rifle sight.   20

Like to the falling of a star
Henry King (1592–1669)

Like to the falling of a star,
Or as the flights of eagles are,
Or like the fresh spring's gaudy hue,
Or silver drops of morning dew,
Or like a wind that chafes the flood,
Or bubbles which on water stood:
Even such is man, whose borrow'd light
Is straight call'd in, and paid to night.

The wind blows out; the bubble dies;
The Spring entomb'd in Autumn lies;   10
The dew dries up; the star is shot;
The flight is past, and man forgot.

Bridgework
Annette Lynch (1922–   )

My teeth dare not trust you.
Somewhere between my schooling
and your begetting
sprawls a chasm crossed

by a swaying rope bridge
which could be
too easily bitten
in two by time
whose teeth I know
I cannot trust.

To His Coy Mistress
Andrew Marvell (1621–1678)

Had we but world enough, and time,
This coyness, Lady, were no crime.
We would sit down and think which way
To walk and pass our long love's day.
Thou by the Indian Ganges' side
Shouldst rubies find; I by the tide
Of Humber would complain. I would
Love you ten years before the Flood,
And you should, if you please, refuse
Till the conversion of the Jews.   10
My vegetable love would grow
Vaster than empires, and more slow;
An hundred years would go to praise
Thine eyes and on thy forehead gaze;
Two hundred to adore each breast,
But thirty thousand to the rest;
An age at least to every part,
And the last age should show your heart.
For, Lady, you deserve this state,
Nor would I love at lower rate.   20

But at my back I always hear
Time's winged chariot hurrying near;
And yonder all before us lie
Deserts of vast eternity.
Thy beauty shall no more be found,

Nor, in thy marble vault, shall sound
My echoing song; then worms shall try
That long preserved virginity,
And your quaint honor turn to dust,
And into ashes all my lust: 30
The grave's a fine and private place,
But none, I think, do there embrace.

Now therefore, while the youthful hue
Sits on thy skin like morning dew,
And while thy willing soul transpires
At every pore with instant fires,
Now let us sport us while we may,
And now, like amorous birds of prey,
Rather at once our time devour
Than languish in his slow-chapped power.   40
Let us roll all our strength and all
Our sweetness up into one ball,
And tear our pleasures with rough strife
Through the iron gates of life:
Thus, though we cannot make our sun
Stand still, yet we will make him run.

Dirge in Woods
George Meredith (1829–1909)

A wind sways the pines,
And below
Not a breath of wild air;
Still as the mosses that glow
On the flooring and over the lines
Of the roots here and there.

The pine-tree drops its dead;
They are quiet, as under the sea.
Overhead, overhead

Rushes life in a race,
As the clouds the clouds chase;
    And we go,
And we drop like the fruits of the tree,
    Even we,
    Even so.

10

Rich Men, Trust Not

Thomas Nashe (1567–1601)

Rich men, trust not in wealth,
Gold cannot buy you health:
Physic[1] himself must fade;
All things to end are made;
The plague full swift goes by.
I am sick, I must die—
    Lord have mercy on us!

Beauty is but a flower
Which wrinkles will devour;
Brightness falls from the air;
Queens have died young, and fair;
Dust hath closed Helen's eye.
I am sick, I must die—
    Lord have mercy on us!

10

Strength stoops unto the grave,
Worms feed on Hector brave;
Swords may not fight with fate;
Earth still holds ope her gate;
Come, come, the bells do cry.
I am sick, I must die—
    Lord have mercy on us!

20

1 The art of medicine.

Death & Co.

Sylvia Plath (1932–1963)

Two, of course there are two.
It seems perfectly natural now—
The one who never looks up, whose eyes are lidded
And balled, like Blake's,
Who exhibits

The birthmarks that are his trademark—
The scald scar of water,
The nude
Verdigris of the condor.
I am red meat. His beak   10

Claps sidewise: I am not his yet.
He tells me how badly I photograph.
He tells me how sweet
The babies look in their hospital
Icebox, a simple

Frill at the neck,
Then the flutings of their Ionian
Death-gowns,
Then two little feet.
He does not smile or smoke.   20

The other does that,
His hair long and plausive.
Bastard
Masturbating a glitter,
He wants to be loved.

I do not stir.
The frost makes a flower,
The dew makes a star,
The dead bell,
The dead bell.   30

Somebody's done for.

Bells for John Whiteside's Daughter

John Crowe Ransom (1888–1974)

There was such speed in her little body,
And such lightness in her footfall,
It is no wonder that her brown study[1]
Astonishes us all.

Her wars were bruited[2] in our high window.
We looked among orchard trees and beyond,
Where she took arms against her shadow,
Or harried unto the pond

The lazy geese, like a snow cloud
Dripping their snow on the green grass,   10
Tricking and stopping, sleepy and proud,
Who cried in goose, Alas,

For the tireless heart within the little
Lady with rod that made them rise
From their noon apple dreams, and scuttle
Goose-fashion under the skies!

But now go the bells, and we are ready;
In one house we are sternly stopped
To say we are vexed at her brown study,
Lying so primly propped.   20

1 The opposite of animated; a state of brooding melancholy. 2 Noised
abroad.

Elegy for Jane

(My student, thrown by a horse)

Theodore Roethke (1908–1963)

I remember the neckcurls, limp and damp as tendrils;
And her quick look, a sidelong pickerel smile;
And how, once startled into talk, the light syllables leaped for
    her.
And she balanced in the delight of her thought,
A wren, happy, tail into the wind,
Her song trembling the twigs and small branches.
The shade sang with her;
The leaves, their whispers turned to kissing,
And the mould sang in the bleached valleys under the rose.

Oh, when she was sad, she cast herself down into such a pure
    depth,
Even a father could not find her:
Scraping her cheek against straw,
Stirring the clearest water.
My sparrow, you are not here,
Waiting like a fern, making a spiney shadow.
The sides of wet stones cannot console me,
Nor the moss, wound with the last light.

If only I could nudge you from this sleep,
My maimed darling, my skittery pigeon.
Over this damp grave I speak the words of my love:
I, with no rights in this matter,
Neither father nor lover.

Song

Christina Rossetti (1830–1894)

When I am dead, my dearest,
  Sing no sad songs for me;
Plant thou no roses at my head,
  Nor shady cypress tree.
Be the green grass above me
  With showers and dewdrops wet;
And if thou wilt, remember,
  And if thou wilt, forget.

I shall not see the shadows,
  I shall not feel the rain;   10
I shall not hear the nightingale
  Sing on as if in pain.
And dreaming through the twilight
  That doth not rise nor set,
Haply[1] I may remember,
  And haply may forget.

1 Perhaps.

Fear no more the heat o' the sun

from CYMBELINE (IV, 2)

William Shakespeare (1564–1616)

Fear no more the heat o' the sun,
  Nor the furious winter's rages;
Thou thy worldly task hast done,
  Home art gone, and ta'en thy wages;
Golden lads and girls all must,
As chimney-sweepers, come to dust.

Fear no more the frown o' the great,
   Thou are past the tyrant's stroke;
Care no more to clothe and eat,
   To thee the reed is as the oak.
The scepter, learning, physic, must
All follow this and come to dust.

Fear no more the lightning flash,
   Nor the all-dreaded thunder-stone;
Fear not slander, censure rash;
   Thou hast finished joy and moan.
All lovers young, all lovers must
Consign to thee and come to dust.

When forty winters shall besiege thy brow

SONNET 2

William Shakespeare (1564–1616)

When forty winters shall besiege thy brow
And dig deep trenches in thy beauty's field,
Thy youth's proud livery, so gaz'd on now,
Will be a tatter'd weed of small worth held.
Then being ask'd where all thy beauty lies,
Where all the treasure of thy lusty days,
To say, within thine own deep-sunken eyes
Were an all-eating shame and thriftless praise.
How much more praise deserv'd thy beauty's use
If thou couldst answer, 'This fair child of mine
Shall sum my count and make my old excuse,'
Proving his beauty by succession thine!
   This were to be new made when thou art old
   And see thy blood warm when thou feel'st it cold.

Since brass, nor stone, nor earth, nor boundless sea,

SONNET 65

William Shakespeare (1564–1616)

Since brass, nor stone, nor earth, nor boundless sea,
But sad mortality o'er-sways their power,
How with this rage shall beauty hold a plea,
Whose action is no stronger than a flower?
O, how shall summer's honey breath hold out
Against the wrackful siege of battering days,
When rocks impregnable are not so stout,
Nor gates of steel so strong, but Time decays?
O fearful meditation! where, alack,
Shall Time's best jewel from Time's chest lie hid?   10
Or what strong hand can hold his swift foot back?
Or who his spoil of beauty can forbid?
   O, none, unless this miracle have might,
   That in black ink my love may still shine bright.

Ozymandias
Percy Bysshe Shelley (1792–1822)

I met a traveler from an antique land
Who said: "Two vast and trunkless legs of stone
Stand in the desert. Near them, on the sand,
Half sunk, a shattered visage lies, whose frown,
And wrinkled lip, and sneer of cold command,
Tell that its sculptor well those passions read
Which yet survive, stamped on these lifeless things,
The hand that mocked them, and the heart that fed:
And on the pedestal these words appear:
'My name is Ozymandias, king of kings: 10
Look on my works, ye Mighty, and despair!'
Nothing beside remains. Round the decay
Of that colossal wreck, boundless and bare
The lone and level sands stretch far away."

Death the Leveller

James Shirley (1596–1666)

The glories of our blood and state
   Are shadows, not substantial things;
There is no armor against fate;
   Death lays his icy hand on kings:
      Scepter and crown
      Must tumble down,
And in the dust be equal made
With the poor crooked scythe and spade.

Some men with swords may reap the field,
   And plant fresh laurels where they kill,   10
But their strong nerves at last must yield;
   They tame but one another still:
      Early or late,
      They stoop to fate,
And must give up their murmuring breath,
When they, pale captives, creep to death.

The garlands wither on your brow;
   Then boast no more your mighty deeds;
Upon death's purple altar now,
   See where the victor-victim bleeds: 20
      Your heads must come
      To the cold tomb;
Only the actions of the just
Smell sweet and blossom in their dust.

Death of a Son

(WHO DIED IN A MENTAL HOSPITAL AGED ONE)

Jon Silkin (1930–   )

Something has ceased to come along with me.
Something like a person: something very like one.
  And there was no nobility in it
   Or anything like that.

Something was there like a one year
Old house, dumb as stone. While the near buildings
  Sang like birds and laughed
   Understanding the pact

They were to have with silence. But he
Neither sang nor laughed. He did not bless silence   10
  Like bread, with words.
   He did not forsake silence.

But rather, like a house in mourning
Kept the eye turned in to watch the silence while
  The other houses like birds
   Sang around him.

And the breathing silence neither
Moved nor was still.

I have seen stones: I have seen brick
But this house was made up of neither bricks nor stone 20
  But a house of flesh and blood
   With flesh of stone

And bricks for blood. A house
Of stones and blood in breathing silence with the other
  Birds singing crazy on its chimneys.
   But this was silence,

This was something else, this was
Hearing and speaking though he was a house drawn

Into silence, this was
Something religious in his silence,   30

Something shining in his quiet,
This was different, this was altogether something else:
Though he never spoke, this
Was something to do with death.

And then slowly the eye stopped looking
Inward. The silence rose and became still.
The look turned to the outer place and stopped,
With the birds still shrilling around him.
And as if he could speak

He turned over on his side with his one year   40
Red as a wound
He turned over as if he could be sorry for this
And out of his eyes two great tears rolled, like stones, and
he died.

Fresh spring the herald of loves mighty king
Edmund Spenser (1552–1599)

Fresh spring the herald of loves mighty king,
In whose cote armour richly are displayed
All sorts of flowers the which on earth do spring
In goodly colours gloriously arrayed.
Go to my love, where she is careless laid,
Yet in her winter's bower not well awake,
Tell her the joyous time will not be stayed
Unless she do him by the forelock take.
Bid her therefore herself soon ready make,
To wait on love amongst his lovely crew   10
Where every one that misseth then her make[1]

1 Mate.

Shall be by him amerced[2] by penance due.
Make haste therefore sweet love, whilst it is prime,[3]
   For none can call again the passéd time.

2 Punished.   3 Blooming.

Song of Bliss

from THE FAERIE QUEENE

Edmund Spenser (1552–1599)

The whiles someone did chant this lovely lay[1];
   Ah see, who so fair thing doest fain[2] to see,
   In springing flower the image of thy day;
   Ah see the Virgin Rose how sweetly she
   Doth first peep forth with bashful modesty,
   That fairer seems, the less ye see her may;
   Lo see soon after, how more bold and free
   Her bared bosom she doth broad display;
Lo see soon after, how she fades, and falls away.

So passeth, in the passing of a day,   10
   Of mortall life the leaf, the bud, the flower,
   Ne more doth flourish after first decay,
   That earst[3] was sought to deck both bed and bower,
   Of many a Lady, and many a Paramour:
   Gather therefore the Rose, whilest yet is prime,[4]
   For soon comes age, that will her pride deflower:
   Gather the Rose of love, whilest yet is time,
Whilest loving thou mayst loved be with equal crime.

1 Song.   2 Desire.   3 Formerly.   4 Blooming.

A Satirical Elegy on the Death of a Late Famous General

Jonathan Swift (1667–1745)

His Grace! impossible! what dead!
Of old age too, and in his bed!
And could that Mighty Warrior fall?
And so inglorious, after all!
Well, since he's gone, no matter how,
The last loud trump must wake him now:
And, trust me, as the noise grows stronger,
He'd wish to sleep a little longer.
And could he be indeed so old
As by the news-papers we're told?   10
Threescore, I think, is pretty high;
'Twas time in conscience he should die.
This world he cumber'd long enough;
He burnt his candle to the snuff;
And that's the reason some folks think,
He left behind *so great a s . . . k.*
Behold his funeral appears,
Nor widow's sighs, nor orphan's tears,
Wont at such times each heart to pierce,
Attend the progress of his herse.   20
But what of that, his friends may say,
He had those honours in his day.
True to his profit and his pride,
He made them weep before he dy'd.

Come hither, all ye empty things,
Ye bubbles rais'd by breath of Kings;
Who float upon the tide of state,
Come hither, and behold your fate.
Let pride be taught by this rebuke,
How very mean a thing's a Duke;   30
From all his ill-got honours flung,
Turn'd to that dirt from whence he sprung.

The Danube to the Severn gave[1]
Alfred, Lord Tennyson (1809–1892)

The Danube to the Severn gave
   The darken'd heart that beat no more;
   They laid him by the pleasant shore,
And in the hearing of the wave.

There twice a day the Severn fills;
   The salt sea-water passes by,
   And hushes half the babbling Wye,
And makes a silence in the hills.

The Wye is hush'd nor moved along,
   And hush'd my deepest grief of all,
   When fill'd with tears that cannot fall,
I brim with sorrow drowning song.

The tide flows down, the wave again
   Is vocal in its wooded walls;
   My deeper anguish also falls,
And I can speak a little then.

10

1 The poet's friend Hallam, the subject of this poem, died in Vienna. He was buried in Clevedon which overlooks the Severn river where it flows into the Bristol Channel. The ebb and flow of the tide up the estuaries of the Severn and its tributary the Wye are applied to Hallam's poetic utterance and silence.

A Refusal to Mourn the Death, by Fire, of a Child in London
Dylan Thomas (1914–1953)

Never until the mankind making
Bird beast and flower
Fathering and all humbling darkness
Tells with silence the last light breaking

And the still hour
Is come of the sea tumbling in harness

And I must enter again the round
Zion of the water bead
And the synagogue of the ear of corn
Shall I let pray the shadow of a sound   10
Or sow my salt seed
In the least valley of sackcloth to mourn

The majesty and burning of the child's death.
I shall not murder
The mankind of her going with a grave truth
Nor blaspheme down the stations of the breath
With any further
Elegy of innocence and youth.

Deep with the first dead lies London's daughter,
Robed in the long friends,   20
The grains beyond age, the dark veins of her mother
Secret by the unmourning water
Of the riding Thames.
After the first death, there is no other.

Do Not Go Gentle into That Good Night
Dylan Thomas (1914–1953)

Do not go gentle into that good night,
Old age should burn and rave at close of day;
Rage, rage against the dying of the light.

Though wise men at their end know dark is right,
Because their words had forked no lightning they
Do not go gentle into that good night.

Good men, the last wave by, crying how bright
Their frail deeds might have danced in a green bay
Rage, rage against the dying of the light.

Wild men who caught and sang the sun in flight,   10
And learn, too late, they grieved it on its way,
Do not go gentle into that good night.

Grave men, near death, who see with blinding sight
Blind eyes could blaze like meteors and be gay,
Rage, rage against the dying of the light.

And you, my father, there on the sad height,
Curse, bless, me now with your fierce tears, I pray.
Do not go gentle into that good night.
Rage, rage against the dying of the light.

Tichborne's Elegy
Chidiock Tichborne (1558?–1586)

Written with his own hand in the Tower before his execution

My prime of youth is but a frost of cares,
My feast of joy is but a dish of pain,
My crop of corn is but a field of tares,
And all my good is but vain hope of gain;
The day is past, and yet I saw no sun,
And now I live, and now my life is done.

My tale was heard and yet it was not told,
My fruit is fallen and yet my leaves are green,
My youth is spent and yet I am not old,
I saw the world and yet I was not seen;   10
My thread is cut and yet it is not spun,
And now I live, and now my life is done.

I sought my death and found it in my womb,
I looked for life and saw it was a shade,

I trod the earth and knew it was my tomb,
And now I die, and now I was but made;
My glass is full, and now my glass is run,
And now I live, and now my life is done.

A Death in the Desert

(IN MEMORY OF HOMER VANCE)

Charles Tomlinson (1927–   )

There are no crosses
on the Hopi graves.   They lie
shallowly
under a scattering
of small boulders.   The sky
over the desert
with its sand-grain stars
and the immense equality
between desert and desert sky,
seem   10
a scope and ritual
enough to stem
death and to be its equal.

"Homer
is the name," he said
the old Hopi doll-maker.
I met him in summer.   He was
dead when I came back that autumn.

He had sat
like an Olympian   20
in his cool room
on the rock-roof of the world,
beyond the snatch
of circumstance

and was to die
beating a burro out of his corn-patch.

"That,"
said his neighbor
"was a week ago." And the week
that lay   30
uncrossably between us
stretched into sand,
into the spread
of the endless
waterless sea-bed beneath
whose space outpacing sight
receded as speechless and as wide as death.

Go, lovely Rose
Edmund Waller (1606–1687)

 Go, lovely Rose,
Tell her that wastes her time and me,
 That now she knows,
When I resemble her to thee,
How sweet and fair she seems to be.

 Tell her that's young,
And shuns to have her graces spied,
 That hadst thou sprung
In deserts where no men abide,
Thou must have uncommended died.   10

 Small is the worth
Of beauty from the light retired:
 Bid her come forth,
Suffer her self to be desired,
And not blush so to be admired.

Then die, that she
The common fate of all things rare
   May read in thee,
How small a part of time they share,
That are so wondrous sweet and faire.   20

Objects

Richard Wilbur (1921–   )

Meridians are a net
Which catches nothing; that sea-scampering bird
The gull, though shores lapse every side from sight, can yet
Sense him to land, but Hanno[1] had not heard

Hesperidean song,[2]
Had he not gone by watchful periploi:[3]
Chalk rocks, and isles like beasts, and mountain stains along
The water-hem, calmed him at last nearby

The clear high hidden chant
Blown from the spellbound coast, where under drifts   10
Of sunlight, under plated leaves, they guard the plant
By praising it. Among the wedding gifts

Of Herë, were a set
Of golden McIntoshes, from the Greek
Imagination. Guard and gild what's common, and forget
Uses and prices and names; have objects speak.

There's classic and there's quaint,
And then there is that devout intransitive eye

---

1 Fifth-century Carthaginian navigator. 2 The Hesperides were maidens
who guarded the golden apples, Gaia's gift to Herë on her marriage to
Zeus, supreme God of the Greeks. 3 Plural of *periplus*, a coastal guide.

Of Pieter de Hooch:[4] see feinting from his plot of paint
The trench of light on boards, the much-mended dry   20

Courtyard wall of brick,
And sun submerged in beer, and streaming in glasses,
The weave of a sleeve, the careful and undulant tile. A quick
Change of the eye and all this calmly passes

Into a day, into magic.
For is there any end to true textures, to true
Integuments; do they ever desist from tacit, tragic
Fading away? Oh maculate,[5] cracked, askew,

Gay-pocked and potsherd world
I voyage, where in every tangible tree   30
I see afloat among the leaves, all calm and curled,
The Cheshire smile—which sets me fearfully free.

4 Seventeenth-century Dutch painter.   5 Stained, blemished.

INSIGHT

*The road of excess leads
to the palace of wisdom.*

William Blake

A Dream of Fair Women

Kingsley Amis (1922–   )

The door still swinging to, and girls revive,
Aeronauts in the utmost altitudes
   Of boredom fainting, dive
Into the bright oxygen of my nod;
Angels as well, a squadron of draped nudes,
   They roar towards their god.

Militant all, they fight to take my hat,
No more as yet; the other men retire
   Insulted, gestured at;
Each girl presses on me her share of what   10
Makes up the barn-door target of desire;
   And I am a crack shot.

Speech fails them, amorous, but each one's look,
Endorsed in other ways, begs me to sign
   Her body's autograph-book;
"Me first, Kingsley: I'm cleverest," each declares,
But no gourmet races downstairs to dine,
   Nor will I race upstairs.

Feigning aplomb, perhaps for half an hour,
I hover, and am shown by each princess   20
   The entrance to her tower,
Open, in that its tenant throws the key
At once to anyone, but not unless
   That anyone is me.

Now from the corridor their fathers cheer,
Their brothers, their young men; the cheers increase
   As soon as I appear;
From each I win a handshake and sincere
Congratulations; from the chief of police
   A nod, a wink, a leer.   30

This over, all delay is over too;
The first eight girls (the roster now agreed)
   Leap on me and undo . . .
But honesty impels me to confess
That this is "all a dream," which was, indeed,
   Not difficult to guess.

But wait: not "just a dream," because, though good
And beautiful, it is also true, and hence
   Is rarely understood;
Who would choose any feasible ideal   40
In here and now's giant circumference
   If that small room were real?

Only the best; the others find, have found
Love's ordinary distance too great,
   And eager, stand their ground;
Map-drunk explorers, dry-land sailors, they
See no arrival that can compensate
   For boredom on the way.

And, seeming doctrinaire, but really weak,
Limelighted dolls guttering in their brain,   50
   They come with me, to seek
The halls of theoretical delight,
The women of that ever-fresh terrain,
   The night after tonight.

Peter Hath Lost His Purse

Anonymous

Peter hath lost his purse, but will conceal it,
Lest she that stole it to his shame reveal it.

Musée des Beaux Arts[1]
W. H. Auden (1907–1973)

About suffering they were never wrong,
The Old Masters: how well they understood
Its human position; how it takes place
While someone else is eating or opening a window or just
    walking dully along;
How, when the aged are reverently, passionately waiting
For the miraculous birth, there always must be
Children who did not specially want it to happen, skating
On a pond at the edge of the wood:
They never forgot
That even the dreadful martyrdom must run its course   10
Anyhow in a corner, some untidy spot
Where the dogs go on with their doggy life and the torturer's
    horse
Scratches its innocent behind on a tree.

In Brueghel's *Icarus*,[2] for instance: how everything turns away
Quite leisurely from the disaster; the ploughman may
Have heard the splash, the forsaken cry,
But for him it was not an important failure; the sun shone
As it had to on the white legs disappearing into the green
Water; and the expensive delicate ship that must have seen
Something amazing, a boy falling out of the sky,   20
Had somewhere to get to and sailed calmly on.

1 Museum of Fine Arts.   2 Mythological character who flew, on **wings of** wax, too near the sun. The wax melted. He fell into the sea and **drowned**.

In Seed Time Learn

from THE MARRIAGE OF HEAVEN AND HELL

William Blake (1757–1827)

In seed time learn, in harvest teach, in winter enjoy.
Drive your cart and your plow over the bones of the dead.
The road of excess leads to the palace of wisdom.
Prudence is a rich, ugly old maid courted by Incapacity.
He who desires but acts not, breeds pestilence.

To a Mouse

Robert Burns (1759–1796)

On turning her up in her nest with the plough, November 1785

Wee, sleekit, cowrin, tim'rous beastie,
O, what a panic's in thy breastie!
Thou need na start awa sae hasty,
　　　　　Wi' bickering brattle![1]
I wad be laith to rin an' chase thee,
　　　　　Wi' murd'ring pattle![2]

I'm truly sorry Man's dominion
Has broken Nature's social union,
An' justifies that ill opinion
　　　　　Which makes thee startle   10
At me, thy poor, earth-born companion,
　　　　　An' fellow-mortal!

I doubt na, whyles, but thou may thieve
What then? poor beastie, thou maun live!
A daimen icker in a thrave[3]
　　　　　'S a sma' request.

1 Hurried scampering. 2 Plow shaft. 3 Occasional ear in 24 sheaves.

I'll get a blessin wi' the lave,
                    And never miss't!

   Thy wee bit housie, too, in ruin!
Its silly wa's the win's are strewin!   20
An' naething, now, to big a new ane,
                    O' foggage green!
An' bleak December's winds ensuin,
                    Baith snell[4] and keen!

   Thou saw the fields laid bare an' waste,
An' weary Winter comin fast,
An' cozie here, beneath the blast,
                    Thou thought to dwell,
Till crash! the cruel coulter past
                    Out thro' thy cell.   30

   That wee bit heap o' leaves an' stibble,
Has cost thee mony a weary nibble!
Now thou's turned out, for a' thy trouble,
                    But house or hald,[5]
To thole[6] the Winter's sleety dribble,
                    An' cranreuch[7] cauld!

   But, Mousie, thou are no thy lane,
In proving foresight may be vain:
The best-laid schemes o' Mice an' Men,
                    Gang aft a-gley,   40
An' lea'e us nought but grief and pain,
                    For promised joy.

   Still thou art blest, compared wi' me!
The present only toucheth thee;
But, Och! I backward cast my e'e,
                    On prospects drear!
An' forward, tho' I canna see,
                    I guess an' fear!

4 Bitter. 5 Possessions. 6 Endure. 7 Frost.

The world is a bundle of hay
George Gordon, Lord Byron (1788–1824)

The world is a bundle of hay,
   Mankind are the asses who pull;
Each tugs in a different way,
   And the greatest of all is John Bull.

For Anne
Leonard Cohen (1934–   )

With Annie gone,
Whose eyes to compare
With the morning sun?

Not that I did compare
But I do compare
Now that she's gone.

Kubla Khan
Samuel Taylor Coleridge (1772–1834)

In Xanadu did Kubla Khan
   A stately pleasure-dome decree:
Where Alph, the sacred river, ran
Through caverns measureless to man
   Down to a sunless sea.
So twice five miles of fertile ground
With walls and towers were girdled round:

And here were gardens bright with sinuous rills,
Where blossomed many an incense-bearing tree,
And here were forests ancient as the hills,
Enfolding sunny spots of greenery.

But oh! that deep romantic chasm which slanted
Down the green hill athwart a cedarn cover!
A savage place! as holy and enchanted
As e'er beneath a waning moon was haunted
By woman wailing for her demon-lover!
And from this chasm, with ceaseless turmoil seething,
As if this earth in fast thick pants were breathing,
A mighty fountain momently was forced,
Amid whose swift half-intermitted burst
Huge fragments vaulted like rebounding hail,
Or chaffy grain beneath the thresher's flail:
And 'mid these dancing rocks at once and ever
It flung up momently the sacred river.
Five miles meandering with a mazy motion
Through wood and dale the sacred river ran,
Then reached the caverns measureless to man,
And sank in tumult to a lifeless ocean:
And 'mid this tumult Kubla heard from far
Ancestral voices prophesying war!

   The shadow of the dome of pleasure
   Floated midway on the waves;
   Where was heard the mingled measure
   From the fountain and the caves.
It was a miracle of rare device,
A sunny pleasure-dome with caves of ice!
   A damsel with a dulcimer
   In a vision once I saw:
   It was an Abyssinian maid,
   And on her dulcimer she played,
   Singing of Mount Abora.
   Could I revive within me
   Her symphony and song,
   To such a deep delight 'twould win me,
That with music loud and long,
I would build that dome in air,

That sunny dome! those caves of ice!
And all who heard should see them there,
And all should cry, Beware! Beware!
His flashing eyes, his floating hair!   50
Weave a circle round him thrice,
And close your eyes with holy dread,
For he on honey-dew hath fed,
And drunk the milk of Paradise.

The Family Goldschmitt
Henri Coulette (1927–   )

Punctual as bad luck,
The aerogramme comes sliding
Under the door, mornings,
Addressed to the Family Goldschmitt.
My landlady puts it there.

My landlady—that blonde aura
of everything Nordic, Clairol
And kroner,[1] the Dowager Queen
Of Inner and Outer Chaos—
Insists that I am Goldschmitt.   10

Coulette, I tell her, Coulette,
Fumbling my money-green passport.
I'm American, gentile,
And there's gas escaping somewhere.
She nods and mutters, Goldschmitt.

There is gas escaping somewhere,
And what does that evil stain
On the mattress signify?

1 A Danish coin.

Are you sure, are you damned sure,
This isn't the train to Deutschland?   20

Suddenly, unaccountably,
I sit down and write a letter
To the world, no! to the people
I love, no! to my family, yes!
The Family Goldschmitt.

I heard a Fly buzz when I died
Emily Dickinson (1830–1886)

I heard a Fly buzz—when I died—
The Stillness in the Room
Was like the Stillness in the Air—
Between the Heaves of Storm—

The Eyes around—had wrung them dry—
And Breaths were gathering firm
For that last Onset—when the King
Be witnessed—in the Room—

I willed my Keepsakes—Signed away
What portion of me be   10
Assignable—and then it was
There interposed a Fly—

With Blue—uncertain stumbling Buzz—
Between the light—and me—
And then the Windows failed—and then
I could not see to see—

Go and catch a falling star

John Donne (1572–1631)

Go and catch a falling star,
    Get with child a mandrake root,
Tell me where all past years are,
    Or who cleft the devil's foot,
Teach me to hear mermaids singing,
Or to keep off envy's stinging,
      And find
      What wind
Serves to advance an honest mind.

If thou be'st born to strange sights,   10
    Things invisible to see,
Ride ten thousand days and nights
    Till age snow white hairs on thee,
Thou, when thou return'st, wilt tell me
All strange wonders that befell thee,
      And swear
      No where
Lives a woman true and fair.

If thou find'st one, let me know;
    Such a pilgrimage were sweet.   20
Yet do not; I would not go,
    Though at next door we might meet.
Though she were true when you met her,
And last till you write your letter,
      Yet she
      Will be
False, ere I come, to two or three.

The Flea

John Donne (1572–1631)

Mark but this flea, and mark in this
How little that which thou deny'st me is;
It sucked me first, and now sucks thee,
And in this flea our two bloods mingled be;
Thou know'st that this cannot be said
A sin, nor shame, nor loss of maidenhead;
   Yet this enjoys before it woo,
   And pampered swells with one blood made of two,
   And this, alas, is more than we would do.

Oh stay, three lives in one flea spare,   10
Where we almost, yea, more than married are.
This flea is you and I, and this
Our marriage bed and marriage temple is;
Though parents grudge, and you, we're met,
And cloistered in these living walls of jet.
   Though use make you apt to kill me,
   Let not to that, self-murder added be,
   And sacrilege: three sins in killing three.

Cruel and sudden, hast thou since
Purpled thy nail in blood of innocence?   20
Wherein could this flea guilty be,
Except in that drop which it sucked from thee?
Yet thou triumph'st and say'st that thou
Find'st not thyself nor me the weaker now;
   'Tis true. Then learn how false fears be:
   Just so much honor, when you yield'st to me,
   Will waste, as this flea's death took life from thee.

I Have Come to the Conclusion
Nelle Fertig (1919–   )

I have come to the conclusion
        she said
that when we fall in love
we really fall in love with ourselves—
that we choose particular people
because they provide
the particular mirrors
in which we wish to see.

And when did you discover
this surprising bit of knowledge?   10
        he asked.

After I had broken a few
very fine mirrors
        she said.

The Dancers Inherit the Party
Ian Hamilton Finlay (1925–   )

When I have talked for an hour I feel lousy —
Not so when I have danced for an hour:
The dancers inherit the party
While the talkers wear themselves out and
        sit in corners alone, and glower.

Fire and Ice
Robert Frost (1874–1963)

Some say the world will end in fire,
Some say in ice.
From what I've tasted of desire
I hold with those who favor fire.
But if it had to perish twice,
I think I know enough of hate
To say that for destruction ice
Is also great
And would suffice.

Nino, the Wonder Dog
Roy Fuller (1912–   )

A dog emerges from the flies[1]
  Balanced upon a ball.
Our entertainment is the fear
  Or hope the dog will fall.

It comes and goes on larger spheres,
  And then walks on and halts
In the centre of the stage and turns
  Two or three somersaults.

The curtains descend upon the act.
  After a proper pause
The dog comes out between them to
  Receive its last applause.

Most mouths are set in pitying smiles,
  Few eyes are free from rheum:

10

---

1 The wings of the stage.

The sensitive are filled with thoughts
Of death and love and doom.

No doubt behind this ugly dog,
Frail, fairly small, and white,
Stands some beneficent protector,
Some life outside the night.   20

But this is not apparent as
It goes, in the glare alone,
Through what it must to serve
Absurdities beyond its own.

My Own Epitaph
John Gay (1685–1732)

Life is a jest; and all things show it.
I thought so once; but now I know it.

The acrobat from Xanadu disdained all nets
Dan Georgakas (1938–   )

The acrobat from Xanadu disdained all nets.
And when we saw him performing the central
twirl of his triple forward roll thru space
we knew his purity went beyond mere pride,
that certain flights require total risk.

After the Quarrel

Barbara Gibson (1930–   )

After the quarrel
I melted
against his back, took
his hand hard in mine,
breathed
SOMEDAY WE'LL BE DEAD
and then oh baby we loved

The Distant Drum

Calvin C. Hernton (1933–   )

I am not a metaphor or symbol.
This you hear is not the wind in the trees,
Nor a cat being maimed in the street.
It is I being maimed in the street.
It is I who weep, laugh, feel pain or joy.
I speak this because I exist.
This is my voice.
These words are my words, my mouth
Speaks them, my hand writes—
I am a poet.   10
It is my fist you hear beating
Against your ear.

Dream Deferred
Langston Hughes (1902–1967)

What happens to a dream deferred?

> Does it dry up
> like a raisin in the sun?
> Or fester like a sore—
> And then run?
> Does it stink like rotten meat?
> Or crust and sugar over—
> like a syrupy sweet?
>
> Maybe it just sags
> like a heavy load.   10
>
> *Or does it explode?*

Ode on a Grecian Urn
John Keats (1795–1821)

Thou still unravished bride of quietness,
  Thou foster-child of Silence and slow Time,
Sylvan historian, who canst thus express
  A flowery tale more sweetly than our rhyme:
What leaf-fringed legend haunts about thy shape
  Of deities or mortals, or of both,
    In Tempe or the dales of Arcady?
  What men or gods are these? What maidens loth?
What mad pursuit? What struggle to escape?
    What pipes and timbrels? What wild ecstasy?   10

Heard melodies are sweet, but those unheard
  Are sweeter; therefore, ye soft pipes, play on;
Not to the sensual ear, but, more endeared,
  Pipe to the spirit ditties of no tone:

Fair youth, beneath the trees, thou canst not leave
  Thy song, nor ever can those trees be bare;
    Bold Lover, never, never canst thou kiss,
Though winning near the goal—yet, do not grieve;
    She cannot fade, though thou hast not thy bliss,
  Forever wilt thou love, and she be fair!   20

Ah, happy, happy boughs! that cannot shed
  Your leaves, nor ever bid the Spring adieu;
And, happy melodist, unweariéd,
  Forever piping songs forever new.
More happy love! more happy, happy love!
  Forever warm and still to be enjoyed,
    Forever panting, and forever young;
All breathing human passion far above,
  That leaves a heart high-sorrowful and cloyed,
    A burning forehead, and a parching tongue.   30

Who are these coming to the sacrifice?
  To what green altar, O mysterious priest,
Lead'st thou that heifer lowing at the skies,
  And all her silken flanks with garlands dressed?
What little town by river or seashore,
  Or mountain-built with peaceful citadel,
    Is emptied of this folk, this pious morn?
And, little town, thy streets forevermore
  Will silent be; and not a soul to tell
    Why thou art desolate, can e'er return.   40

O Attic shape! Fair attitude! with brede[1]
  Of marble men and maidens overwrought,
With forest branches and the trodden weed;
  Thou, silent form, dost tease us out of thought
As doth eternity: Cold Pastoral!
  When old age shall this generation waste,
    Thou shalt remain, in midst of other woe
Than ours, a friend to man, to whom thou say'st,
  "Beauty is truth, truth beauty,"—that is all
    Ye know on earth, and all ye need to know.   50

1 Woven pattern, braid.

On First Looking into Chapman's Homer
John Keats (1795–1821)

Much have I travelled in the realms of gold
   And many goodly states and kingdoms seen;
   Round many western islands have I been
Which bards in fealty to Apollo hold.
Oft of one wide expanse had I been told
   That deep-browed Homer ruled as his demesne;[1]
   Yet did I never breathe its pure serene
Till I heard Chapman[2] speak out loud and bold.

Then felt I like some watcher of the skies
   When a new planet swims into his ken;   10
Or like stout Cortez when with eagle eyes
   He stared at the Pacific, and all his men
Looked at each other with a wild surmise—
   Silent, upon a peak in Darien.

1 Domain.   2 An Elizabethan poet.

The Old Wife
(for JBB)

Rolly Kent (1946–   )

I WAS THE CHOICE of many old men when I was
   young.
My husband was proud to give me—
whenever I lay with the old men, he said, buffalo
   would come.

The first old man I lay with, I thought only of the
   honor.

Later on, I used to giggle, those heaving old bellies!
I went to the lodges of seven of them, seven different
    years,
and only once did a man not lay with me.

He wasn't like the other elders. The village
suspected him because he kept to himself.
I quaked as I walked behind him, afraid I would not   10
    be pretty.
The bed of robes waited in the center of the lodge,
beneath the smoke hole. The stars were out, so big and
    bright,
the bed floated in a circle of silver.
There was no place for a scared girl to hide,
so I turned my back to him and let my things fall away.
I felt him looking as I slipped beneath the robes.
Then he sat down beside me and lit a pipe.
He never took his eyes from me or spoke a word,
and I fell asleep confused with waiting.
In the morning he was still there, only   20
dressed now in beautiful white skins.
When I sat up I saw that I too had new clothes on,
soft skins with beadwork the colors of day.
I pulled the robes over my head, ashamed.
When I thought him gone, I popped up.
He was still there. He took my head and rubbed
fine-scented bear oil on my hair, smiled, and let me go.

Later, people thought him a wealthy man,
I a lucky girl. My husband was the envy of the village.
I lied for my looks and told my sisters   30
what a sweaty old bull he was.

For several days after, no one saw him.
Then some hunters found him frozen up on a hill,
watching for the herds to come, dead in the same
    clothes.

For a long time I made sense of that old man
by thinking I brought him what he needed before he
    could die.

It has cost me my body to know I was wrong,
that when he smiled, it was for an ignorant girl
who would wake up one day, a cold day like this,
feel someone's hands make her hair shine again,
and find just the sun on a dry, old head.

Poetry of Departures
Philip Larkin (1922–   )

Sometimes you hear, fifth-hand,
As epitaph:
He chucked up everything
And just cleared off,
And always the voice will sound
Certain you approve
This audacious, purifying,
Elemental move.

And they are right, I think.
We all hate home
And having to be there:
I detest my room,
Its specially-chosen junk,
The good books, the good bed,
And my life, in perfect order:
So to hear it said

He walked out on the whole crowd
Leaves me flushed and stirred,
Like *Then she undid her dress*
Or *Take that you bastard;*
Surely I can, if he did?
And that helps me stay
Sober and industrious.
But I'd go today,

Yes, swagger the nut-strewn roads,

Crouch in the fo'c'sle[1]
Stubbly with goodness, if
It weren't so artificial,
Such a deliberate step backwards
To create an object: 30
Books; china; a life
Reprehensibly perfect.

1 Forecastle of a ship.

A Wish

Laurence Lerner (1925–   )

Often I've wished that I'd been born a woman.
It seems the one sure way to be fully human.
Think of the trouble—keeping the children fed,
Keeping your skirt down and your lips red,
Watching the calendar, and the last bus home,
Being nice to all the dozens of guests in the room;
Having to change your hairstyle and your name
At least once; learning to take the blame;
Keeping your husband faithful, and your char.
And all the things you're supposed to be grateful for   10
—Votes and proposals, chocolates and seats in the train—
Or expert with—typewriter, powderpuff, pen,
Diaphragm, needle, chequebook, casserole, bed.
It seems the one sure way to be driven mad.

So why would anyone want to be a woman?
Would you rather be the hero or the victim?
Would you rather win, seduce, and read the paper
Or be beaten, pregnant, and have to lay the table?
Must we dismiss as a kind of masochism
This longing to feel submission's sharp orgasm?   20
Nothing is free: in order to pay the price
Isn't it simpler, really, to have no choice?

Only ill-health, recurring, inevitable,
Can teach the taste of what it is to be well.

No man is frigid: must we take that to mean
Passion can never matter to a man?
No man has ever felt his daughter tear
The flesh he had earlier torn to plant her there.
Men know the pain of birth by a kind of theory:
No man has been a protagonist in the story,
Lying back bleeding, exhausted and in pain,
Waiting for stitches and sleep and to be alone,
And woken with tender breasts to the hesitant croak
At the bedside growing continuous as you wake.
That is the price: that is what love is worth.
It will go on twisting your heart like an afterbirth;
Whether you choose to or not you will pay and pay
Your whole life long: nothing on earth is free.

No Country You Remember

Robert Mezey (1935–   )

But for the steady wash of rain,
The house is quiet now. Outside,
Occasional cars move past the lawn
And leave the stillness purified.

I find myself in a dark chair
Idly picking a banjo, lost
In reveries of another time,
Thinking of what heavy cost

I came to this particular place,
This house in which I let my life
Play out its subterranean plot,
My Christian and enduring wife.

What if I paid for what I got?
Nothing can so exhaust the heart
As boredom and self-loathing do,
Which are the poisons of my art.

All day I resurrect the past.
This instrument I love so ill
Hammers and rings and, when I wish,
Lies in its coffin and is still.   20

I think of winter mornings when
Between bare woods and a wrecked shack
I came down deep, encrusted slopes,
A bag of dead birds at my back;

Then let my mind go blank and smile
At what small game the mind demands,
As dead time flickers in the blind
Articulation of my hands.

I know you must despise me, you
Who judge and measure everything   30
And live by little absolutes—
What would you like to hear me sing?

A strophe on the wasted life?
Some verses dealing with my fall?
Or would you care to contemplate
My contemplation of the wall?

I write from down here, where I live.
In the cold light of a dying day,
The covered page looks cold and dead.
And then, what more is there to say   40

Except, you read this in a dream.
I wrote nothing. I sat and ate
Some frozen dinner while I watched
The Late Show, and the Late Late.

Is this the Region, this the Soil, the Clime

from PARADISE LOST

John Milton (1608–1674)

Is this the Region, this the Soil, the Clime
Said then the lost Arch Angel, this the seat
That we must change for Heav'n, this mournful gloom
For that celestial light? Be it so, since hee
Who now is Sovran can dispose and bid
What shall be right: fardest from him is best
Whom reason hath equald, force hath made supream
Above his equals, Farewel happy Fields
Where Joy for ever dwells: Hail horrours, hail
Infernal world, and thou profoundest Hell   10
Receive thy new Possessor: One who brings
A mind not to be chang'd by Place or Time.
The mind is its own place, and in it self
Can make a Heav'n of Hell, a Hell of Heav'n.

Poetry

Marianne Moore (1887–1972)

I, too, dislike it: there are things that are important beyond all
          this fiddle.
     Reading it, however, with a perfect contempt for it, one
               discovers in
     it after all, a place for the genuine.
          Hands that can grasp, eyes
          that can dilate, hair that can rise
               if it must, these things are important not because a

high-sounding interpretation can be put upon them but because
          they are
     useful. When they become so derivative as to become
               unintelligible,

the same thing may be said for all of us, that we
          do not admire what   10
          we cannot understand: the bat
                    holding on upside down or in quest of something to
eat, elephants pushing, a wild horse taking a roll, a tireless wolf
                    under
          a tree, the immovable critic twitching his skin like a horse
                    that feels a flea, the base-
          ball fan, the statistician—
                    nor is it valid
                              to discriminate against "business documents and

school-books"; all these phenomena are important. One must
                    make a distinction
          however: when dragged into prominence by half poets,
                    the result is not poetry,
          nor till the poets among us can be   20
                    "literalists of
                    the imagination"—above
                              insolence and triviality and can present

for inspection, imaginary gardens with real toads in them, shall
                    we have
          it. In the meantime, if you demand on the one hand, the
                    raw material of poetry in
                    all its rawness and
                    that which is on the other hand
                              genuine, then you are interested in poetry.

Cowards

from JULIUS CAESAR (II, 2)

William Shakespeare (1564–1616)

Cowards die many times before their deaths
The valiant never taste of death but once.
Of all the wonders that I yet have heard,
It seems to me most strange that men should fear,
Seeing that death, a necessary end,
Will come when it will come.

Not marble, nor the gilded monuments

SONNET 55

William Shakespeare (1564–1616)

Not marble, nor the gilded monuments
Of princes, shall outlive this powerful rhyme;
But you shall shine more bright in these contents
Than unswept stone besmeared with sluttish time.
When wasteful war shall statues overturn,
And broils[1] root out the work of masonry,
Nor Mars his sword nor war's quick fire shall burn
The living record of your memory.
'Gainst death and all-oblivious enmity
Shall you pace forth; your praise shall still find room   10
Even in the eyes of all posterity
That wear this world out to the ending doom.
   So, till the judgment that yourself arise,
   You live in this, and dwell in lover's eyes.

1 Noisy quarrels.

Disillusionment of Ten O'Clock
Wallace Stevens (1879–1955)

The houses are haunted
By white night-gowns.
None are green,
Or purple with green rings,
Or green with yellow rings,
Or yellow with blue rings.
None of them are strange,
With socks of lace
And beaded ceintures.[1]
People are not going   10
To dream of baboons and periwinkles.
Only, here and there, an old sailor,
Drunk and asleep in his boots,
Catches tigers
In red weather.

1 Belts.

So Careful of the Type?
Alfred, Lord Tennyson (1809–1892)

"So careful of the type?" but no
  From scarpèd cliff and quarried stone
  She cries, "A thousand types are gone;
I care for nothing, all shall go.

"Thou makest thine appeal to me:
  I bring to life, I bring to death;
  The spirit does but mean the breath:
I know no more." And he, shall he,

Man, her last work, who seem'd so fair,
  Such splendid purpose in his eyes,   10

Who roll'd the psalm to wintry skies,
Who built him fanes of fruitless prayer,

Who trusted God was love indeed
    And love Creation's final law—
    Tho' Nature, red in tooth and claw
With ravine,[1] shriek'd against his
        creed—

Who loved, who suffer'd countless ills,
    Who battled for the True, the Just,
    Be blown about the desert dust,
Or seal'd within the iron hills?

No more? A monster then, a dream,
    A discord. Dragons of the prime,
    That tare[2] each other in their slime,
Were mellow music match'd with him.

O life as futile, then, as frail!
    O for thy voice to soothe and
        bless!
    What hope of answer, or redress?
Behind the veil, behind the veil.

1 Plundering.   2 Tore.

The Eagle

Alfred, Lord Tennyson (1809–1892)

He clasps the crag with crooked hands;
Close to the sun in lonely lands,
Ringed with the azure world, he stands.

The wrinkled sea beneath him crawls;
He watches from his mountain walls,
And like a thunderbolt he falls.

The Owl
Edward Thomas (1878–1917)

Downhill I came, hungry, and yet not starved;
Cold, yet had heat within me that was proof
Against the North wind; tired, yet so that rest
Had seemed the sweetest thing under a roof.

Then at the inn I had food, fire, and rest,
Knowing how hungry, cold, and tired was I.
All of the night was quite barred out except
An owl's cry, a most melancholy cry

Shaken out long and clear upon the hill,
No merry note, nor cause of merriment,   10
But one telling me plain what I escaped
And others could not, that night, as in I went.

And salted was my food, and my repose,
Salted and sobered, too, by the bird's voice
Speaking for all who lay under the stars,
Soldiers and poor, unable to rejoice.

The Black Panther
John Hall Wheelock (1886–   )

There is a panther caged within my breast;
But what his name, there is no breast shall know
Save mine, nor what it is that drives him so,
Backward and forward, in relentless quest—
That silent rage, baffled but unsuppressed,
The soft pad of those stealthy feet that go
Over my body's prison to and fro,
Trying the walls forever without rest.
All day I feed him with my living heart:

But when the night puts forth her dreams and stars,   ¹⁰
The inexorable Frenzy reawakes:
His wrath is hurled upon the trembling bars,
The eternal passion stretches me apart,
And I lie silent—but my body shakes.

Composed upon Westminster Bridge
William Wordsworth (1770–1850)

Earth has not anything to show more fair:
Dull would he be of soul who could pass by
A sight so touching in its majesty:
This city now doth, like a garment, wear
The beauty of the morning; silent, bare,
Ships, towers, domes, theatres, and temples lie
Open unto the fields, and to the sky;
All bright and glittering in the smokeless air.
Never did sun more beautifully steep
In his first splendour, valley, rock, or hill;   ¹⁰
Ne'er saw I, never felt, a calm so deep!
The river glideth at his own sweet will:
Dear God! the very houses seem asleep;
And all that mighty heart is lying still!

Trouble
James Wright (1927–   )

Well, look, honey, where I come from,
when a girl says she's in trouble, she's in trouble.
                                    Judy Holliday

Leering across Pearl Street,
Crum Anderson yipped:
"Hey Pugh!
I see your sister

Been rid bareback.
She swallow a watermelon?
Fred Gordon! Fred Gordon! Fred Gordon!"

"Wayya mean? She can get fat, can't she?"

Fat? Willow and lonesome Roberta, running
Alone down Pearl Street in the rain the last time   10
I ever saw her, smiling a smile
Crum Anderson will never know,
Wondering at her body.

Sixteen years, and
All that time she thought she was nothing
But skin and bones.

Leda[1] and the Swan
William Butler Yeats (1865–1939)

A sudden blow: the great wings beating still
Above the staggering girl, her thighs caressed
By the dark web, her nape caught in his bill,
He holds her helpless breast upon his breast.

How can those terrified vague fingers push
The feathered glory from her loosening thighs?
And how can body, laid in that white rush,
But feel the strange heart beating where it lies?

A shudder in the loins engenders there
The broken wall, the burning roof and tower   10
And Agamemnon dead.

1 Ravished by Zeus, chief Greek god, who took the form of a swan. Leda
gave birth to Helen of Troy, whose kidnapping caused the Trojan War,
and to Clytemnestra, who murdered her husband Agamemnon upon his
return from the Trojan War.

> Being so caught up,
> So mastered by the brute blood of the air,
> Did she put on his knowledge with his power
> Before the indifferent beak could let her drop?

Sailing to Byzantium
William Butler Yeats (1865–1939)

That is no country for old men. The young
In one another's arms, birds in the trees,
—Those dying generations—at their song,
The salmon-falls, the mackerel-crowded seas,
Fish, flesh, or fowl, commend all summer long
Whatever is begotten, born, and dies.
Caught in that sensual music all neglect
Monuments of unaging intellect.

An aged man is but a paltry thing,
A tattered coat upon a stick, unless   10
Soul clap its hands and sing, and louder sing
For every tatter in its mortal dress,
Nor is there singing school but studying
Monuments of its own magnificence;
And therefore I have sailed the seas and come
To the holy city of Byzantium.

O sages standing in God's holy fire
As in the gold mosaic of a wall,
Come from the holy fire, perne in a gyre,
And be the singing-masters of my soul.   20
Consume my heart away; sick with desire
And fastened to a dying animal
It knows not what it is; and gather me
Into the artifice of eternity.

Once out of nature I shall never take
My bodily form from any natural thing,

But such a form as Grecian goldsmiths make
Of hammered gold and gold enameling
To keep a drowsy Emperor awake;
Or set upon a golden bough to sing   30
To lords and ladies of Byzantium
Of what is past, or passing, or to come.

PROSODY

The Shaping Force of Poetry

Reading a poem is a process of discovery and revelation. The simplest way to respond to a poem is through the emotions. One first *feels* a poem, comprehending what it is about without necessarily understanding it. During the first reading, the reader should be open and loose, allowing the rhythms, the images, and the flow of the poem to impress themselves. Since most of the poems in this book are short, they can be read three or four times in the span it might take to read three or four pages of prose. Additional readings after the first will bring increased comprehension, then understanding. Theme, logical structure, syntax, image, symbol, and prosodic form contribute to the reading of a poem. The first five elements involve arrangement and meaning (denotative and connotative) of words and to a greater or lesser degree are involved in all writing. The sixth, prosody, is unique to poetry. Some knowledge of *prosody,** the study of meter, rhyme, and versification, is valuable to increase the reader's sensibility.

Meter (measurement) is based upon the syllable: *quantitative meter* is based on the duration of the syllable, *accentual meter* on the *accent* or *stress* of the syllable, and *syllabic meter* on the number of syllables. Since duration of syllables has little significance in English, English poetry is measured by stressed and unstressed sounds, combining the accentual and syllabic systems. The unit of measurement is the *foot*, a group of two or three syllables, one of which is accented or stressed.

Counting and identifying syllabic stress is called *scansion*. When poetry is scanned, its metrical pattern is shown by marks placed over the individual syllables: / for a stressed syllable and − for an unstressed syllable. The feet found in English poetry are illustrated and named below:

iambic	ālóne	dactylic	lónelīnēss
trochaic	lónelȳ	amphibrachic	ālónenēss
anapestic	b̄y m̄ysélf	amphimacic	áll alóne

Two feet found only as *substitutions* in series of the above feet are

spondaic	Stáy, stáy
pyrrhic	ōf thē

Metered poetry is called *verse*. Poetry without a fixed metrical pattern is called *free verse*—"Song of Solomon" from the King James Bible for example.

---

* Italicized terms appear in the Glossary.

Poetry is usually divided into lines. A line of poetry is a *verse*, not to be confused with *verse* meaning metered poetry, nor with a *stanza*. The number and kinds of feet in a line define the meter of that line:

monometer	one foot
dimeter	two feet
trimeter	three feet
tetrameter	four feet
pentameter	five feet
hexameter	six feet
heptameter	seven feet
octameter	eight feet
nonameter	nine feet
decameter	ten feet

The line is identified by a combination name derived from the kind of foot and the number of times it is repeated. Some common lines in English poetry are

iambic pentameter	My mis | tress' eyes | are no | thing like | the sun.
trochaic tetrameter	Back and | side go | bare, go | bare
anapestic tetrameter	The Assyr | ian came down | like a wolf | on the fold

Some less common lines are

dactylic dimeter	Corpse clad with | carefulness
iambic trimeter	The whis | key on | your breath

"Meter" and "rhythm" are often used interchangeably in discussion of poetry. However, there is a distinct difference in the meanings of the two terms. Whereas *meter* is solely a mechanical measurement of the number and types of feet in a line, rhythm is much more complex. *Rhythm* in poetry is the pattern or quality of movement of the whole line, and can be affected by duration of vowel sounds, punctuation, articulation, and semantic meaning, as well as by meter.

Each of the following are iambic pentameter lines, but the rhythm differs markedly. "When I do count the clock that tells the time" has a slow, even tempo. "Of systems possible, if 'tis confest" has a rapid, broken rhythm. Several elements contribute to the slowness of the first line's movement: many of the vowel sounds are of long duration; all the words are monosyllabic, requiring a slight pause between each; clear enunciation of words ("count-the," "clock-that," "that-tells") which begin with a sound similar to the end sound of the previous word demands a longer pause (*hiatus*). Most of the words are of approximately the same duration, adding regularity to the slow rhythm.

In contrast, the second line contains only vowel sounds of short duration; three of the words are polysyllabic, hence there is no pause between the syllables; there is no pause between the words "systems possible" and " 'tis confest" because of the linking "s" at the end of the first word in each pair; the words "if 'tis" slide together in a similar manner. This line consists of two distinct phrases of rapid utterance, separated by the pause (*caesura*) enforced by the punctuation at midpoint of the line, and thus has a rapid, broken rhythm quite unlike that of the first line.

A line, then, is slowed by long vowel sounds, monosyllabic words, hiatus, and caesura, and speeded by short vowel sounds and polysyllabic or linked words. Other elements also contribute to the speed of a line.

Metrical silence is related to hiatus and caesura in slowing the line. It occurs when the poet omits the unaccented syllables his metrical pattern has led us to expect, as in the last line of the opening stanza of Keats's "La Belle Dame Sans Merci"

Ō whát căn aíl thēe, Kníght āt árms
Ālóne ănd pálelȳ loítērīng?
Thē sédge hās wíthēred fróm thē Láke
Ānd nó (⁻) bírds (⁻) síng (⁻).

Successive stresses are also used to slow a line. These make it impossible to hurry over the line, as in Tennyson's "Bréak, bréak, bréak" and Shelley's "Ān óld, mád, blínd, dēspiséd ānd dýīng kíng." On the other hand, Byron's line of trisyllabic feet is fast and tripping: "Ānd thē shéen ōf thēir spéars wās līke stárs ōn thē séa."

If a line contains words that are difficult to articulate, it is slow, as in Pope's "When Ajax strives some rock's vast weight to throw." Conversely, if the words flow together easily, the line speeds up, as in Pope's "Soft is the strain when Zephyr gently blows." Alliteration also helps speed a line.

Finally, the meaning of the words themselves affects the tempo of the lines. If the line contains a restful image, it is slow, as in Keats's "Thou watchest the last oozings hours by hours."

Meter, the most common prosodic technique, has many functions. One of the simplest is mnemonic. Before the invention of writing, poetry survived through oral transmission because metered verse was easier to memorize than prose. Meter has other connections with primitive man, with its ritualistic repetition; its very difference from everyday language gives it importance and immediacy. We respond more strongly because it is "special."

Meter also sets us apart from the poet. At the same time that we respond to it, we are aware, through the meter, that it is an ordered, formal art. This saves us from becoming too involved. The very artificiality of meter tempers the emotion aroused by the poem. We might find the emotions expressed in Dylan Thomas's "Do Not Go Gentle Into That Good Night" or Sir Thomas Wyatt's "They Flee from Me" too intense if we were not distracted from the emotion by the artistry. On the other hand, meter serves to heighten emotion when the subject of the poem is commonplace. This *aesthetic distance* prevents us from confusing art with real life; it gives us "a sort of half-consciousness of unsubstantial existence." Prose gives us neither the immediacy nor the distance of metered verse.

Since meter demands that words be arranged according to sound and stress, as well as to their *denotative* and *connotative* value, poetry may take on overtones not possible in prose, such as the trancelike effect induced by the easy rhythm of Coleridge's "Kubla Khan." Indeed the choice of meter permits an *ambiguity*, a multiplicity of meanings, not acceptable in prose. This ambiguity can be seen in Justice's "Counting the Mad," which imitates the singsong meter and playful repetition of "This little pig went to market." One of the questions raised by this technique is about our attitude to disturbed human beings. Do we regard mad people as a joke, a source of fun, as a child's toes are a source of fun when we play "This little pig"? Another is the relationship between the madmen and the "ordinary man." Are they as similar as the toes in the game? Such effects could not be achieved in eighteen lines of prose. Thus meter plays its part in making poetry "language functioning at its highest efficiency."

Another function of meter is that it satisfies man's "blessed rage for order," as well as his love of variety. Meter gives us variety within an orderly structure and, at the same time, allows the poet to emphasize the point he wishes to make. Within the framework of a particular meter, any variations from that meter take on a significance impossible to achieve in *free verse* or prose. For example, the opening line of Shelley's "Ozymandias" sets up the meter—iambic pentameter—

which we expect to continue. Hence when the meter changes in line two, with the substitution of a *spondee* in the second foot, the impact is immediate.

Ī mét ā tráveller fróm an antique lánd
Whō saíd: Twō vást and trúnkless legs ōf stóne
Stánd īn the desert. . . .

We know at once that the "two vast and trunkless legs" are of far greater significance than the traveller.

Indeed, a change in meter can become a *symbol*, as in Wordsworth's "Westminster Bridge," where the structure of some of the lines resembles the structure of the subject itself.

This city now doth, like a garment wear
The beauty of the morning; silent, bare
Shíps, tówers, dómes, théatrēs, and tempēs líe
Open unto the fields. . . .

The crowding together of heavily stressed words or syllables, disrupting the iambic pentameter meter, imitates the crowded buildings described. In Matthew Arnold's "Dover Beach," the meter and line length imitate the subject, which is the ceaseless ebb and flow of waves on the beach.

But now I only hear
Its melancholy, long, withdrawing roar,
Retreating, to the breath
Of the night wind, down the vast edges drear
And naked shingles of the world.

In conclusion, meter functions in various ways. It enriches a strong tradition and satisfies our need for ritual repetition. It draws us into and separates us from art. It surprises and delights us by its variety while it gains emphasis from that variety. Finally it takes on a symbolic value.

Rhyme is the correspondence of sound in two or more words. Its varieties can be categorized as *full rhyme, slant rhyme, alliteration, consonance,* and *assonance.*

Full rhyme consists of different initial sounds and identical following sounds. Ring-sing, design-resign, reader-leader, and invention-convention are full rhymes. Full rhymes fall into two classes, *masculine* and *feminine.* When the final syllable in rhyming words is the stressed one, the rhyme is masculine. Thus all monosyllabic rhymes are masculine: sun-done, rage-wage, must-dust. The following poly-syllabic rhymes are also masculine: inspect-reflect, champagne-campaign, require-enquire. Masculine rhymes are strong (emphatic) because of the stress on the final syllable. Feminine rhymes occur when the stressed and rhymed syllables are not in the final position. Warmer-former, marry-tarry, and getting-setting are feminine rhymes. These are weak (unemphatic) rhymes because they are followed by a drop in pitch. Full rhymes occur rarely in the initial position in the line, occasionally as internal rhymes within the line, and most often in the terminal position.

Slant rhyme consists of sounds which correspond imperfectly or approximately. Dice-piece, even-heaven, hearth-earth, death-birth are slant rhymes. When slant rhyme appears from the spelling to be full rhyme, as in Wordsworth's "Westminster Bridge":

Dull would he be of soul who could pass by
A sight so touching in its majesty.

it is called *eye rhyme*. There are many varieties of slant rhyme, which occur rarely in the initial position of the line, occasionally in the ter-minal position, and most frequently internally.

Assonance, very similar to slant rhyme, is the resemblance of accented vowel sounds but not of consonants. The opening lines of Melville's "The Portent" substitute assonance for terminal rhyme:

Hanging from the beam
Slowly swaying (such the law)
Gaunt the shadow on your green
Shenandoah!

Alliteration occurs when two or more words in a line or two have the same initial sound or sound-cluster.

O *w*ild *W*est *W*ind thou *b*reath of Autumn's *b*eing
"Ode to the West Wind"—Shelley

Consonance is a form of rhyme involving resemblance among con-sonants in stressed syllables. They do not necessarily occupy the initial position. MacLeish's lines contain consonant s's and alliterative w's:

The *w*ave *w*ithdrawing
*W*ithers with *s*eaward ru*s*tle of flim*s*y *w*ater
" 'Dover Beach'—a Note to That Poem"

The pattern or sequence in which terminal rhyme sounds occur is known as the *rhyme scheme*. Each similar end sound is assigned the same letter. The following rhyme scheme is *a b a b*.

Whenever Richard Cory went to t*own*,   *a*
We people on the pavement looked at h*im*: *b*
He was a gentleman from sole to cr*own*,   *a*
Clear favored, and imperially sl*im*.   *b*

"Richard Cory"—Edward Arlington Robinson

Rhyme is used to gain aesthetic distance, for its musical quality, for emphasis, and as a structural device.

Aesthetic distance is achieved in two ways. Since rhyme is obviously not the sound of everyday language, the listener recognizes that what he hears has been artistically shaped, hence he does not expect it to be "true," and will be willing to suspend his disbelief as he confronts the art. The poet distances himself from his emotions by the fact of his search for rhyme. It forces him to shape his point rather than to merely present it.

The musical quality of rhyme may serve both as an end in itself and as a means to an end. It is an end joyous in itself in such poems as "Sumer Is Icumen In" with its repeated sound of "cuccu." It is a means to an end when it adds to the point the poet is trying to make. The euphonious rhyme of Burns's "My Luve Is Like a Red, Red Rose" is particularly appropriate in a poem celebrating love and beauty. The harsh internal rhyme in Hopkins's "God's Grandeur" entirely suits the bitter questioning tone.

Why do men then now not reck his rod?
Generations have trod, have trod, have trod;
And all is seared with trade; bleared, smeared with toil;
And wears man's smudge and shares man's smell: the soil
Is bare now, nor can foot feel, being shod.

Since rhyme makes words conspicuous, it is a natural device for emphasizing important words. It can also be used to emphasize the tone of the poem. No one can doubt the satiric intent of Byron in *Don Juan* when he uses such outrageous rhymes as

But oh ye lords and ladies intellectual
Inform us truly have they not henpecked you all?

As a structural device, rhyme unifies words and lines which belong together. In the *English Sonnet* each quatrain is distinguished from the other two by its rhyme scheme, although all have the same basic pattern, *a b a b c d c d e f e f*, while the couplet is set apart by a different rhyme, *g g*. The *octave* of the *Italian Sonnet* is bound by its rhyme scheme, *a b b a a b b a*, while the *sestet* is set apart by its rhyme scheme, *c d e c d e*, or a variation.

In conclusion, rhyme, like meter, gains our attention while it sets us apart from the poem as a work of art and emphasizes ideas and tone. It is also valuable for its musical quality. Finally, it contributes to the architecture, the overall plan, of the poem.

The final prosodic device is versification, which can be divided into undifferentiated, aggregative, and integral forms.[1]

Blank verse, consisting of lines of unrhymed, iambic pentameter, is an undifferentiated form of poetry. The line is its only shaping device. The poet can write as long or as short a poem as he pleases. This form is particularly suitable for such descriptive/reflective poetry as Wordsworth's "Lines Composed above Tintern Abbey," and for Milton's great epic on the fall of man, *Paradise Lost.* The form is flexible, and is used by Shakespeare and Marlowe in the drama.

The aggregative form is the stanza, a repeatable unit grouping two or more lines in terms of length, meter, and, often, rhyme scheme. Aggregative stanzas commonly range in English poetry from the *couplet* to the *Spenserian stanza.*

The simplest stanza is the couplet, two lines, unrhymed or rhymed. The unrhymed couplet is rare in English. The rhymed couplet is found in a variety of meters. When it is in iambic pentameter, it is called a *heroic couplet.*

That's my last Duchess painted on the wall,
Looking as if she were alive. I call

"My Last Duchess"—Browning

A poem may consist of a single couplet or a series of couplets. When the meaning is complete within the couplet, it is called a *closed couplet.*

In men we various ruling passions find;
In women two almost divide the kind.

"Epistle II"—Pope

1 Charles B. Wheeler, *Design of Poetry*, W. W. Norton & Company, Inc., New York, 1966.

When the meaning carries over to the next couplet, the poem consists of *open couplets.*

> Thou by the Indian Ganges' side
> Shouldst rubies find; I by the tide
> Of Humber would complain. I would
> Love you ten years before the flood,
> And you should, if you please, refuse
> Till the conversion of the Jews.
>
> "To His Coy Mistress"—Marvell

The *tercet* or *triplet* is a three-line stanza. It may have three consecutive rhyming lines, or it may have a rhyme scheme which interlocks with other tercets throughout the poem. This latter form is known as *terza rima,* used by Shelley in "Ode to the West Wind" which rhymes *a b a, b c b, c d c, d e d,* etc.

The four-line stanza, the *quatrain,* has many varieties. Probably the oldest form in English is the *ballad stanza.* This usually consists of iambic tetrameter in lines one and three, and iambic trimeter in lines two and four, with a rhyme scheme of *a b c d.*

> The king sits in Dumferling toune
> Drinking the blude-reid wine:
> "O whar will I get a guid sailor
> To sail this schip of mine?"
>
> "Sir Patrick Spens"—Anonymous

The *heroic quatrain* consists of iambic pentameter lines rhyming *a b a b:*

> A sudden blow: the great wings beating still
> Above the staggering girl, her thighs caressed
> By the dark webs, her nape caught in his bill,
> He holds her helpless breast upon his breast.
>
> "Leda and the Swan"—Yeats

Five-, six-, and seven-line stanzas are known as *cinquains, sixains,* and *septets,* respectively. When a septet of iambic pentameter lines rhymes *a b a b b c c,* it is known as *rhyme royal* or *Chaucerian stanza.* Shelley's "To a Skylark" is in cinquains, Thomas's "A Refusal . . ." is in sixains, and Wyatt's "They flee from me" is in rhyme royal.

The *octave,* or eight-line stanza, is known as a common octave when it consists of two joined quatrains. The iambic pentameter octave which rhymes *a b a b a b c c* is known as *ottava rima*. Byron's *Don Juan* and Yeats's "Sailing to Byzantium" are written in ottava rima.

The *Spenserian stanza* is a nine-line stanza rhyming *a b a b b c b c c*. It has eight iambic pentameter lines followed by an *alexandrine*, an iambic hexameter line. It is used by Spenser in *The Faerie Queene*.

Longer stanzas are relatively rare.

Integral stanzaic forms have a definite shape. Instead of having a series of stanzas, the whole poem is delimited in terms of number of lines, rhyme scheme, and, often, line length. The *sonnet* is the most common form in English poetry, followed by the *limerick* ("There Was an Old Party of Lyme"). The *rondeau* ("Help Me to Seek" by Wyatt) and the *villanelle* ("Do Not Go Gentle" by Thomas) are exemplified in this text, as are the other common forms. Other integral forms, such as the ballade, triolet, and sestina are relatively rare in English poetry.

The sonnet is a fourteen-line *lyric* poem, usually of iambic pentameter following one of several set rhyme schemes. The *Italian*, or *Petrarchan*, form is divided into an *octave*, rhyming *a b b a a b b a* and a *sestet*, rhyming *c d e c d e* or a variation. The *English*, or *Shakespearean*, form is divided into three quatrains and a couplet, usually rhyming *a b a b c d c d e f e f g g*. Spencer used interlocking rhymes between the quatrains, *a b a b b c b c c d c d*.

The limerick is a five-line form having anapestic lines. Lines one, two, and five are trimeter; lines three and four are dimeter. The rhyme scheme is *a a b b a*.

The rondeau is a fifteen-line form having a refrain in lines nine and fifteen. Except for the refrain, (c), it has only two rhymes, *a a b b a a a b c a a b b a c*.

The villanelle is a nineteen-line form divided into five tercets, rhyming *a b a*, and a final quatrain rhyming *a b a a*. Lines one, six, twelve, and eighteen are identical, as are lines three, nine, fifteen, and nineteen.

Prosody then, is the shaping force. It is the physical form which adds impact to the content. Form and content together become poetry, stirring emotion, intellect, and imagination.

GLOSSARY

Accent or **Stress**   The emphasis given a syllable or word: méntiōn, amen.

See **Scansion, Accentual Meter.**

Accentual Meter   A system of measurement based on number of syllables.

See **Sprung Rhythm, Accentual-Syllabic Meter.**

Accentual-Syllabic Meter   A system of measurement based on both number of syllables and number of accents. The meter of English poetry.

See **Syllabic Meter.**

Aesthetic Distance   The effect produced when an emotion or experience is tempered by being rendered in an artificial form such as poetry. Meter and rhyme contribute to this, giving "a sort of half-consciousness of unsubstantial existence." It prevents the confusion of art with real life.

Alexandrine   An iambic hexameter line.

See **Spenserian Stanza.**

Alliteration   The occurrence in close proximity of two or more words having the same initial sound. The following line contains alliterative w's and s's:

The wave withdrawing/Withers with seaward rustle
of flimsy water.

Allusion   A reference, often indirect, to a Biblical, mythological, or historical event, to another work of art, etc., which, if recognized, will recall its context and thus enhance the present work. Arnold alludes to Sophocles in "Dover Beach" p. 177.

Ambiguity   Multiplicity of meaning giving rise to varied, even opposed interpretations.

Analogy   Resemblance in certain aspects between dissimilar things. In "A Valediction Forbidding Mourning" p. 122, Donne likens two parting lovers to the two points of a compass.

Anapest   A metrical foot consisting of two unstressed syllables followed by a stressed syllable:

Thē Āssýriān cāme dówn līke ā wólf ōn thē fóld.

Apostrophe   A figure of speech in which a person (often absent or nonexistent), an abstract quality, or a god is addressed directly as though he were present:

Milton! thou shouldst be living at this hour.

Assonance The resemblance of accented vowel sounds but not of consonants: main-came, fire-time.

Ballad A dramatic narrative poem by an anonymous poet often intended to be sung. Characteristically, it deals with an episode of love or adventure in an understated tone without much development of character or description; supernatural elements are often involved; the stanza form is simple, and there is often a **refrain.** "Sir Patrick Spens," p. 207; "Frankie and Johnnie," p. 111.

Ballad Stanza A **quatrain** having lines one and three in iambic pentameter and lines two and four in iambic trimeter with a **rhyme scheme** of *a b c b.*

Blank Verse Unrhymed iambic pentameter used for long dramatic, narrative, and reflective poems. "Lines Composed above Tintern Abbey," p. 198.

Caesura A pause or break within a line of **verse,** usually in the middle but occasionally in other positions.

Chaucerian Stanza See **Rhyme Royal.**

Common Octave An eight-line **stanza** consisting of two joined **quatrains.** "Lines: When the Lamp Is Shattered," p. 102.

Connotation Emotional implications carried in words or phrases in addition to the literal meaning. They may be individual, group, or universal implications. Helen of Troy connotes womanly beauty and infidelity.

Consonance A resemblance among consonants in stressed syllables. These do not necessarily, as in **alliteration,** occupy the initial position:

> The *m*oan of doves in *imm*emorial el*ms.*

Couplet A two-line **stanza.**

> **Heroic couplet** A rhymed couplet of iambic pentameter:
>
> > Be not the first by whom the new are tried,
> > Nor yet the last to lay the old aside.
>
> **Closed Couplet** A couplet in which a complete thought is presented:
>
> > Had we but world enough and time
> > This coyness, lady, were no crime.
>
> **Open Couplet** A couplet whose meaning carries over into the next couplet:

> That's my last duchess painted on the wall,
> Looking as if she were alive. I call
> That piece a wonder now: Fra Pandolph's hands
> Worked busily a day, and there she stands.

Dactyl   A metrical foot consisting of one stressed syllable followed by two unstressed syllables:

> Hálf a léague, hálf a léague

See **Foot, Meter, Scansion.**

Decameter   A line of poetry having ten feet. See **Foot, Meter, Scansion.**

Denotation   The specific meaning of a word independent of all **connotation.**

Diction   The use, choice, and arrangement of words.

Dimeter   A line of poetry having two feet:

> Some say | in ice.

See **Foot, Meter, Scansion.**

Dissonance   Harsh, inharmonious sounds.

Double Rhyme   See **Feminine Rhyme.**

Dramatic Poetry   Poetry which reveals tense situations and emotional conflict through dramatic techniques such as monologue and dialogue, rather than through description.

See **Dramatic Monologue.**

Dramatic Monologue   A lyric poem in which the character speaking addresses a present but silent listener *in the poem.* The speaker reveals his character through his words. "The Love Song of J. Alfred Prufrock," p. 84; "My Last Duchess," p. 148; "Ulysses," p. 47.

Elegy   A serious meditative poem on death or some other grave theme. "Elegy for Jane," p. 296; "A Death in the Desert," p. 308.

End Stopped Line   A line in which the sense and the grammatical structure are complete, hence followed by a period or other clear pause:

> O stay, sweet love; see here the place of sporting.

English Sonnet   See **Sonnet.**

Enjambment   The running of the sense and grammatical structure of one line to the next:

> Old Eben Flood, climbing alone one night

Over the hill between the town below
And the forsaken upland hermitage
That held as much as he should ever know
On earth again of home, paused warily.

Epic   A long narrative poem in elevated style presenting the adventures of gods, heroes, or other important characters.

Epigram   A short, pithy saying, often clever and witty: "Of Treason," p. 147.

Euphony   Pleasant and agreeable sounds.

Eye Rhyme   Rhyme that appears from spelling to be **full rhyme,** but whose words are pronounced differently:

> Dull would he be of soul who could pass by
> A sight more touching in its majesty.

See **Slant Rhyme**

Feminine Ending   An extra, unstressed syllable added to the end of an iambic or anapestic line:

> Nōr fáme, nōr pówēr, nōr lóve, nōr léisūre.

Feminine Rhyme   A double rhyme in which the stressed rhyming syllable is not in the final position: warmer-former, marry-tarry, getting-setting.

Foot   The unit of measurement of poetic meter. A group of two or three syllables, one of which is accented or stressed. The various feet found in English poetry, together with their names are illustrated below:

Iambic	ālóne
Trochaic	lónelȳ
Anapestic	by̆ mȳsélf
Dactylic	lónelīnēss
Amphibrachic	ālónenēss
Amphimacic	áll ālóne

Two other feet are found only as substitutions in series of the above feet, since they are hardly possible in a series.

Spondaic	stáy, stáy
Pyrrhic	ōf thē

The name of the foot and the number of feet per line combine to name metrical lines, i.e., iambic pentameter, anapestic hexameter, etc.

Free Verse   Verse without regular metrical pattern: "from 'Song of Solomon'," p. 114; "Poets to Come," p. 28.

Full Rhyme   Different initial sounds and identical following sounds: ring-sing, design-resign, reader-leader, invention-convention.
See **Masculine** and **Feminine Rhymes.**

Half Rhyme   See **Slant Rhyme.**

Heptameter   A line of poetry having seven feet.
See **Foot, Meter, Scansion.**

Hexameter   A line of poetry having six feet.
See **Alexandrine, Foot, Meter, Scansion.**

Hiatus   A pause compelled when the end sound of one syllable and the beginning sound of the next are similar:

A Sena*te*-*T*ime's wors*t S*tatute unrepealed.

Hyperbole   Deliberate exaggeration for effect:

And I will love thee still my dear
Till a' the seas gang dry.

Iamb   A metrical foot consisting of one unstressed syllable followed by a stressed syllable:

The Kíng | sīts ín | Dūmfer´ | līng toúne.

See **Foot, Meter, Scansion.**

Imagery   The evocation of any sensory experience or mental impression through concrete representation. Images may be literal or figurative. Arnold's sea in the opening lines of "Dover Beach," p. 177, is a literal image—the meaning of the words is obvious and evokes a sensory representation of the scene:

The sea is calm tonight.
The tide is full, the moon lies fair
Upon the straights . . .

Later in the poem the sea becomes a figurative image of the human condition, ". . . the turbid ebb and flow / Of human misery", then, metaphorically, the "Sea of Faith." Keats uses clusters of tactile, visual, and sound imagery in "To Autumn," p. 37.
See **Analogy, Apostrophe, Hyperbole, Irony, Metaphor, Metonymy, Personification, Simile,** and **Synecdoche.**

Irony A figure of speech in which the words carry the opposite meaning of the actual intent, often using words of praise to imply blame and vice versa:

> He missed the medieval grace
> Of iron clothing.

Italian Sonnet See **Sonnet.**

Limerick A five-line verse pattern having anapestic lines. Lines one, two, and five are trimeter and three and four are dimeter. Rhyme scheme is *a a b b a.* "There Was an Old Party of Lyme," p. 231.

Lyric Poetry A brief, subjective poem expressing powerful emotion. "They Flee from Me," p. 107; "Do Not Go Gentle," p. 306; "Western Wind," p. 113.

Masculine Rhyme A **full rhyme** in which the final syllable is the stressed syllable. All monosyllabic rhymes are masculine; sun-done, rage-wage, must-dust; the following polysyllabic rhymes are masculine: inspect-reflect, champagne-campaign, require-enquire.

Metaphor A figure of speech in which two objects are equated. An implied comparison:

> The crowds upon the pavement
> Were fields of harvest wheat.

Meter The recurrence of a regular rhythmic pattern in poetry. The unit of measurement is the **foot.** The number and kinds of feet in the line are used to describe the meter, e.g.:

Iambic pentameter

> When Í | hāve séen | bȳ Timé's | fēll hánd | dēfácéd

Dactylic dimeter

> Córpse clād wīth | cárefūlnēss

Trochaic tetrameter

> Cóme yōu | préttȳ | fálse-ēyed | wántōn

See **Accent, Anapest, Dactyl, Decameter, Dimeter, Foot, Heptameter, Hexameter, Iamb, Monometer, Nonameter, Octameter, Pentameter, Pyrrhic, Scansion, Spondee, Trimeter, Tetrameter, Trochee.** For a full discussion of meter, see pp. 351–355.

Metonymy A figure of speech in which a term closely associated with the object to be described is substituted for the object itself.

Thus when Wordsworth writes "altar, sword, and pen" he means clergymen, soldiers, and writers.

Metrical Silence The omission of unaccented syllables expected because of the preceding metrical pattern.

Monometer A line of poetry having one foot. (The following is said to be the shortest poem on the antiquity of microbes.)

Á̆dām
Hắd 'ēm.

See **Foot, Meter, Scansion.**

Narrative Poetry A nondramatic poem which tells a story. "The Destruction of Sennacherib," p. 252.

Oblique Rhyme See **Slant Rhyme.**

Octameter A line of poetry having eight feet.

See **Foot, Meter, Scansion.**

Octave An eight-line stanza. See **Ottava Rima, Common Octave.** The first eight line of an Italian sonnet rhyming *a b b a a b b a*. See **Sonnet.**

Ode An elaborate lyric poem in sincere, dignified language on a serious theme. "Ode on a Grecian Urn," p. 330 is a derivative of the classic form.

Off Rhyme See **Slant Rhyme.**

Onomatopoeia The use of words which suggest their meaning in their sound. The following suggests the hiss of the sea:

"It keeps eternal whisperings around / Desolate shores."

Ottava Rima An iambic pentameter **octave** which rhymes *a b a b a b c c.* "Sailing to Byzantium," p. 346.

Overstatement See **Hyperbole.**

Paradox The deliberate statement of what seems to be absurd or contradictory, yet is in fact reasonable or consistent in the context:

Thus, though we cannot make our sun
Stand still, yet we will make him run.

Until I labor, I in labor lie.

Parody An imitation, through subject, style, or technique of another work for the purpose of ridicule or criticism. "Sumer is icumen in," p. 4, is parodied in "Ancient Music," p. 23; "This Is Just to Say," p. 29—in "Variations on a theme by William Carlos Williams," p. 20.

Pentameter   A line of poetry having five feet:

My mís | trèss' eyés | a͞re nó | th� líke | thͤe sún.

See **Foot, Meter, Scansion.**

Personification   A figure of speech which endows nonhuman objects, animals, and abstractions with personality or with human traits: "He [the eagle] clasps the crag with crooked hands;" "the City's voice;" "Devouring Time;" etc.

Petrarchan Sonnet   See **Sonnet.**

Prosody   The theory and principles of versification: **Accent, Meter, Rhyme,** and **Stanza.**

See **Foot, Scansion.**

Pyrrhic   A metrical foot consisting of two unstressed syllables: "of thͤe," found as a substitution in iambic or trochaic lines, often in conjunction with a **spondee.** The following line substitutes a pyrrhic for the third foot:

"Whén tͦo | thͤe sés | sͬiͦons ͦof | swéet sí | lͤent thóught."

See **Foot, Meter, Scansion, Substitution.**

Quatrain   A four-line **stanza.**

See **Ballad Stanza.**

Refrain   A group of words repeated at intervals throughout a poem. "Do not go gentle into that good night," p. 306.

Rhyme   The correspondence of sound in two or more words.

See **Full Rhyme, Slant Rhyme, Alliteration, Consonance, Assonance, Eye Rhyme.** For a full discussion of rhyme, see pp. 355–360.

Rhyme Royal (Chaucerian Stanza)   A **septet** of iambic pentameter lines rhyming *a b a b b c c.* "They Flee from Me," p. 107; "Troilus Soliloquizes," p. 120.

Rhyme Scheme   The pattern or sequence in which rhyme sounds occur. Each similar end sound is assigned the same letter:

> Out upon it! I have loved   *a*
> Three whole days together;   *b*
> And am like to love three more, *c*
> If it proves fair weather.   *b*

Rhythm   The pattern or quality of movement of the whole line. For a full discussion of rhythm see pp. 352–353.

Rondeau A fifteen-line form having a refrain in lines nine and fifteen. Except for the refrain *c*, it has only two rhymes, *a a b b a a a b c a a b b a c*. "Help Me to Seek," p. 143.

Run-on Line   See **Enjambment.**

Scansion   The act of counting accents and identifying syllabic stress. When poetry is scanned, its metrical pattern is made evident to the eye by the following conventional marks placed over the appropriate syllable: for a stressed syllable, for an unstressed one. These marks form a pattern of repeated units, feet, divided by the mark | as in the following line:

"Ī find | nō péace, | ānd all | mȳ wár | īs dóne"

Septet   A seven-line **stanza.**
See **Rhyme Royal.**

Sestet   The last six lines of an **Italian Sonnet** rhyming *c d e c d e, c d c c d c*, or *c d e d c e*.

Shakesperian Sonnet   See **Sonnet.**

Simile   A figure of speech introduced by "like" or "as" in which a similarity between two things is directly expressed: "My love is like a red, red rose"; "My love is as a fever. . . ."

Sixian   A six-line **Stanza.** "A refusal to mourn," p. 305.

Slant Rhyme   An imperfect or approximate correspondence of sound: dice-piece, even-heaven, hearth-earth, death-birth.
See **Eye Rhyme.**

Sonnet   A fourteen-line **lyric** poem, usually of iambic pentameter, following one of several set rhyme patterns. The **English** or Shakespearean form is divided into three quatrains and a couplet, usually rhyming *a b a b, c d c d, e f e f, g g*. Spenser used linking rhymes between the quatrains, *a b a b, b c b c, c d c d*. The **Italian** or Petrarchan form is divided into an **octave,** rhyming *a b b a, a b b a* and a **sestet** rhyming *c d c, c d c*, or a variation.

Spenserian Stanza   A nine-line stanza rhyming *a b a b b c b c c* having eight iambic pentameter lines followed by an **Alexandrine,** an iambic hexameter line. "Song of Bliss," p. 303.

Spondee   A metrical foot consisting of two stressed syllables, thus: "héartbréak." Since most polysyllabic English words carry only one stress, the spondaic foot is rare except as a **substitution** for iambic or trochaic feet; a spondee is substituted in the fourth **foot** of the following line:

"Ā súd | dēn blów. | Thē gréat | wíngs béat | īng stíll."

See **Foot, Meter, Scansion, Substitution.**

Sprung Rhythm A term coined by Gerald Manley Hopkins to designate a metrical system in which a **foot** consists of one stressed syllable followed by a varying number of unstressed syllables. See **Accentual Meter.**

Stanza A repeatable unit of two or more lines, having the same meter, length, and often the same **rhyme scheme.** In thought, similar to a paragraph in prose. Common stanzas in English poetry are the **couplet,** the **tercet** or **triplet,** the **quatrain,** the **septet,** the **octave,** and the **Spenserian** stanza.

Stress See **Accent.**

Substitution The use of a different **foot** from the one demanded by the metrical pattern. A **spondee** is substituted for the second **iamb** in line two below and a **trochee** for the first iamb in line three:

> "Ī mét | ā trá | veller fróm | ān án | tique lánd
> Whō saíd: | Twó vást | ānd trúnk | lēss légs | ōf stóne
> Stánd īn | the dé | sērt. . . ."

Syllabic Meter A system of measurement based on the number of syllables in a line.
See **Accentual-Syllabic Meter.**

Symbol An object used to represent or suggest another, evoking a meaning beyond the literal object.

Synecdoche A figure of speech in which part of the object to be described is substituted for the object itself. Thus when Shakespeare writes, "When forty winters shall besiege thy brow," he means forty years.

Syntax The arrangement and interrelationship of words in phrases and sentences.

Tercet or **Triplet** A three-line **stanza.** "For Anne," p. 320.
See **Terza Rima.**

Terza Rima Three line stanzas with an interlocking rhyme scheme *a b a, b c b, c d c, d e d,* etc.

Tetrameter A line of poetry having four feet:

> "Whȳ shoúld | ā foól | īsh már | riàge vów

See **Foot, Meter, Scansion.**

Theme In a literary work, the central or dominating idea, not to be confused with subject—the vehicle through which the theme is expressed. For example, the mythological Greek hero Ulysses is the subject of Tennyson's poem of that name, but the theme of the poem is that man must search for and perform deeds worthy of himself.

Tone   The implied attitude in a literary work toward the subject and the audience. It can be formal, informal, serious, satiric, ironic, etc.

Trimeter   A line of poetry having three feet:

"Thāt sa͞ils | ūpón | t͞he sēa"

See **Foot, Meter, Scansion.**

Triplet   See **Tercet, Terza Rima.**

Trochee   A metrical foot consisting of a stressed syllable followed by an unstressed syllable:

"Gó and | cátch ā | fálli͞ng | stár"

It is often used as a substitution for the first foot in an iambic line:

"Whén īn | dīsgráce | wīth fór | tūne and | mēn's eyés."

See **Foot, Meter, Scansion, Substitution.**

Understatement   A form of **irony** in which something is intentionally represented as less than it actually is. There is great understatement in the line, "I do not think that they [the mermaids] will sing for me," since there is not the remotest chance that they will.

Verse   Metered poetry, not to be confused with a "verse" meaning a line of poetry, nor with a **"stanza"** for which it is popularly used synonymously.

Villanelle   A verse pattern of nineteen lines divided into five **tercets** rhyming *a b a* and a final **quatrain** rhyming *a b a a*. Lines one, six, twelve, and eighteen are identical, as are lines three, nine, fifteen, and nineteen. "Do not go gentle," p. 306.

ACKNOWLEDGMENTS

AI, "Everything: Eloy, Arizona, 1956," from *Cruelty*, copyright © 1973 by AI. Reprinted by permission of Houghton Mifflin Company.

Brian Aldiss, "Progression of the Species," reprinted with the kind permission of the poet.

Kingsley Amis, "A Dream of Fair Women," reprinted with the permission of Curtis Brown, Ltd.

A. R. Ammons, "Auto Mobile," from *Collected Poems 1951–1971* by A. R. Ammons. Copyright © 1972 by A. R. Ammons. Reprinted by permission of W. W. Norton & Company, Inc.

Maya Angelou, "Chicken-Licken," from *Oh Pray My Wings Are Gonna Fit Me Well* by Maya Angelou, copyright © 1975. Reprinted by permission of Random House, Inc.

W. H. Auden, "As I Walked Out One Evening," "Musée des Beaux Arts," and "The Unknown Citizen," copyright © 1940 and renewed 1968 by W. H. Auden. Reprinted from *Collected Shorter Poems 1927–1957* by W. H. Auden, by permission of Random House, Inc.

Robert Bagg, "Soft Answers," copyright © 1960 by Robert Bagg. Reprinted from *Madonna of the Cello* by Robert Bagg, by permission of Wesleyan University Press.

Donald Baker, "Formal Application," from *Saturday Review* (5/11/76). Reprinted by permission of *Saturday Review*.

George Barker, "To My Mother," from *Collected Poems 1930 to 1965*. Copyright © 1957, 1962, and 1965 by George Granville Barker. Reprinted by permission of October House, Inc.

Martha Beidler, "Mohammed Ibrahim Speaks," from *The Honey and the Gall*, ed. by Chad Walsh. Reprinted with the kind permission of the poet.

Martin Bell, "The Songs," from *Penguin Modern Poets 3*. Copyright © Penguin Books Ltd., 1962. Reprinted by permission of Penguin Books Ltd.

Lerone Bennett, "Blues and Bitterness," from *New Negro Poets: U.S.A.*, edited by Langston Hughes. Copyright © 1964 by the editor. Reprinted by permission of Indiana University Press.

Wendell Berry, "Earth and Fire," copyright © 1970 by Wendell Berry. Reprinted by permission of Harcourt Brace Jovanovich, Inc.

John Berryman, Stanzas 19, 20, and 21 from *Homage to Mistress Bradstreet* by John Berryman, copyright © 1956 by John Berryman. "The Ball Poem," from *The Dispossessed* by John Berryman, copyright ©

1948 by John Berryman. Reprinted by permission of Farrar, Straus and Giroux.

Robert Bly, "The Puritan on His Honeymoon," copyright © 1958 by Robert Bly. Reprinted by permission of the poet.

Alan Bold, "That's Life?" from *To Find the New* by Alan Bold. Reprinted by permission of Chatto and Windus, Ltd.

Julian Bond, "Rotation," from *New Negro Poets: U.S.A.*, edited by Langston Hughes. Copyright © 1964 by the editor. Reprinted by permission of Indiana University Press.

Arna Bontemps, "Southern Mansion," from *Personals*, published by Paul Breman, London. Copyright © 1963 by Arna Bontemps. Reprinted by permission of Harold Ober Associates Incorporated.

D. E. Borrell, "Another Death," from *New Poems: 1971–1972*, published by Hutchinson of London. Originally published in *New Coin*, edited by Prof. Guy Butler, University of Rhodes, Grahamstown, South Africa. Reprinted with kind permission of the poet.

Gwendolyn Brooks, "We Real Cool," copyright © 1959 by Gwendolyn Brooks, from *Selected Poems* by Gwendolyn Brooks; "When You Have Forgotten Sunday: The Love Story" and *"Kitchenette Building,"* from *A Street in Bronzeville* by Gwendolyn Brooks. Copyright © 1944 by Gwendolyn Brooks Blakely. Reprinted by permission of Harper and Row, Publishers, Inc.

Jim Burns, "The End Bit," reprinted with kind permission of the poet.

Howard Byatt, "Death," from *New Poems: 1971–1972*, published by Hutchinson of London. Reprinted with kind permission of the poet.

Charles Causley, "Envoi" of "Ballad of Five Continents," from *Collected Poems 1951–1975*. Copyright © 1975 by Charles Causley. Reprinted by permission of Harold Ober Associates Incorporated.

Lucille Clifton, "Good Times," from *Good Times* by Lucille Clifton. Reprinted by permission of Random House, Inc.

Leonard Cohen, "For Anne" and "The Music Crept by Us," from *Collected Poems: 1956–1968* by Leonard Cohen. Copyright © 1964 by Leonard Cohen. All rights reserved. Reprinted by permission of The Viking Press, Inc.

Gregory Corso, "Uccello," from *Gasoline* by Gregory Corso. Copyright © 1958 by Gregory Corso. Reprinted by permission of City Lights Books.

John Cotton, "Old Movies," from *Old Movies* by John Cotton. Copyright © 1971 by John Cotton. Reprinted from *Old Movies* by permission of Wesleyan University Press.

Henri Coulette, "The Family Goldschmitt" from *The Family Goldschmitt* by Henri Coulette. Copyright © 1971 by Henri Coulette. "EMERITUS, n." Both poems reprinted with the kind permission of the poet.

Robert Creeley, "The Crisis," is reprinted with the permission of Charles Scribner's Sons from *For Love* by Robert Creeley. Copyright © 1962 by Robert Creeley.

Victor Hernandez Cruz, "going uptown to visit miriam," from *Snaps*. Copyright © 1969 by Victor Hernandez Cruz. Reprinted by permission of Random House, Inc.

376 **Acknowledgments**

Connery Lathem. Copyright 1916, 1923, 1930, 1939, © 1969 by Holt, Rinehart and Winston, Inc. Copyright © 1967 by Lesley Frost Ballentine. Reprinted by permission of Holt, Rinehart and Winston, Inc.

Jean Overton Fuller, "Not Marching Away to be Killed," copyright 1969. Corgi Books: *Doves of the 70's*. Reprinted by permission of Transworld Publishers, Ltd.

Roy Fuller, "Nino the Wonder Dog," from *Collected Poems* by Roy Fuller. Reprinted by permission of Andre Deutsch.

Javier Gálvez, "This Morning," reprinted with the kind permission of the poet.

Dan Georgakas, "The acrobat from Xanadu disdained all nets," reprinted with the kind permission of the poet.

Barbara Gibson, "After the Quarrel," from *In a Time of Revolution*, ed. by Walter Lowenfels. Reprinted with kind permission of the poet.

Morgan Gibson, "Beyond the Presidency," reprinted with the kind permission of the poet.

Walker Gibson, "The Killer Too," from *The Reckless Spenders* by Walter Gibson. Copyright © 1954 by the author. Reprinted by permission of Indiana University Press. "The Killer Too" previously copyright © 1945 by *Harper's Magazine*.

Allen Ginsberg, "Uptown," from *Planet News* by Allen Ginsberg. Copyright © 1968 by Allen Ginsberg. Reprinted by permission of City Lights Books.

Paul Goodman, "Surfers at Santa Cruz," copyright © 1966 by Paul Goodman. Reprinted from *Hawkweed* by Paul Goodman, by permission of Random House, Inc.

Donald Hall, "Questions (1)," "Questions (2)," and "Your voice on the telephone" from *The Yellow Book: Love Poems.* Copyright © 1971 by Donald Hall. Reprinted by permission of Harper & Row, Publishers, Inc.

Michael Hamburger, "Squares," published by Fulcrum Press. Reprinted with kind permission of the poet.

Thomas Hardy, "Epitaph on a Pessimist," from *Collected Poems* by Thomas Hardy. Copyright 1925 by The Macmillan Company, renewed 1953 by Lloyds Bank Ltd. "The Man He Killed," from *Collected Poems* by Thomas Hardy. Both poems reprinted with permission of The Macmillan Company.

Robert Hayden, "Night, Death, Mississippi" and "Those Winter Sundays" from *Selected Poems* by Robert Hayden, copyright © 1966 by October House, Inc. Reprinted by permission of October House, Inc.

Calvin Hernton, "The Distant Drum," from *New Negro Poets: U.S.A.*, edited by Langston Hughes. Copyright © 1964 by the editor. Reprinted by permission of Indiana University Press.

Ruth Herschberger, "Song," in *Aphra* (Fall, 1969). Reprinted with the kind permission of the poet.

Robert Hershon, "How to Walk in a Crowd," reprinted with the kind permission of the poet.

William Hoffman, "Screw Spring," reprinted with the kind permission of the poet.

A. E. Housman, "Loveliest of Trees," from *A Shropshire Lad*—Authorized

Edition—from *The Collected Poems of A. E. Housman.* Copyright 1939, 1940, © 1959 by Holt, Rinehart and Winston, Inc. Copyright © 1967, 1968 by Robert E. Symons. Reprinted by permission of Holt, Rinehart and Winston, Inc.

Langston Hughes, "I, Too" and "Midnight Dancer," copyright 1926 by Alfred A. Knopf, Inc., renewed 1954 by Langston Hughes. "Dream Deferred," copyright 1951 by Langston Hughes; reprinted from *The Panther and the Lash* by Langston Hughes. Reprinted by permission of Alfred A. Knopf, Inc.

Ted Hughes, "That Moment," from *Crow* by Ted Hughes. By permission of Harper & Row, Publishers, Inc.

David Ignatow, "The Bagel," copyright © 1966 by David Ignatow, reprinted from *Rescue the Dead.* "The Sky Is Blue" by David Ignatow, copyright © 1964. Reprinted from *Figures of the Human* by David Ignatow, by permission of Wesleyan University Press.

Randall Jarrell, "The Death of the Ball Turret Gunner" and "Eighth Air Force," from *The Complete Poems of Randall Jarrell*, reprinted with the permission of Farrar, Straus & Giroux, Inc.

Robinson Jeffers, "Shine, Perishing Republic," copyright 1925 and renewed 1953 by Robinson Jeffers. Reprinted from *The Selected Poetry of Robinson Jeffers* by permission of Random House, Inc.

James Joyce, from *Ulysses* by James Joyce. Copyright 1914, 1918 by Margaret Caroline Anderson and renewed 1942, 1946 by Nora Joseph Joyce. Reprinted by permission of Random House, Inc.

Donald Justice, "Counting the Mad," from *The Summer Anniversaries* by Donald Justice. Copyright © 1957 by Donald Justice. Reprinted by permission of Wesleyan University Press.

X. J. Kennedy, "Down in Dallas," copyright © 1964 by X. J. Kennedy, from *Growing into Love* by X. J. Kennedy. "The Aged Wino's Counsel to a Young Man on the Brink of Marriage," copyright © 1961 by X. J. Kennedy, from *Nude Descending a Staircase* by X. J. Kennedy. Both poems reprinted by permission of Doubleday & Company, Inc.

Kenneth Koch, "Variations on a Theme by William Carlos Williams," from *Thank You and Other Poems*, copyright © 1962 by Kenneth Koch. Reprinted by permission of Grove Press, Inc.

Angela Langfield, "Living With You," is reprinted with kind permission of the poet.

Joseph Langland, "War," is reprinted with the permission of Charles Scribner's Sons from *The Green Town: Poems* by Joseph Langland. Copyright © 1956 by Joseph Langland. *(Poets of Today III).*

Philip Larkin, "Poetry of Departures," is reprinted from *The Less Deceived*, copyright © The Marvell Press, 1955, 1971. By permission of the Marvell Press, Hessle, Yorkshire, Eng.

Carl Larsen, "The Plot to Assassinate the Chase Manhattan Bank," reprinted with the kind permission of the poet.

D. H. Lawrence, "Love on the Farm," from *The Complete Poems of D. H. Lawrence*, Volume I, edited by Vivian de Sola Pinto and F. Warren Roberts. Copyright 1920 by B. W. Huebsch, Inc., renewed 1948 by Frieda Lawrence. Reprinted by permission of The Viking Press, Inc.

Eliot. "I May, I Might, I Must," from *The Complete Poems of Marianne Moore*, copyright © 1959 by Marianne Moore. Reprinted by permission of The Viking Press, Inc.

Edwin Morgan, "In the Snack Bar," reprinted from Edwin Morgan's *The Second Life* (Edinburgh: Edinburgh Univ. Press, 1968). Copyright 1968 by Edwin Morgan and Edinburgh Univ. Press. "INSTAMATIC Fort Benning, Georgia, April 1971," from *Lines Review* # 42/43. Reprinted with the kind permission of the poet.

Jean Morgan, "The Misogynist" is reprinted by permission of *The New Republic*. Copyright © 1972 The New Republic, Inc.

Pablo Neruda, "The Fickle One," from *The Captain's Verses*, translated by Donald D. Walsh. Copyright © 1972 by Pablo Neruda and Donald D. Walsh. Reprinted by permission of New Directions Publishing Corporation.

John Frederick Nims, "Love Poem," copyright © by John Frederick Nims. Reprinted by permission of William Morrow & Co. from *The Iron Pastoral* by John Frederick Nims.

Gregory Orr, Part 7 of "Before We Met," ("Like Any Other Man") in *Gathering the Bones Together* by Gregory Orr, copyright © 1975 by Gregory Orr. Reprinted by permission of Harper & Row, Publishers, Inc.

Wilfred Owen, "Disabled" and "Dulce et Decorum Est," from *The Collected Poems of Wilfred Owen*. Copyright © Chatto & Windus, Ltd. 1946, 1963. Reprinted by permission of New Directions Publishing Co.

Robert Pack, "Don't Sit under the Apple Tree with Anyone Else but Me," from *Home from the Cemetery*, published by Rutgers University Press and reprinted with the permission of the publisher and the poet.

Brian Patten, "Where Are You Now Superman?" from *Little Johnny's Confession* by Brian Patten. Copyright © 1967 by Brian Patten. Reprinted by permission of Hill and Wang, Inc.

Raymond Patterson, "I've Got a Home in That Rock," reprinted with the permission of Universal Publishing and Distributing Corporation.

Octavio Paz, "The Street," reprinted from *Spanish-American Literature in Translation*, edited by Willis Knapp Jones, with the permission of Frederick Ungar Publishing Co., Inc.

Marge Piercy, "Learning Experience," from *Hard Loving* by Marge Piercy. Copyright © 1969 by Marge Piercy. Reprinted by permission of Wesleyan University Press.

Sylvia Plath, "Death & Co.," copyright © 1963 by Ted Hughes, from *Ariel* by Sylvia Plath. Reprinted by permission of Harper & Row, Publishers, Inc.

Ezra Pound, "Ancient Music," "Portrait d'une Femme," and "Hugh Selwyn Mauberly" (Parts IV and V) from Ezra Pound's *Personae*. Copyright 1926 by Ezra Pound. Reprinted by permission of New Directions Publishing Corporation.

Dudley Randall, "A Different Image," from *Cities Burning*, copyright © 1968 by Dudley Randall. Reprinted by permission of Broadside Press.

John Crowe Ransom, "Bells for John Whiteside's Daughter," copyright 1924 by Alfred A. Knopf, Inc., and renewed 1952 by John Crowe

Ransom. Reprinted from *Selected Poems*, 3rd edition, by John Crowe Ransom, by permission of the publisher.

Henry Reed, "Naming of Parts," from *A Map of Verona*, published by and reprinted by permission of Jonathan Cape, Ltd.

Ismael Reed, "Skirt Dance," from *Chattanooga* by Ishmael Reed. Copyright © 1973 by Ishmael Reed. Reprinted by permission of Random House, Inc.

Adrienne Rich, "Living in Sin," from *Poems: Selected and New, 1950–1974* by Adrienne Rich. Copyright © 1975, 1973, 1971, 1969, 1966 by W. W. Norton & Co., Inc. Copyright © 1967, 1963, 1962, 1961, 1960, 1959, 1958, 1956, 1955, 1954, 1953, 1952, 1951 by Adrienne Rich. Reprinted by permission of W. W. Norton & Co., Inc.

Edwin Arlington Robinson, "Miniver Cheevy" (copyright 1907 by Charles Scribner's Sons; renewed copyright 1935) is reprinted with the permission of Charles Scribner's Sons from *The Town Down the River* by Edwin Arlington Robinson; "Richard Cory" is reprinted with the permission of Charles Scribner's Sons from *The Children of the Night* by Edwin Arlington Robinson. "Mr. Flood's Party" is reprinted with permission of Macmillan Co. from *Collected Poems* by Edwin Arlington Robinson. Copyright 1921 by Edwin Arlington Robinson, renewed 1949 by Ruth Nivison.

Theodore Roethke, "My Papa's Waltz," copyright © 1942 by Hearst Magazine, Inc. "Elegy for Jane," copyright © 1950 by Theodore Roethke. Both poems from *The Collected Poems of Theodore Roethke.* Reprinted by permission of Doubleday & Co., Inc.

Alan Ross, "Radar," from *Something of the Sea* by Alan Ross, reprinted with the permission of Derek Verschoyle, Publishers.

Muriel Rukeyser, "Rondel," from *Breaking Open*, published by Random House. Copyright © 1973 by Muriel Rukeyser. Reprinted by permission of Monica McCall, ICM.

Luís Omar Salinas, "Pedro," from *Crazy Gypsy*, copyright © 1970 by Luís Omar Salinas. Reprinted with kind permission of the poet.

Louis B. Salomon, "Univac to Univac," reprinted with the kind permission of the poet.

Siegfried Sassoon, "Base Details," from *Collected Poems* by Siegfried Sassoon. Copyright 1918 by E. P. Dutton & Co., renewed 1946 by Siegfried Sassoon. Reprinted by permission of The Viking Press, Inc.

Alexander Scott, "Problems," copyright © 1974 by Alexander Scott, from *Selected Poems 1943–1974*, published by Akros Publications, Preston, England. Used with the kind permission of the poet.

Anne Sexton, "Her Kind," and "Ringing the Bells," from *To Bedlam and Part Way Back.* Copyright © 1960 by Anne Sexton. Reprinted by permission of the publisher, Houghton Mifflin Company.

Karl Shapiro, "Auto Wreck," copyright 1942 by Karl Shapiro. Reprinted from *Selected Poems* by Karl Shapiro, by permission of Random House, Inc.

Martin Staples Shockley, "Crossedroads," reprinted from *The University Review* with the kind permission of the poet.

Jon Silkin, "Death of a Son," from *Poems New and Selected*, copyright

1954 by Jon Silkin. Reprinted by permission of Wesleyan University Press.

Stevie Smith, "Not Waving but Drowning," copyright © 1962, 1964 by Stevie Smith. Reprinted by permission of New Directions Publishing Corporation.

William Jay Smith, "American Primitive," reprinted from *New and Selected Poems* by William Jay Smith. Copyright © 1944, 1946, 1948, 1949, 1950, 1951, 1953, 1956, 1957, 1959, 1961, 1962, 1963, 1964, 1965, 1966, 1967, 1970 by William Jay Smith. A Seymour Lawrence Book/Delacorte Press. Used by permission.

W. D. Snodgrass, "Mementos, I" and "Leaving the Motel," from *After Experience*, copyright © 1960 by W. D. Snodgrass. Reprinted by permission of Harper & Row, Publishers, Inc.

Gary Snyder, "Looking at Pictures to Be Put Away," from *The Back Country* by Gary Snyder. Copyright © 1968 by Gary Snyder. Reprinted by permission of New Directions Publishing Corporation.

Stephen Spender, "An Elementary School Classroom in a Slum," copyright © 1942 by Stephen Spender. Reprinted from *Selected Poems* by Stephen Spender, by permission of Random House, Inc.

William Stafford, "Adults Only," from *Traveling through the Dark*. Copyright © 1960 by William Stafford. Reprinted by permission of Harper & Row, Publishers, Inc.

Wallace Stevens, "Disillusionment of Ten O'Clock," "The Emperor of Ice-Cream," and "The Plot Against the Giant," copyright 1923 and renewed 1951 by Wallace Stevens. "The Idea of Order at Key West," copyright 1936 and renewed 1964 by Holly Stevens Stephenson. Reprinted from *The Collected Poems of Wallace Stevens* by permission of Alfred A. Knopf, Inc.

Laura St. Martin, "as i look out" and "the ocean," copyright 1977 by Laura St. Martin. Reprinted with kind permission of the poet.

Muriel Stuart, "In the Orchard," from *Selected Poems* by Muriel Stuart. Reprinted by permission of Jonathan Cape, Ltd.

May Swenson, "All That Time," from *Half Sun Half Sleep*, copyright © 1967 by May Swenson is used by kind permission of the poet.

James Tate, "The Professor Waking," copyright © 1970 by and used with permission of *The Atlantic Monthly*.

Dylan Thomas, "Do Not Go Gentle into That Good Night", "A Refusal to Mourn the Death, by Fire, of a Child in London," and "If I Were Tickled by the Rub of Love," from *The Collected Poems* by Dylan Thomas. Copyright 1939 by New Directions Publishing Corporation, 1952 by Dylan Thomas. Reprinted by permission of New Directions Publishing Corporation.

R. S. Thomas, "Over," from *New Poems 1971–72*, published by Macmillan of London. Reprinted with kind permission of the poet.

Charles Tomlinson, "A Death in the Desert," from *American Scenes and Other Poems* by Charles Tomlinson, copyright © 1966 by Oxford University Press. Reprinted by permission of Oxford University Press.

Kathryn Van Spanckeren, "Muse Poem," reprinted from *The American Poetry Review* with the kind permission of the poet.

Peter Viereck, "Kilroy," from *New and Selected Poems, 1932–1967*,

INDEX OF AUTHORS, TITLES, AND FIRST LINES OF POETRY

No separate entry is given for a title when it is identical with the opening words of the first line.

Sexton, Anne, 43, 159
Shakespeare, William, 24, 25, 44, 101, 137, 138, 160, 222, 244, 271, 297–299, 340
Shapiro, Karl, 68
She died turning aside from the sink, 281
She dwelt among the untrodden ways, 142
She had thought the studio would keep itself, 158
Shelley, Percy Bysshe, 69, 102, 272, 299
She packs the flower beds with leaves, 242
She sang beyond the genius of the sea, 224
She walks in Beauty, like the night, 118
She was afraid of men, 79
"Shiloh," 262
"Shine, Perishing Republic," 65
Shiny record albums scattered over, 92
Shirley, James, 300
Shockley, Martin Staples, 192
Sigh no more, ladies, sigh no more! 25
Silkin, Jon, 301
Since brass, nor stone, nor earth, nor boundless sea, 299
"Sir Patrick Spens," 207
Skimming lightly, wheeling still, 262
"Skirt Dance," 24
Sleep, angry beauty, sleep, and fear not me, 119
Smith, Stevie, 161
Smith, William Jay, 103
Snodgrass, W. D., 223, 245
Snyder, Gary, 44
"So careful of the type?" but no, 341
"Soft Answers," 113
"Soft Snow," 6
Some say the world will end in fire, 327
Something has ceased to come along with me, 301
Sometimes you hear, fifth-hand, 334
"Song," (Behn), 279
"Song," (Herschberger), 129
"Song," (Rossetti), 297
"Song of Bliss," 303
Sorting out letters and piles of my old, 245
So squeezed, wince you I scream? I love you & hate, 5
"Southern Mansion," 281
So we'll go no more a-roving, 34
Spender, Stephen, 70
Spenser, Edmund, 104, 138, 302, 303
"Spring and Fall: To a Young Child," 36
"Squares," 183
Stafford, William, 26
Stevens, Wallace, 27, 161, 224, 341
Still to be neat, still to be dressed, 219
"Stopping by Woods on a Snowy Evening," 287
Stuart, Muriel, 46
Suckling, Sir John, 141
"Suicide," 106
Sumer is icumen in, 4
Sundays too my father got up early, 35

Sunset and evening star, 192
"Surfers at Santa Cruz," 151
Swenson, May, 139
Swift, Jonathan, 71, 304

Tate, James, 162
Tell me not, Sweet, I am unkind, 259
Tennyson, Alfred, Lord, 47, 104, 163, 192, 225, 305, 341, 342
Testubicles spill blood across the page, 192
That is no country for old men. The young, 346
"That Moment," 218
"That's Life?" 211
That's my last Duchess painted on the wall, 148
That time of year thou mayst in me behold, 44
That which her slender waist confined, 142
The ache of marriage, 241
The acrobat from Xanadu disdained all nets, 328
The age, 188
"The Aged Wino's Counsel to a Young Man on the Brink of Marriage," 238
The Assyrian came down like the wolf on the fold, 252
"The Bagel," 20
"The Ball Poem," 33
"The Banjo," 168
The beauty of Israel is slain upon thy high places . . . , 251
"The Black Panther," 343
The boy sits in the classroom, 99
The buzz saw snarled and rattled in the yard, 286
"The Chimney Sweeper," 147
"The Crisis," 234
"The Dancers Inherit the Party," 326
The Danube to the Severn gave, 305
"The Death of the Ball Turret Gunner," 258
"The Destruction of Sennacherib," 252
"The Distant Drum," 329
The door still swinging to, and girls revive, 315
"The Eagle," 342
"The Emperor of Ice-Cream," 161
"The End Bit," 212
"The Family Goldschmitt," 322
The father raised words, 38
"The Fickle One," 131
The first cold front came in, 83
"The Flea," 325
"The Fury of Aerial Bombardment," 254
The glories of our blood and state, 300
"The Good-Morrow," 123
The gray sea and the long black land, 117
"The Great Day," 75
The haill warld waited, 270
"The Harlem Dancer," 94